Beginning Investing
How To Succeed Investing In Stocks And Other Wealth Building Strategies

By John Molvar

Cover Photo: Wall Street Bull Photo courtesy of <u>BostInno</u>

Text copyright © 2015, John Molvar, All Rights Reserved
No part of this publication may be reproduced or transmitted in any form or by any means, or transmitted electronically without direct written permission in writing from the author. While all attempts have been made to verify the information provided herein, neither the authors nor publisher assume any responsibility for errors, omissions or misuse of the subject matter contained in this Book.

This eBook is for entertainment purposes only, and the views expressed are those of the author alone, and should not be taken as expert instruction. The reader is responsible for his or her own actions. Adherence to applicable laws and regulations, including international, federal, state, and local governing professional licensing business practices, advertising, and all other aspects of doing business in the U.S.A. or any other jurisdiction is the sole responsibility of the purchaser or reader. Previous Title: Fundamental Stock Investing And Wealth Building

Table Of Contents

FOREWORD   15

CHAPTER 1   TO BUILD WEALTH YOU MUST INVEST AND SAVE   19

CHAPTER 2   WHY INVEST INSTEAD OF "STARTING MY OWN BUSINESS"?   20

CHAPTER 3   WHY STOCKS ARE THE BEST FORM OF INVESTING OVER THE LONG HAUL   22

CHAPTER 4   WHAT PERSONAL TRAITS ARE NECESSARY TO MAKE IT IN STOCK INVESTING?   24

CHAPTER 5   SHOULD I GO WITH INDIVIDUAL STOCKS OR WITH FUNDS?   28

CHAPTER 6   BEFORE INVESTING IN STOCKS, STEP 1: CONSIDER BUYING A HOME   29

CHAPTER 7   BEFORE INVESTING IN STOCKS IN A TAXABLE ACCOUNT, STEP 2: GET THE MAXIMUM MATCHING FUNDS FROM YOUR 401K/403B/TSP PLAN   37

CHAPTER 8   BEFORE INVESTING IN STOCKS IN A TAXABLE ACCOUNT, STEP 3: ELIMINATE CREDIT CARD DEBT   38

CHAPTER 9   BEFORE INVESTING IN STOCKS IN A TAXABLE ACCOUNT, STEP 4: PUT MAXIMUM ALLOWABLE INTO YOUR 401K/403B/TSP PLAN   40

CHAPTER 10   BEFORE INVESTING IN STOCKS IN A TAXABLE ACCOUNT, STEP 5: PUT AS MUCH AS YOU CAN INTO A ROTH IRA   43

CHAPTER 11   WHAT FUNDS DO I PUT MY 401K/403B/TSP/IRA MONEY INTO?   46

CHAPTER 12   I HAVE MAXED OUT AVAILABLE 401K/403B/TSP, MAXED OUT ROTH IRA AND HAVE NO CREDIT CARD DEBT AND STILL HAVE MONEY LEFT OVER   48

CHAPTER 13   HOW TO PICK A STOCK MUTUAL FUND   66

CHAPTER 14   WHAT ABOUT INTERNATIONAL FUNDS?   70

CHAPTER 15   CHECKLIST FOR STARTING IN INDIVIDUAL STOCKS VIA FUNDAMENTAL STOCK INVESTING   72

CHAPTER 16   FUNDAMENTAL STOCK INVESTING PHILOSOPHY   74

CHAPTER 17   FUNDAMENTAL STOCK INVESTING BASICS   75

CHAPTER 18   EARNINGS ARE THE KEY, THERE IS NOTHING RANDOM ABOUT IT   81

CHAPTER 19   WHEN IS A GOOD TIME TO START INVESTING IN STOCKS?   83

CHAPTER 20   I AM OVER 50, IS IT TOO LATE TO START INVESTING?   85

CHAPTER 21   I AM AFRAID TO START NOW BECAUSE THE STOCK MARKET MIGHT CRASH   86

CHAPTER 22 WHAT IF THE MARKET ENVIRONMENT IS TOO UNCERTAIN TO INVEST IN? 88

CHAPTER 23 IGNORE THE EXPERTS 90

CHAPTER 24 IGNORE ALL THE SILLY STOCK MARKET SAYINGS THAT HAVE NO MEANING 92

CHAPTER 25 MORE DETAILS ON STOCK INVESTING: ANALYZING GROWTH STOCK'S GROWTH RATE IN RELATION TO P/E 95

CHAPTER 26 MORE DETAILS ON STOCK INVESTING: ANALYZING THE BALANCE SHEET 101

CHAPTER 27 MORE DETAILS ON STOCK INVESTING: MORE ON INVESTING IN RETAILERS AND RESTAURANTS 103

CHAPTER 28 MORE DETAILS ON STOCK INVESTING: HOW TO MAKE MONEY IN CYCLICAL STOCKS 105

CHAPTER 29 MORE DETAILS ON STOCK INVESTING: MORE INFORMATION ON CYCLICAL AUTO STOCK INVESTING 112

CHAPTER 30 MORE DETAILS ON STOCK INVESTING: HOW TO MAKE MONEY IN TURNAROUNDS 115

CHAPTER 31 MORE DETAILS ON STOCK INVESTING: EVALUATING BANK STOCKS 119

CHAPTER 32 MORE DETAILS ON STOCK INVESTING: EVALUATING INSURANCE STOCKS 123

CHAPTER 33 MORE DETAILS ON STOCK INVESTING: ANALYZING STOCK BUY BACKS 124

CHAPTER 34   MORE DETAILS ON STOCK INVESTING: SECONDARY OFFERINGS   127

CHAPTER 35   MORE DETAILS ON STOCK INVESTING: INSIDER BUYING AND SELLING   128

CHAPTER 36   MORE DETAILS ON STOCK INVESTING: INSTITUTIONAL OWNERSHIP   129

CHAPTER 37   MORE DETAILS ON STOCK INVESTING: NUMBER OF ANALYSTS FOLLOWING A STOCK   130

CHAPTER 38   MORE DETAILS ON STOCK INVESTING: INSIDER OWNERSHIP   131

CHAPTER 39   MORE DETAILS ON STOCK INVESTING: CAREFULLY EVALUATE ACQUISITION ANNOUNCEMENTS   133

CHAPTER 40   MORE DETAILS ON STOCK INVESTING: WHAT IF THERE ARE NO ANALYST ESTIMATES?   135

CHAPTER 41   MORE DETAILS ON STOCK INVESTING: BOOK VALUE   136

CHAPTER 42   MORE DETAILS ON STOCK INVESTING: CASH FLOW AND RETURN ON EQUITY AND EBITDA   137

CHAPTER 43   MORE DETAILS ON STOCK INVESTING: DIVIDENDS   139

CHAPTER 44   MORE DETAILS ON STOCK INVESTING: DON'T SELL A FAST GROWTH STOCK JUST BECAUSE THE STOCK HAS BECOME EXPENSIVE   141

CHAPTER 45   MORE DETAILS ON STOCK INVESTING: WHERE DO I GET NEW STOCK IDEAS?   143

CHAPTER 46   MORE DETAILS ON STOCK INVESTING: DON'T BUY CHEAP STOCKS WITH DETERIORATING FUNDAMENTALS   145

CHAPTER 47   MORE DETAILS ON STOCK INVESTING: DON'T BUY A STOCK THAT HAS NEVER BEEN PROFITABLE   146

CHAPTER 48   MORE DETAILS ON STOCK INVESTING: IGNORE SHORT SELLERS   147

CHAPTER 49   MORE DETAILS ON STOCK INVESTING: ALWAYS EVALUATE EARNINGS REPORTS IN ABSOLUTE TERMS, NOT WITH RESPECT TO "ANALYSTS EXPECTATIONS"   152

CHAPTER 50   MORE DETAILS ON STOCK INVESTING: WHAT ABOUT IPOS?   155

CHAPTER 51   MORE DETAILS ON STOCK INVESTING: TREAD LIGHTLY IN HIGH TECH   156

CHAPTER 52   MORE DETAILS ON STOCK INVESTING: BEWARE OF CONCENTRATED SUPPLIERS   158

CHAPTER 53   MORE DETAILS ON STOCK INVESTING: WHAT ABOUT A COMPANY THAT IS "RESTRUCTURING"?
                            159

CHAPTER 54   MORE DETAILS ON STOCK INVESTING: ANALYST'S UPGRADES/DOWNGRADES OF STOCKS   160

CHAPTER 55   MORE DETAILS ON STOCK INVESTING: WHAT ABOUT SO-CALLED CHANNEL CHECKERS?   162

CHAPTER 56   MORE DETAILS ON STOCK INVESTING: WRITE DOWN THE REASON YOU BOUGHT A STOCK   164

CHAPTER 57   MORE DETAILS ON STOCK INVESTING: THE EFFECT OF MAINSTREAM MEDIA NEWS ON YOUR INVESTING ABILITY   173

CHAPTER 58   MORE DETAILS ON STOCK INVESTING: ONLY WATCH FINANCIAL SHOWS FOR ENTERTAINMENT, NOT FOR ADVICE OR EDUCATION   175

CHAPTER 59   MORE DETAILS ON STOCK INVESTING: WHAT ABOUT FRAUD?   177

CHAPTER 60   MORE DETAILS ON STOCK INVESTING: EXPECT TO MAKE LOTS OF MISTAKES   180

CHAPTER 61   MORE DETAILS ON STOCK INVESTING: DO NOT TRY TO TIME THE MARKET BECAUSE THE BULK OF STOCK MARKET GAINS HAPPEN IN JUST A FEW DAYS PER YEAR   182

CHAPTER 62   MORE DETAILS ON STOCK INVESTING: IGNORE ALL OPINIONS AND STICK EXCLUSIVELY TO FUNDAMENTAL FACTS   183

CHAPTER 63   MORE DETAILS ON STOCK INVESTING: SHORT TERM STOCK MOVEMENTS MEAN NOTHING   184

CHAPTER 64   MORE DETAILS ON STOCK INVESTING: THE DOLLAR PRICE A STOCK IS SELLING FOR IS IRRELEVANT UNLESS COMPARED TO P/E   185

CHAPTER 65   MORE DETAILS ON STOCK INVESTING: SPIN-OFFS   186

CHAPTER 66   MORE DETAILS ON STOCK INVESTING: AVOID PENNY STOCKS LIKE THE PLAGUE   187

CHAPTER 67   MORE DETAILS ON STOCK INVESTING: STOCK SPLITS   189

CHAPTER 68   MORE DETAILS ON STOCK INVESTING: WHEN EVALUATING A STOCK, WHERE THE STOCK PRICE HAS BEEN IN THE PAST IS COMPLETELY IRRELEVANT   191

CHAPTER 69   MORE DETAILS ON STOCK INVESTING: SEEK OUT SHAREHOLDER FRIENDLY COMPANIES   192

CHAPTER 70   MORE DETAILS ON STOCK INVESTING: DON'T BOTHER CALLING THE COMPANY   193

CHAPTER 71   MORE DETAILS ON STOCK INVESTING: HOW CAN THE LITTLE GUY COMPETE IN TODAY'S MARKET?   194

CHAPTER 72   MORE DETAILS ON STOCK INVESTING: HOW TO EXECUTE A BUY ORDER   198

CHAPTER 73   MORE DETAILS ON STOCK INVESTING: HOW TO EXECUTE A SELL ORDER   199

CHAPTER 74   MORE DETAILS ON STOCK INVESTING: WHAT ABOUT CORPORATE RAIDERS/ACTIVISTS?   202

CHAPTER 75   MORE DETAILS ON STOCK INVESTING: WHAT ABOUT THE TAX IMPLICATIONS OF BUYING AND SELLING STOCKS?   203

CHAPTER 76   MORE DETAILS ON STOCK INVESTING: ANOTHER TAX SAVINGS STRATEGY   204

CHAPTER 77   MORE DETAILS ON STOCK INVESTING: IN A DOWN YEAR LOOK FOR FANTASTIC BARGAINS IN MID OCTOBER TO EARLY DECEMBER IN SMALL STOCKS AND/OR CYCLICAL STOCKS   205

CHAPTER 78   MORE DETAILS ON STOCK INVESTING: NEVER BUY DRUG STOCKS WITH ONLY ONE DRUG   206

CHAPTER 79   MORE DETAILS ON STOCK INVESTING: WHAT ABOUT BUYING STOCKS ON MARGIN?   207

CHAPTER 80   MORE DETAILS ON STOCK INVESTING: WHAT ABOUT STOP LOSS ORDERS?   208

CHAPTER 81   MORE DETAILS ON STOCK INVESTING: WHAT ABOUT SHORTING STOCKS?   209

CHAPTER 82   MORE DETAILS ON STOCK INVESTING: HOW DO I KNOW IF THE STOCK MARKET IS CHEAP OR EXPENSIVE?   210

CHAPTER 83   MORE DETAILS ON STOCK INVESTING: HOW MANY STOCKS SHOULD I OWN?   215

CHAPTER 84   MORE DETAILS ON STOCK INVESTING: WHAT TYPE OF RETURNS SHOULD I EXPECT FROM INDIVIDUAL STOCK PICKING?   217

CHAPTER 85   MORE DETAILS ON INVESTING: WHAT ABOUT COMMODITIES?   219

CHAPTER 86   MORE DETAILS ON INVESTING: WHAT ABOUT CURRENCY TRADING?   224

CHAPTER 87   MORE DETAILS ON STOCK INVESTING: WHAT ABOUT OPTIONS TRADING?   225

CHAPTER 88   MORE DETAILS ON INVESTING: I JUST HEARD ABOUT AN INVESTMENT WHERE MY FRIEND IS GETTING 20% ANNUAL RETURNS!   226

CHAPTER 89   MORE DETAILS ON STOCK INVESTING:
HOW LONG DO I STAY FULLY INVESTED IN STOCKS?   229

CHAPTER 90   MORE DETAILS ON STOCK INVESTING:
HOW MUCH MONEY DO I NEED TO RETIRE?   230

CHAPTER 91   MORE DETAILS ON STOCK INVESTING:
HOW LONG DOES IT TAKE TO RETIRE EARLY?   231

CHAPTER 92   MORE DETAILS ON STOCK INVESTING:
COMPLETELY IGNORE POLITICS   233

CHAPTER 93   A DIFFERENT AND MORE POSITIVE TAKE
ON THE OUT OF CONTROL GROWTH OF GOVERNMENT
DEBT   235

CHAPTER 94   MORE DETAILS ON STOCK INVESTING:
WHAT ABOUT OTHER INVESTING TECHNIQUES?   240

CHAPTER 95   SAVING MONEY IS CRITICAL FOR
BUILDING WEALTH   242

CHAPTER 96   SAVING MONEY: THE ULTIMATE SAVINGS
TOOL IS THE 401K/403B/TSP   243

CHAPTER 97   SAVING MONEY: IF PRACTICABLE, PICK A
LOW TAX STATE TO LIVE AND WORK IN   244

CHAPTER 98   SAVING MONEY: CARS ARE THE SINGLE
BIGGEST MONEY SINK   246

CHAPTER 99   SAVING MONEY: BUY A HOUSE WHEN THE
TIMING IS RIGHT   249

CHAPTER 100   SAVING MONEY: THE EFFECT OF
MARRIAGE AND DIVORCE ON WEALTH BUILDING   250

CHAPTER 101   SAVING MONEY: DON'T MARRY A BIG SPENDER   254

CHAPTER 102   SAVING MONEY: WHAT IF I AM ALREADY MARRIED TO A BIG SPENDER?   255

CHAPTER 103   SAVING MONEY: DON'T PAY TOO MUCH FOR COLLEGE   256

CHAPTER 104   SAVING MONEY: SAVING FOR COLLEGE USING COVERDELL ESA ACCOUNTS AND 529 COLLEGE SAVINGS PLANS   259

CHAPTER 105   SAVING MONEY: DO IT YOURSELF WHEN IT COMES TO HOME MAINTENANCE   261

CHAPTER 106   SAVING MONEY: THE COST OF SMOKING
                                                                                                                         263

CHAPTER 107   SAVING MONEY: PACK A LUNCH   264

CHAPTER 108   SAVING MONEY: ATTENTION COFFEE DRINKERS   265

CHAPTER 109   SAVING MONEY: EATING OUT   266

CHAPTER 110   SAVING MONEY: THE COST OF GOING OUT TO THE MOVIES   267

CHAPTER 111   SAVING MONEY: THE CLUB SCENE   268

CHAPTER 112   SAVING MONEY: VACATIONS   269

CHAPTER 113   SAVING MONEY: DON'T CHEAT ON YOUR INCOME TAXES   270

12

CHAPTER 114   SAVING MONEY: LIFE INSURANCE   271

CHAPTER 115   SAVING MONEY: DON'T BE AN
UPGRADER   272

CHAPTER 116   SAVING MONEY: GYM/CLUB
MEMBERSHIPS   273

CHAPTER 117   SAVING MONEY: ADDITIONS AND OTHER
HOME IMPROVEMENT PROJECTS   274

CHAPTER 118   SAVING MONEY: CHANGE YOUR LIFE
PHILOSOPHY   275

CHAPTER 119   SAVING MONEY: HOME EQUITY LOANS
                                                   277

CHAPTER 120   SAVING MONEY: IF YOU LACK
DISCIPLINE, GET RID OF YOUR CREDIT CARDS   278

CHAPTER 121   SAVING MONEY: DON'T REPLACE A
CAR/HEATING SYSTEM/CENTRAL
AIR/REFRIGERATOR/ROOM AIR CONDITIONER/ETC. THAT
IS STILL OPERATING FINE WITH A MORE ENERGY
EFFICIENT MODEL   279

CHAPTER 122   SAVING MONEY: BEFORE YOU BUY
ANYTHING, ALWAYS CHECK ONLINE FIRST   280

CHAPTER 123   SAVING MONEY: BUYING GROCERIES 281

CHAPTER 124   SAVING MONEY: CLOTHES   282

CHAPTER 125   SAVING MONEY: DON'T WASTE MONEY
ON ENERGY BILLS   283

CHAPTER 126   SAVING MONEY: BARTER WITH
TELECOMMUNICATION COMPANIES   284

CHAPTER 127   SAVING MONEY: CHANGE ELECTRICITY
PROVIDERS   285

CHAPTER 128   SAVING MONEY: DRAW UP A BUDGET 286

CHAPTER 129   SAVING MONEY: DON'T SPEED   287

CHAPTER 130   SAVING MONEY: WATCH OUT FOR
CAMERAS AT INTERSECTIONS AND ON HIGHWAYS   289

CHAPTER 131   SAVING MONEY: ATTENDING PRO
SPORTS GAMES   290

CHAPTER 132   SAVING MONEY: NEVER PAY TOO MUCH
FOR ANYTHING   292

CHAPTER 133   SUMMARY OF MY STOCK INVESTING
RETURNS   293

CHAPTER 134   EPILOGUE   294

BACK COVER OF BOOK   296

14

Foreword

This book will set you on the path towards achieving financial independence. It is for both the beginner and the experienced investor who has been burned in investing by using popular but foolish methods that treat investing as if it were a game. This book is unique because it is the only book that addresses how to build wealth over time with techniques for saving money and investing in stocks using *Fundamental Stock Investing*. Stop wasting time and negative emotional energy complaining about the so called "One Percenters" and start working towards financial independence!

Fundamental Stock Investing which is defined as buying stocks as if you were buying a business, is a simple and common sense method that is vastly superior over the long haul as proven by investing legends Warren Buffett, who became the richest man in the world, and Peter Lynch, who averaged staggering 29.2% annual returns over a 13 year period and beat the S&P 500 by an average of 13.4 percentage points per year during that period. That 29.2% remains unprecedented for any money manager over such a long period of time. Using *Fundamental Stock Investing* the past 15 years, I have averaged 16.1% annual returns versus 3.1% for the S&P 500, also beating the index by 13 percentage points per year. Not only that, because the method generally involves holding stocks for longer time periods, transactions costs are lower but most importantly gains are taxed at much lower rates and the gains are also deferred, all of which results in much higher increases in wealth than the official gains compared to ALL other investing methods. There are many systems you can use to make money in stocks but when you combine the returns with the huge tax advantages, *Fundamental Stock Investing* becomes the superior method. It is also the simplest and easiest to learn method and the only method that uses common sense. What is unique about this book is that it also explains how you must combine savings with successful stock investing to build significant wealth over the long haul and it outlines critical techniques to save money so you have more to invest. This book will set you on the path towards achieving financial independence.

The reason *Fundamental Stock Investing* works so well is it is the only method that attempts to correlate a company's future profits (over the next 1-3 years) to the current stock price and determines if the stock is cheap, fairly valued or overpriced. In fact, it uses the exact criteria one would use when deciding if you were going to buy a business or not. It is the only method that makes actual business sense. In the short run anything can and will happen to a company's stock price, but in the long run a company's stock price correlates exactly with its profits. This difference between a stock's price in the short run and the long run is where you make money by *Fundamental Stock Investing*.

Here is why the other methods are inferior. The *Price and Earnings Momentum* method completely ignores price. Who would buy a company while ignoring the price it is selling for? *Technical Analysis* is studying charts and graphs of stock prices and completely ignores how the actual business is doing and ignores the price! Who would buy a company while ignoring how the business is doing and the price it is selling for?! The *Options* method is treating stock investing as if you were playing a game and is essentially gambling. The *Price Momentum* method also ignores both how the business is doing and the price. The *CANSLIM* method ignores price and tries to time the stock market and tries to use technical analysis with some fundamental analysis simultaneously that has you constantly jumping in and out of the market and in and out of stocks suffering endless stop losses in the hope you might catch a big momentum winner to make up for all the constant losses from jumping in and out of the market and in and out of stocks. The *Buy And Hold Forever* method is like buying a business and then never once checking on how the business is actually doing for the rest of your life. How dumb is that? The *Value Investing* method does consider price but ignores how the company is actually doing and the future prospects for the company. The *Hedging* method attempts to balance investing long in stocks with short investing against stocks which almost guarantees mediocre or worse returns which explains the horrendous performance by Hedge Funds the past 5 years. None of these methods make any "business sense".

Fundamental Stock Investing makes perfect business sense and that combined with the huge tax advantages, it is always superior to all other methods over the long run. While other methods come in and out of favor, *Fundamental Stock Investing* is ageless because it treats stock investing as if you were actually buying a business.

- John Molvar

John Molvar is also the co-author of:

THE YOUTH AND TEEN RUNNING ENCYCLOPEDIA

http://www.amazon.com/dp/B00AG7CXJ8

Disclaimer

Before following any advice in this book, you need to have a certified financial advisor review your financial situation and you should first clear any investment decisions you make based on this book with your financial advisor.

Chapter 1 To Build Wealth You Must Invest And Save

To build wealth you must invest and save. Doing one without the other will fail to build significant wealth over time. I know of many great savers who live off of a remarkably small amount of money and save the rest. The problem is without investing this savings, they can't build wealth over time. The interest on their savings account has always been and always will be below the rate of inflation. Therefore their real rate of return is always going to be negative, meaning the value of their hard earned savings is going down each year so they never get anywhere as far as wealth building. You can admire their thriftiness and their tenacious saving techniques and even copy some of them, but without investing they won't build wealth.

Conversely I know of many very good investors who fail to build significant wealth. The reason is simply that they are not saving enough money to have enough to invest to reach a critical mass such that they really start building wealth. Many of them blow any investment gains by taking the profits and spending it as soon as they make it. Others never have enough savings to begin with.

You must use a combination of saving and investing to build significant wealth. One without the other won't work very well. Fantastic, yet simple and easy to follow saving techniques are outlined in the second half of the book.

Chapter 2   Why Invest Instead Of "Starting My Own Business"?

Most of the very richest people in the world got that way by successfully starting their own business, growing that business by leaps and bounds over a very long time and eventually becoming a publicly traded stock company and at some point seeing their stock rise to an astronomical level. This is how you get on the **Forbes 400 Richest People In America** list. Additionally, hundreds of thousands of Americans have become rich by successfully starting their own business. If you want to build wealth fairly rapidly and successfully, starting your own business is the best and fastest way to do it.

So why am I here advocating investing instead of starting your own business? The reason is simply that a sizable minority of people can successfully build significant wealth by investing, whereas only a tiny percentage of people can successfully start their own business. Your odds of succeeding as an investor are over 100 times better than succeeding at starting your own business.

If you are one of the tiny, tiny percentage of Americans capable of starting up a successful business, by all means go for it. In fact, this freedom to start one's own business is what has made America the greatest and richest nation on earth and we all are blessed to have a system that allowed these remarkable people to succeed and the rest of us to benefit from all the great products and services and jobs they have provided the rest of us. In addition, the rest of us are able to invest in the public companies these people created by buying stock so we too can reap some of the rewards of their success.

The simple fact is that most people lack the talent, the drive, the disciplined focus, the willingness to work extraordinarily hard and long hours over years and even decades, the courage, the sacrifice, the entrepreneurial skill, the ability to secure start-up money and often being in the right era at the right time and at the right location to succeed. If you lack any of those attributes, you are likely doomed. Indeed, this is why up to 70% of all start-up businesses fail within the first 2 years and 75% of restaurants (the most often tried start up business) fail within the first 5 years.

You will often hear extraordinarily talented/successful people such as Steve Jobs and Bill Gates and Warren Buffett telling you to pursue your passion. That is great advice if you happen to have that one in a million talent in the field you are passionate about or have a very wealthy relative funding the pursuit of your passion, but for the vast majority of us, pursing our passion as a main career is disastrously costly for us economically both in actual cost and time/opportunity cost lost. The majority of us are far better off working in practical fields while pursing our passions on the side as hobbies if time permits or pursing them AFTER we have built sufficient wealth.

The odds of succeeding at investing are far greater than starting your own business, especially through *Fundamental Stock Investing*, although you must possess some personal qualities to succeed that are outlined in **Chapter 4**. Therefore be aware that not everyone can make it at investing, although a sizable minority of the population is capable of doing it.

Chapter 3   Why Stocks Are The Best Form Of Investing Over The Long Haul

Stocks are the best method of investing over the long term. Over and over the data confirms this although we are talking the long haul. Here are the long term average annual returns of various investments from 1926 to 2013.

Long Term Investment Returns

Small Stocks	12%
Large Stocks	10%
Real Estate	4-8% *
Long Term Bonds	5.7%
Short term Treasuries	3.5%
Inflation	3.0%
Cash	2.5%

* A range is given for real estate because most studies and most experts vary widely on the long term average return for real estate due to the fact that there are so many variables to factor in.

Therefore, you want to be invested in stocks over the long term because of the incredible power of **compound interest**.

Here is what 1 dollar would have grown to in the various investments over that time period:

Small Stocks	$19000
Large Stocks	$4000
Real Estate	$160
Long Term Bonds	$125
Short term Treasuries	$20
Inflation	$13
Cash	$9

As you can see, a 1 or 2 percentage point advantage can result in a huge wealth building increase over the long haul due to the power of compound interest. Granted over shorter time frames i.e. less than 10 years, other investments have and will continue to outperform stocks, but over the long term, stocks will always win out. So if your goal is to build wealth over the long haul, which this book is all about, you must have the vast majority of your investment money in stocks most of the time.

Even in the 19th Century stocks were also the place to be. According to a study by Goetzsmann, Ibbotson and Peng, estimated average annual total returns for stocks for the 100 year period from 1825 to 1925 were between 6.0% and 8.5%. Therefore, for nearly 200 years, stocks have been the best long term investment.

Need further proof, just look at the Forbes 400 Richest People In America list and you will find the list is dominated by people who invested in stock in their own company or other companies and they did it over a very long period of time. As the above data indicates, you will also find some people in real estate on that list because it is generally the second best form of investing, but note that no one in the top 30 got there via real estate. Also note that no one made the top 400 via investing in bonds.

Chapter 4   What Personal Traits Are Necessary To Make It In Stock Investing?

This is a critical point in the book. Right now you need to honestly assess your personal traits to determine if you can make it as a stock investor. You should also ask some people who know you well to independently assess your personal traits to make sure you are being objective enough to make the correct decision. While a sizable minority of the population (i.e. tens and tens of millions of Americans) armed with the right knowledge can succeed, a lot of people cannot succeed if they don't possess the right qualities. If you do not possess the right qualities, you should not be investing in stocks or stock funds and should pursue other avenues to build wealth.

Here are the qualities:

1) Patience - To build wealth by investing literally takes years. You have to have the patience to recognize this and commit yourself to it for the rest of your life or until you feel you have made enough money. This is not a get rich quick scheme. No get rich quick schemes work. It you want to get rich quick, you need to make it in one of the following fields (with the percentage odds of success at making it rich in the field):

Lottery Winner	0.0018%
Successful Gambler	0.05%
Pro Athlete	0.03% basketball, 0.1% hockey, 0.08% football, 0.6% baseball
Actor	0.013%
Music Pop Star	0.01%
Struck by Lightening	0.03%

When using *Fundamental Stock Investing*, you will encounter long periods where the stock market goes nowhere or even goes down and the same for individual stocks you own and you must have the patience to stick with stocks (when appropriate as described later in the book) over long periods of time. If you don't have this type of patience, you won't make it in stocks.

2) **Ability To Ignore What Everyone Else Is Doing** - You must be your own person and not a follower. You have to forever ignore the non-stop deafening roar of what other people are saying about individual stocks, the stock market, interest rates, what the Fed might do, the price of oil and the direction of the economy. You must ignore all "experts" and their stock market predictions, their individual stock picks, their upgrades and downgrades of stocks, their economic forecasts, their interest rate predictions, their price of oil and other commodity predictions, etc. You need to do your own stock research (which this book will show you is much easier than the experts make it out to be) and ignore everyone else, including those so called "experts" you see on business channels, read about in newspapers and on the internet and on message boards and hear on the radio, etc. If you can't ignore everyone else, you won't make it in investing.

3) **Humility** - You must be able to admit when you are wrong and sell (or buy) stocks when necessary. If 5 out of 10 stocks you buy end up making money, you will make money in stocks and it will be profitable for you over the long haul. If 6 out of 10 of the stocks you buy end up making money for you, you will be very successful at stock investing and make a lot of money over the long haul. If 7 out of 10 of your picks make it, you will make a ton of money. What does this mean? If you are the best of the best, you are still going to be wrong at least 30% of time. That is a lot of mistakes and you have to admit every one of them by selling when it becomes apparent. If you don't have the humility to admit your mistakes over and over again, you won't make it in investing. If you are a "perfectionist", you will never be able to deal with the 30-40% failure rate that comes with successful individual stock investing and you should not go near stock investing.

4) **Toughness** - You must be tough enough to endure the pain of losses and the pain of a declining stock market. Many people can follow the simple rules of *Fundamental Stock Investing* and cite them by heart after reading this book, but when the real life action begins and the stock market declines, if you can't take the pain and get scared out (usually right at the bottom), you will never make it as a stock investor. Similarly, if you cannot take the pain and humility of being wrong 30-40% of the time, you will not make it at individual stock picking.

5) Decisiveness - When using *Fundamental Stock Investing*, you won't be doing as much buying and selling of stock as all other methods, but when appropriate to buy and sell, you must be decisive and act. If you have trouble making decisions like this, and a lot of people do, you won't make it in individual stock investing. The combination of being decisive when required and patient when required are seemingly contradictory personal traits that will eliminate many people from being able to make it in individual stock investing.

6) Ability To Make Decisions With Imperfect Information - You must be able to buy or sell stocks based on following the simple rules of this book, but always with imperfect information. By the time everything is known about a company, all the money has already been made or lost in the stock. If you are the type who needs to know EVERYTHING before you act, you won't make it in stock investing. That is not to say don't research stocks following all the rules of this book, but I am pointing out that the information will never be perfect.

7) Will You Need This Money Within The Next 5 Years? - Stocks are by far the best investment over the long term. However, anything can and will happen within any given 5 year period. If you need the money within the next 5 years, you could buy right before a major Bear Market decline of 20-50% and then need to pull out of stocks with a huge loss and spend the money on something else and not benefit from the ultimate recovery of the market. Therefore, no money that you will need within the next five years should be invested in stocks or stock funds.

8) Can You Emotionally Handle A Big Stock Market Decline? - There have been 205 stock market declines of 5% or more since 1926. There have been 44 stock market "**corrections**" (defined as a 10% decline in the S&P 500) since 1926. There have been 16 **Bear Markets** (defined as a 20% or greater decline in the S&P 500) since 1926. There have been 5 "**Stock Market Collapses**" (defined as a 40% or greater decline in the S&P 500) since 1926. For 100% of these declines, stocks have always come back and ultimately gone higher. But if you panic and abandon stocks during these scary times, you will get killed investing in stocks. If you don't have the stomach to ride these declines out (and buy more when stocks are way down), you won't

make it in stock investing. Every one of these Bear Markets and Stock Market Collapses have been scary and they are assigned scary reasons for the decline (after the fact) and when they are happening everything will be doom and gloom with no end in sight and every time you will hear "experts" saying "this time it is different and it won't ever come back" and they will sound convincing. At what turned out to be the bottom of every one of these scary events, there were multiple "experts" sounding very convincing and saying that the market would continue to fall much further. Do you have the emotional might to ignore these people? Before you start investing in stocks, you must know the answer to that question. When you start investing, a Correction will almost certainly happen within the first 3 years or so, a Bear Market will happen within 8 years or so and a Market Collapse will happen sometime within 20 years and you and everyone else won't see it coming. Count on it. But before you invest, you must ask yourself if you will be able to handle it emotionally when it actually is happening to you.

In summary, you need to possess all of the 8 above qualities to make it in stock investing. You don't have to be a superhero in all of them, but you need to possess all of them to some degree. If not, you are better off not investing in stocks.

Chapter 5   Should I Go With Individual Stocks Or With Funds?

If you posses all the qualities outlined in chapter 4, you should go with investing in individual stocks because you will likely outperform most fund managers and the market over the long haul following the simple rules of this book. As we saw earlier, even outperforming by an average of 1-2 percentage points per year can make a huge difference in wealth accumulation over a long period of time.

To make it in Hedge Funds or Stock Mutual Funds or Exchange Traded Funds, you don't have to possess all 8 of the qualities that an individual stock investor requires, but you need to possess numbers 1 (Patience), 2 (Ability To Ignore What Everyone Else Is Doing), 4 (Toughness), and especially 7 (not needing the money in the next 5 years) and 8 (Emotionally handling a big stock market decline). Review these qualities in **Chapter 4**. If you posses these qualities, you can make it as a stock fund investor. Later in the book I cover on how to pick funds. If you don't possess these qualities, you need to forget about any form of stock investing at all because you won't succeed.

Chapter 6   Before Investing In Stocks, Step 1: Consider Buying A Home

Unlike most stock investing books, this book is also about how to build wealth and also how to save money.

The number one obstacle to wealth building is taxes and close behind as number two is the inability to control reckless spending habits which will be discussed later in the book. To build wealth, you must use every legal means to minimize your taxes because your returns will be greatly reduced by taxes if you fail to do so. In America, home ownership is massively subsidized by the government by huge tax breaks. At some point you need to take advantage of this huge tax saving. All other investments are taxed as heavily as possible, but in most cases you can buy and sell your home for a profit and pay no taxes. Furthermore, the government also subsidizes home ownership by allowing you to deduct the mortgage interest, i.e. the interest is **tax deductible**. Additionally, as noted earlier in the book, real estate appreciates at an average rate of 4-8% per year over the very long term which is a good rate of return. Finally, in periods of high inflation, real estate is usually the best performing investment. So if you don't already own a home, you should eventually buy one as part of your overall wealth building strategy. To succeed as a home owner, you need to buy at the right time by following a couple of simple rules.

Before buying a house, the single most important thing to do is determine where we are in the real estate cycle. Real Estate goes up for many years in a row, followed by a cyclical decline of a couple years and then the next up cycle begins again. Real estate down cycles tend to coincide with recessions but not always. Simply put, you want to buy your home (or upgrade to a more expensive house) right after we have been in a down cycle for 2 years. You don't want to buy a house when we have been in an up cycle for more than 4 years in a row, because it is impossible to predict when the real estate market will top so you may end up "buying at the top" just before the next downturn and soon be "**underwater**", meaning you will owe more on your mortgage than the house is worth and be unable to sell if you need to.

So how do you know what part of the real estate cycle are we in? You can never know exactly where we are or time the top or bottom, but you can estimate as explained below by using a couple of simple rules that will shift the odds of success greatly in your favor.

Rule 1: Don't buy real estate when we have been in an up cycle for 4 or more years. Wait until after the next down cycle.

Rule 2: Buy real estate after we have been in a down cycle for 2 years. Buy as soon as possible after the 2 year mark.

Let's look at past real estate cycles and see how this strategy worked in real life the past 55 years.

1960-1961 Down cycle. After 2 years would be 1962, so buy real estate from 1962-1965. Don't buy real estate from 1966 until 2 years after beginning of next down cycle. Strategy worked extremely well, as real estate market peaked in 1968.

1962-1968 Up Cycle

1969-1970 Down cycle. After 2 years would be 1971, so buy real estate from 1971-1974. Don't buy real estate from 1975 until 2 years after beginning of next down cycle. Strategy worked just ok because if you waited until 1974 to buy, you ended up buying at the top. However, if you didn't sell during the downturn, the runaway inflation of the 1970s, combined with the next recovery, caused your house to nearly double in value in just 5 years, while your mortgage remained the same.

1971-1973 Up cycle

1974-1975 Down cycle. After 2 years would be 1976, so buy real estate from 1976-1979. Don't buy real estate from 1980 until 2 years after beginning of next down cycle. Strategy worked just ok because if you waited to buy until 1979, you ended up buying near the 1980 top. However, if you didn't sell during the downturn, inflation combined with the 1980s boom caused your house to nearly double in value by 1988, while your mortgage remained the same.

1976-1980 Up cycle

1981-1982 Down cycle. After 2 years would be 1983, so buy real estate from 1983-1986. Don't buy real estate from 1987 until 2 years after beginning of next down cycle. Strategy worked perfectly, as real estate market peaked in 1988.

1983-1988 Up cycle

1989-1990 Down cycle. After 2 years would be 1991, so buy real estate from 1991-1994. Don't buy real estate from 1995 until 2 years after beginning of next down cycle. Strategy worked extremely well for those who bought during 1991-1994, as they saw their home prices soar almost uninterrupted until 2007. However, prices continued to rise from 1995 through 2000, so you still could have bought real estate between 1996 and 1998 and done well, as this turned out to be the longest up cycle for real estate in US history.

1991-2000 Up cycle

2001 Down cycle. After 2 years would be 2003, so buy real estate from 2003-2006. Don't buy real estate from 2007 until 2 years after beginning of next down cycle. Strategy worked fairly well. The 2001 down cycle only lasted 1 year compared to the normal 2 years and was very mild and home prices only declined slightly, so you actually could have bought in 2002 and that would have been the best year to buy and not wait until 2003. If you bought from 2003 through 2005 you saw massive appreciation in your home value. However, if you bought in 2006, you bought just 1 year from the top and therefore didn't make out that well, especially if you needed to sell in 2008 or 2009.

2002-2007 Up cycle

2008-2009 Down cycle. After 2 years would be 2010, so buy real estate from 2010-2013. Don't buy real estate from 2014 until 2 years after beginning of next down cycle. Strategy has worked perfectly so far as 2010-2012 turned out to be a fantastic time to buy real estate. According to the strategy, 2013 is the last safe year to buy real estate, because the odds of the next downturn grow with each passing year after 2013. Time will tell.

2010-2013+ Up cycle

As you can see from the above real world data, the strategy works fairly well but is not perfect, because no one can predict the end of a real estate up cycle (or for that matter an economic up cycle or stock market up cycle). It definitely increases your odds of success if you buy as soon as possible after the end of the 2 year period from the beginning of the downturn. In this current cycle, you should have been buying real estate in early 2010. After 2013, your odds of succeeding at buying a house starts going down and the odds get worse with each passing year.

The best indicator of the beginning of the next downturn is when the **National Bureau of Economic Research** declares a start date of a recession. Usually they declare the start many months after it actually occurs but that is ok, because when you get that date, simply add 2 years to that date and you will have close to the ideal time to buy real estate and it is usually still good to buy for the first 4 years after that time.

There are a few more secondary rules you need to know before buying real estate:

Rule 3: Ignore What Everyone Else Is Doing And Saying Regarding Real Estate. As with stocks, you must be your own person and not a follower. You have to forever ignore the non-stop deafening roar of what other people are saying about real estate, interest rates, and the economy. You must ignore all "experts" and their real estate cycle predictions, their economic forecasts, their interest rate predictions, etc. You need to simply follow Rules 1 & 2 above and ignore everyone else including those so called "experts" you see on business channels, read about on the internet and in newspapers, hear on the radio, etc. If you can't do this, you will be too scared to buy at the bottom of the real estate cycle and will buy at the top of the real estate cycle and be convinced the up real estate cycle will go on forever.

Remember, no one knows when the cycle bottoms and when it tops. There is no bell that goes off and says "this is the bottom" and "this is the top". We only know the bottom and the top well after the fact when it is too late. Keep in mind the following contradictory signals. At the bottom, all the real estate data, news and headlines will be horrible and most "experts" will be saying the bad times will go on forever. At the top, all real estate data, news and headlines will be great and most "experts" will be predicting "several more good years". At the bottom, when it is best to buy, here is what the headlines will be saying:

- "Real Estate Prices Down For The 15th Month In A Row"
- "New Home Starts At Lowest Level In 6 Years"
- "Foreclosures Hit Record Level"
- "Why It Makes Much More Sense To Rent"
- "This Housing Downturn Is Different"
- "New Restrictive Lending Requirements Keeping First Time Buyers Out"
- "Real Estate Expert Sees No End To Downturn"
- "You Can No Longer Think Of Homeownership As An Investment, Just A Place To Live"
- "Mortgage Meltdown Threatens Very Survival Of Many Banks"
- "Americans Starting Household Formation Later Bodes Poorly For Real Estate"

At the top, when you definitely don't want to be buying, here is what the headlines will be saying:

- "New Home Starts Reach Record Level"
- "Real Estate Prices Rise For 5th Consecutive Year"
- "Homebuilders Trying To Cope With Shortage Of Buildable Lots"
- "Expert Says We Are Only In The 3rd Inning Of Housing Boom"
- "Why Homeownership Is The Perfect Investment"
- "Best Selling Author Of 'How To Flip Real Estate In 90 Days' "
- "Why Renting Is Just Throwing Away Money"
- "Banks Now Offering 40 Year Loans And Other Innovative New Lending Products"
- "Above Asking Price Deals Are The New Normal"
- "Demographic Trends Mean Housing Boom Can Last Much Longer This Time"

As you can see above, you can't be a follower and you need to ignore the noise and be your own person. For instance, following the Rule 2 above you would have bought real estate in 2010. Meanwhile in 2009 after big declines in real estate prices, an Ivy League professor who is considered one of the top real estate "experts" in America, predicted a further 33% catastrophic collapse of real estate prices from 2009 to 2014 to validate his personal theory that over the long term real estate doesn't appreciate at all when factoring in inflation. What really happened? Instead of falling 33% as he predicted, real estate prices confounded the "experts" and proceeded to rise 25% between 2009 and 2013.

Rule 4: Do not buy real estate in any jurisdiction that has above average property taxes. Again, taxes are the number one obstacle to wealth creation and you don't want your real estate gains eaten away year after year by a huge property tax bill.

Nearly 100% of cities in America have given unsustainable contracts to public employee unions in wages and benefits, especially retirement benefits over the past 60 years. If you have any doubt about this, simply type in "unsustainable public employee benefits" in your search engine and you will get links to over 1000 articles from all across the USA explaining the unsustainable nature of these benefits in city after city. Although these benefits are unsustainable, politicians will never try to tackle this issue and instead will try to put off the day of reckoning as long as possible by massive increases in property taxes, special assessments, overrides of laws capping rates, higher property value assessments, higher water/sewer fees, new and higher user and service fees, increases in traffic fines and increase in writing of fines, installation of traffic fine cameras at traffic lights and on highways, etc. to collect more and more revenue by any means possible. As I am writing this, I just got hit with a whopping 9% increase in my property taxes despite the fact that we have been in a low inflation and anemic growth environment for years.

No matter where you live in America, expect huge increases in local taxes, fees and fines over the next several years. Therefore, it is critical that you buy real estate in a city that is starting at a much lower overall taxes/fees base compared to the average city. If you don't, any profit you make on your home will be eaten away by ever increasing taxes, services fees, fines, etc.

Also don't go by rates and city assessments, as city politicians play all kinds of games to mask the true cost of taxes. Simply determine the full actual annual tax bill including all "special assessments" and "overrides" and compare it to what the property is worth on the open market, i.e. what is could actually sell for right now. Also find out the current annual water/sewer bill, trash collection bill, etc. and include all those in the total as that is just another game politicians use by issuing separate bills to hide the true overall tax bill.

Rule 5:

Do not buy real estate in an area with exceptionally high property insurance costs. This includes property in flood zones, hurricane zones, tornado zones, high crime zones, etc. A huge insurance bill year after year will wipe out any profits you can expect to make on your real estate.

Rule 6:

Watch out for high maintenance costs. If you plan on doing none of the work yourself, forget about making any money through real estate. If you hire people to cut lawns and do landscaping and clean your house, shovel snow, maintain a pool, do all repairs etc., those costs can pile up year after year and wipe out any profits you make on owning a home. Also, if you do none of the work yourself and are in a high blue collar labor cost area, those renovations, "new kitchens" and additions you put on "to increase the value of your home" will cost way more than any actual increase in the value of your home.

Rule 7:

Don't buy real estate in a "Company Town". By Company Town I mean a city where a major plant or factory or government installation or military base is located in which a large portion of the population generates their income from working at the facility and/or from selling products and services to the facility. If the company suddenly has a major layoff, goes under or relocates the plant overseas or into a cheaper Red State or the government moves the facility or closes the base, this can devastate property values for years and even decades to come. It is safer to extend your commute and buy a home a few cities away from the facility. The last thing you need is to lose your job AND have your home value collapse simultaneously, a fate millions of short sighted Americans have experienced over and over again.

Rule 8:

Once you know you are buying at the right time following Rules 1 & 2, and considering rules 3 through 7, to pick out a specific house to buy, you need to then follow general real estate rules on home buying such as location-location-location, not buying the most expensive house on the street, consider buying a duplex and triplex and renting out the units you are not living in, never buying a condominium unless you can hit the ocean/lake with rock thrown from the roof of the condo, etc. These general real estate rules are outside of the scope of this book and you need to learn them from other sources. Of course do not buy such an expensive house that you have no money left over for savings and investments. In fact if you have 2 incomes it may be prudent to buy a house in which you can make the mortgage payment with only 1 income in case one of you loses their job.

Chapter 7   Before Investing In Stocks In A Taxable Account, Step 2: Get The Maximum Matching Funds From Your 401k/403b/TSP Plan

If the place you work for offers a **401k/403b/TSP** plan, put at least as much into your 401k/403b/TSP plan as necessary to get all the matching funds. For example, with the Federal Thrift Savings Plan (TSP), if you put in at least 5%, they will match another 5%, plus the 1% automatic contribution for a total of 6%. The reason is a no-brainer. They are handing you free money! Not only that, it grows tax free (**sheltered**) so you pay no taxes until you retire and start taking the money out. Not only that, your contributions are **tax deductible** so you make a 30% profit right off the bat in typical Federal (25%) and typical state tax (5%) savings. When looking for a job, one of the highest priorities should always be taking a job with an outstanding 401k/403b/TSP plan. You want a plan that matches at least up to 3% and up to 6% is awesome. You also want no limits on how much you can contribute (up to the IRS limit which was $17,500 in 2014 and $23,000 for those over age 50). A superior plan is far more important over the long run than small or even moderate differences in salary. Where you put the money within your plan is discussed in a later chapter. If you have a job that doesn't have a plan, then use the IRA as your primary savings vehicle per **Chapter 10**.

Also remember, if you leave a job, don't get the money as cash, have it transferred into a **Rollover Individual Retirement Account (IRA)**. There are two reasons. If you don't put it in an IRA, the government will take 10% of it off the top. The second reason is that your money will continue to grow tax free in the Rollover IRA. Also, a Rollover IRA has unlimited investing options including investing in individual stocks, compared to leaving it in a 401k/403b/TSP which is limited to the options offered by your employer.

Also note, many plans have a **vesting requirement** that means the minimum time you have to stay with the job to keep the matching funds when you leave. Before taking a new job and before deciding to leave a job voluntarily, carefully review your plan's vesting requirements and stay on the job at least long enough to be vested.

Chapter 8   Before Investing In Stocks In A Taxable Account, Step 3: Eliminate Credit Card Debt

If you are carrying over a credit card debt balance from month to month, you need to focus next on this with your money. You also need to incorporate the savings methods outlined in the second half of the book to get your spending under control. The ideal is to have a card with a grace period and that has no annual fee and pay for everything with a credit card and pay it off at the end of the month so you pay no finance charge. If you do this, get a card that pays you back such as Discover or USAA MasterCard, which give you 1% back on all your purchases. If you are not paying it off at the end of the month you need to consider 3 options.

The first one is to tear up the card if you have a spending problem and cut back on spending by following every savings technique outlined later in this book and pay the thing off even if it takes years. The reason is that they are charging you 10-24% in interest (14.9% was the average rate in 2013) and you cannot expect to make that on investments. So any extra cash should be used to pay it off instead of investing that money. Also, you need to find the lowest interest rate you can get and transfer to that card. They vary widely in rates but you have to read the fine print.

A second option is to play the "new card every 6 months game". What you can do is keep transferring to a new card that offers 6 months of zero finance AND continue to pay it off. Beware of course of the **Balance Transfer Fee**, which could be so high that it is not worth transferring. Also, some of these cards only offer zero percent on the transferred balance and charge outrageously high interest rates on new purchases. Also, the switching game can hurt your credit rating which may make it hard to get a loan down the road. Of course if you don't remember to transfer to a new card, the rates after 6 months are outrageous so this is a tricky game so watch out.

The third option is to tear up the card and if possible get a home equity loan to pay off the credit card. There are two advantages; the rate will be much lower (for example 6% compared to 15%) and you can deduct the interest because it is a home loan, so the after tax rate is close to 4%. The main thing of course is to get your spending under control and the second half of this book is loaded with saving methods.

Chapter 9   Before Investing In Stocks In A Taxable Account, Step 4: Put Maximum Allowable Into Your 401k/403b/TSP Plan

If you have any money left over, put the maximum allowable or as much as you can afford into your 401k/403b/TSP. In 2014 the Federal pre-tax limit was $17,500 and $23,000 if over age 50. There are two reasons. Firstly, any contributions you make are tax deductible. So say you make $40,000 a year and you put $2000 into your TSP, you will be taxed as if you only make $38,000 that year. Suppose the money you invested gets a return of only 1% in the first year. You actually gained 31% on your investment! How? A 1% gain, plus the typical 25% saved in Federal taxes and the typical 5% saved in state taxes for a total gain of 31%. You will likely never make enough in a taxable account to overcome the first year 30% advantage of new money put into your plan. The second reason is that any gains you make over the years will grow tax free until you withdraw it when you retire.

Another great advantage of these plans over pensions is you can change jobs often and can always transfer the money into a new plan or preferably put the money into a Rollover IRA. You could have many different jobs in your career and yet be constantly building your nest egg. On the other hand, if you leave a job with a pension it is disastrous from a retirement wealth building standpoint in lost money and lost time in retirement wealth building and the longer you stay in a job with a pension the worse the consequences if you leave or are forced to leave before you are eligible to collect a pension.

NEVER take a loan from your plan. This is defeating everything you are trying to accomplish in your wealth building quest.

Over the years, the limit on contributions has been raised and is now $17,500 (and $23,000 for those over age 50).   Many lower income workers cannot afford to put the maximum into their 401k. If this is the case, it means you won't have any extra cash to invest in individual stocks via an IRA or a taxable account. That is ok though because a 401k/403b/TSP can be a powerful wealth builder. For example, If you make $40,000 per year in a job that has a good plan and you contribute 7% of your pay per year ($2,800) to your plan and your company matches 6% and you earn an average annual return of 10% per year (the long term average return of stocks since 1926), and you start at age 21, you will have a million dollars in your plan by age 52. The fact that someone making a relatively modest salary can become a millionaire by age 52 shows you how critically important it is to take advantage of your employer's retirement plan. The initial typical 30% gain you make due to the Federal and state tax deductibility is nearly impossible to overcome by doing individual stocks in a taxable account. That is why you want to fund your 401k/403b/TSP as much as possible first. Also note when you leave a job and rollover your (vested) 401k/403b/TSP money into a Rollover IRA, you will then be able to invest in individual stocks in that Rollover IRA.

Type in your search engine "**401k retirement calculator**" and a long list of these calculators are available on the internet and you should bookmark one in your favorites and frequently use these to see the possibilities and also so that you become aware of the amazing power of **tax free compound interest wealth building**.

Here is a stunning example of how powerful of a wealth building tool this can be. A family member of mine started work in 1989 as an engineer until she got laid off in 1996. From 1996 through 1999 she worked as a mailman. All during this time she put the maximum amount allowable into her plan, which is much lower than current maximum limits. When she quit working in 1999, she transferred it into a Rollover IRA. Despite only working 10 years and never contributing again after that 10 years of work, her Rollover IRA was worth $640,000 at the end of 2013. All this despite the fact that 2 of the 5 Stock Market Collapses since 1926 happened during that time span. The power of the free matching funds, the tax deduction from Federal and state taxes, the tax sheltering of gains until retirement and the power of compound interest when investing in stocks over the long term is a potent combination and should never be underestimated.

I recommend using the traditional 401k/403b/TSP over the **Roth 401k/403b/TSP**. The traditional 401k/403b/TSP is pre-tax money so it is tax deductible. The Roth 401k/403b/TSP is after taxes so is not deductible. The advantage of the Roth 401k/403b/TSP is that you pay no taxes when you withdraw the money. As stated repeatedly throughout this book, taxes are the number one obstacle to wealth creation and you always want to legally delay paying them as long as possible, so therefore the traditional 401k/403b/TSP will allow you to build wealth much faster than a Roth 401k/403b/TSP. You want the size of your account to be as big as possible, as soon as possible. Ignore any fanciful advice about trying to figure out what tax bracket you are going to be in 30 years from now, because no one knows what the politicians will have come up by then other than the fact it will be onerous, convoluted, overly complicated and make no economic sense. You will be lucky to even be able to figure out what your current marginal tax rate is right now due to the complicated mess the politicians have created of the tax system, let alone guess what it will be 30 years from now. The one exception is if your income is so low that after deductions you pay little or no Federal and state income taxes, then the traditional 401k/403b/TSP tax deduction does you no good, so you would be better off in a Roth. If that is the case, put what is necessary in your Roth 401k/403b/TSP to get all the matching funds. However, if you still have more money to save, then put any extra money (beyond the amount necessary to get the maximum matching funds) into a Roth IRA (up to the Roth limit) per the next chapter, instead of a Roth 401k/403b/TSP, because you have more investment options in a Roth IRA. Also note that when you go with the Roth 401k/403b/TSP, your contributions go into a Roth account, but any matching funds go into a separate traditional account, thanks to the convoluted laws the politicians have come up with.

Chapter 10   Before Investing In Stocks In A Taxable Account, Step 5: Put As Much As You Can Into A Roth IRA

If you have any money left over, put as much as you can into a **Roth IRA** (maximum in 2014 was $5,500 if under age 50 and $6500 if over 50). The reason is that it will grow sheltered tax free and when you retire and start taking it out the withdrawals are also tax free. You don't get the initial tax deduction you get from 401k/403b/TSP plans but you pay no taxes at the end when you withdraw. As shown earlier in the book, the incredible power of compound interest over time makes having as much money in early more important, which is why I always say fund your 401k/403b/TSP before you fund your Roth IRA. However, you will find some well respected advisors who say fund the Roth IRA first, because you have more investment options including doing individual stocks. Regardless, fund both as much as possible! Also, fund it as early in the year as possible, as you will have more time overall for the money to grow tax free.

Note that you can only contribute to an IRA if you are working (i.e. have **Earned Income**) and your income has to be at least as much as you contribute to the IRA.

As of 2014, if you are single and your adjusted gross income is over $114,000 ($181,000 for married couples), you cannot contribute to a Roth IRA or the amount will be restricted by **Phase Out** rules based on your income. In this case contribute to a Traditional IRA and then as soon as it is in the account, convert it to a Roth IRA, also known as a **Backdoor Roth IRA Conversion**. This can be tricky if you already have another existing Traditional IRA that has tax deductible money in it, because the convoluted tax laws makes you convert all of your Traditional IRAs at once. In that case, consult a tax expert to determine the best course of action.

What About A **Traditional IRA**?

Due to the convoluted and steeply progressive state of our current tax system, very little new money is going into the Traditional IRA compared to the Roth IRA. That is because you have to pay taxes on money withdrawn from the Traditional IRA whereas withdrawals from the Roth IRA are tax free. Therefore, the only reason one would go with a Traditional IRA is if initial contributions are tax deductible and there are income restrictions (and Phase Out amounts) on who can deduct contributions to Traditional IRAs. If you fall below these income restrictions, you will also likely be in a situation where you are paying little or no income taxes anyway, so the deductibility does you no good and therefore you would still be better off in a Roth IRA. Our tax system is so steeply progressive that nearly half of all USA households no longer pay any income tax. If you are in that group, don't even consider going with a Traditional IRA, go with a Roth IRA. Here are the rules for who is eligible to deduct contributions to a Traditional IRA:

1) If you are single and your job does not have a 401k or 403b plan or married and neither spouses' jobs have a plan, your contributions to a Traditional IRA are tax deductible (there is no income limit), therefore, put an amount into the Traditional IRA equal to what you actually pay in income taxes and put the rest into a Roth IRA (up to the IRA contribution limit which applies to Traditional contributions and Roth contributions combined). If you pay no income taxes, go with the Roth IRA.

2) If you are single and your job has a 401k or 403b and your **modified adjusted gross income** is less than $60,000, your contributions to a Traditional IRA are tax deductible, therefore, put an amount into the Traditional IRA equal to what you actually pay in income taxes and put the rest into a Roth IRA (up to the IRA contribution limit which applies to Traditional contributions and Roth contributions combined). If you pay no income taxes, go with the Roth IRA.

3) If you are married and filing jointly and your job does not have a 401k or 403b but your spouse's job does have a plan and your modified adjusted gross income is less than $181,000, your contributions to your Traditional IRA are tax deductible, therefore, put an amount into your Traditional IRA equal to what you actually pay in income taxes and put the rest into your Roth IRA (up to the IRA contribution limit which applies to Traditional contributions and Roth

Contributions combined). If you pay no income taxes, go with the Roth IRA.

4) If you are married and filing jointly and both your jobs have a 401k or 403b and your modified adjusted gross income is less than $95,000, your contributions to a Traditional IRA are tax deductible, therefore, put an amount into the Traditional IRA equal to what you actually pay in income taxes and put the rest into a Roth IRA (up to the IRA contribution limit which applies to Traditional contributions and Roth contributions combined). If you pay no income taxes, go with the Roth IRA.

Chapter 11   What Funds Do I Put My 401k/403b/TSP/IRA Money Into?

If you have money in a 401k/403b/TSP/IRA, you need to decide where to put it. First, go back to **Chapters 4 and 5** and honestly determine if you have the personal traits to invest in individual stocks or stock funds or neither. If the answer is neither or if you will need the money within the next 5 years, then you CANNOT invest in individual stocks or stock funds and if you do, you will likely pull your money out at the worst possible time and lose a ton of money. If this is the case, the only place to put your money is in a Cash/Money Market/Fixed Income type of fund. Your gains will barely keep up with inflation or fail to keep up with inflation but as described above, the tax advantages will give you far better overall returns than if you had the money in a Cash/Money Market/Fixed Income type of fund in a taxable account outside of the 401k/403b/TSP/IRA plan, where you will trail inflation AND still have to pay taxes on the money every year.

If you have the personal traits to invest in stock funds and won't need the money within 5 years, the best long term investments are **small cap value stock** funds. As we showed earlier in the book, stocks out perform all other asset classes over the long term. Within stocks, **small cap** stocks outperform **large cap** stocks by a 12% versus 10% average annual return since 1926. Within stock funds, **value funds** have outperformed **growth funds** on average with small cap value outperforming small cap growth by several percentage points over the past 85 years (13.9% versus 9.0% between 1928 and 2009 according to data compiled by Eugene Fama and Ken French). If they don't offer a small cap value fund, simply go with a small cap fund that is offered. If they don't offer a small cap fund, simply go with whatever US stock fund is offered. If your plan offers multiple stock funds to choose from in each category, you will have to pick the "best performing fund" in that category. See **Chapter 13** on how to pick a specific fund.

If you have an IRA, you can invest in Funds or Individual Stocks. If you meet all the criteria for investing in individual stocks in **Chapter 4**, you should go that route instead of Funds because you can likely beat the typical fund and the market by following the simple rules of *Fundamental Stock Investing* that follow in later chapters. You transfer your IRA to a **discount brokerage** company and start investing in individual stocks. Later in the book we will get into how to pick individual stocks. If not, stick with stock funds.

Warning: If the company you work for offers company stock as part of matching contributions, by all means put in the required amount to get the "free" matching company stock. However, do not put *any* additional money in your 401k into your company stock, put it in a stock fund. You already have huge job risk associated with the company by simply working there. Meaning, in this day and age you can get let go from your job for any reason including a downturn in business for the company resulting in a big decline in the company stock price AND by you getting laid off. This double whammy has devastated the life savings of many workers who not only lost their job but suffered a huge hit to their retirement account because they had most of their 401k invested in their company stock. This can become a triple whammy if as I warned against in an earlier chapter, you also own a home in a "company town" in that you could lose your job, have your company stock collapse and the value of your house plunge all at once.

Chapter 12   I Have Maxed Out Available 401k/403b/TSP, Maxed Out Roth IRA And Have No Credit Card Debt And Still Have Money Left Over

Once you have maxed out all the tax shelters available to you as described above, the rest of your investing money has to go into some form of **taxable account**. You have to choose among individual stocks, ETFs, index funds, stock mutual funds, bond funds, Hedge Funds or "cash". Let's take a look at these options:

Cash - If you don't meet the criteria of **Chapters 4 or 5** and therefore should not be investing in individual stocks or stock funds, your only place to put your money is in "**Cash**" or bonds. "Cash" is the generic term that covers **Money Market Funds**, **Certificates of Deposit (CDs)**, **Savings Accounts**, **Checking Accounts** and hiding paper money in Safe Deposit Boxes or safes and the proverbial "hide it under the mattress".

Hiding paper money is not recommended because it earns zero interest, can be stolen or lost and it is not "insured by the government".

Checking and saving accounts pay interest but it is usually negligible when compared to the prevailing inflation rate. They are insured by the Federal Government up to 250K per bank. Obviously if you have more than 250K, you need to spread it out over several banks.

CDs and Money Markets pay a higher interest rate, but ALWAYS at least a little below the prevailing inflation rate and often well below the prevailing inflation rate. In some economic situations, CDs pay more and in other economic situations, Money Markets pay more. CDs are also insured up to 250K per bank. Money markets are not insured and losses, also called "**Breaking The Buck**", are extremely rare (only 4 funds out of thousands ever lost money in US history and losses were brief and tiny on the order of 1-3%), but the possibility of losing money in them exists. Money market funds rates change instantly when short term interest rates change which can be good if rates go up or bad if rates go down. With CDs you are locked into a rate for the term of the CD which can be good if rates go down or bad if rates go up. Many money market funds also offer the advantage of check writing for amounts above a certain minimum.

While Cash is the safest place to put your money in the short run, it is the absolute worst place to put your money in the long run. It is important to remember that the value of all Cash savings will *always* be slowly declining and the magnitude of the decline is enormous over a long period of time. To add insult to injury, you still have to pay taxes on those tiny interest payments you get even though you are losing to inflation.

Just how bad is the decline of cash over the long haul? Pretty bad. The **US Federal Reserve** or **"Fed"** as they are called is assigned the job of keeping the value of the US Dollar stable. Unfortunately, the Fed has always been and always will be mostly made up of politically appointed academics/bureaucrats with no real world experience at managing money and it is also highly politicized, which has resulted in the Fed's absolutely miserable performance. Under the Fed's "leadership" the dollar has lost 95% of its value since the Fed was created by Congress in 1913. Therefore, if you are in cash, don't expect the Fed to keep the dollar stable; count on them to be systematically wiping out the value of cash over time. You will hear various fancy and technical and benign sounding terms the Fed uses to describe the policies they are using that change over the years such as "expanding the monetary base", "expanding the money supply", "reverse repos", "money supply growth", "Quantitative Easing", "Operation Twist", "loose money supply", "M1 growth", "M2 growth", "M3 growth", "Fed Bond Buying Program", "Fed easing", "accommodative Fed policy", "expanding the Fed's balance sheet" etc. and they will invent new terminology as time goes on, but in the end what the Fed does is print money which causes inflation, which destroys the value of the dollar, which makes cash the worst possible long term "investment". As I am writing this, the politicians have appointed yet another academic/bureaucrat with zero real world experience at managing money to head the Fed. I won't bother mentioning her name because it doesn't matter and she is sure to be a "Fed Dove" which means, expect more debasing of the buying power of the dollar to try to bail out, the out of control spending of the politicians who appointed her.

However, if you don't meet the criteria of **Chapters 4 or 5** or you will need the money within 5 years, you are better off slowly losing money in cash than being in stocks and panicking at the worst possible time in the middle of a stock market crash and selling and quickly losing half your money in short order.

Bonds - Bonds are simply loans or money borrowed by the government or corporations with the promise to pay back the **principle** or borrowed amount, plus **interest**. As detailed earlier in the book, **long term bonds** (with maturities of 10 to 30 years or longer) return an average of 5.7% over the long term which is better than inflation (3%) but inferior to stocks (10%) and have been slightly better or slightly worse than real estate (4-8%), depending on which real estate study you believe. **Short term bonds** or "Treasury Bills" (with maturities of 3 years or less) return an average of 3.5% over the long term or slightly stay ahead of inflation.

The Federal government, state governments, city/town governments and government utilities are constantly borrowing more and more money via bonds. State/city/town/government utility bonds are called **Municipal Bonds** or "Munis" and by law are exempt from Federal taxes.

Corporations can also borrow money by issuing **Corporate Bonds** and when they are riskier they are called **Corporate High Yield Bonds** or "**Junk Bonds**" which pay a higher interest rate to compensate for the higher risk of the company **defaulting**, i.e. failing to pay the money back. They can also issue **Convertible Bonds** which are bonds that ultimately can be converted into the company's stock.

In general, I do not recommend investing in bonds as part of your wealth building strategy. This may sound radical, especially since you will hear most financial planners and experts recommend you "diversify" over several **asset classes** and also to increase the bond percentage of your portfolio as you get older. Here is why in general you should not be investing in bonds:

1) The main reason is simply the immovable fact that stocks have far better returns than bonds over the long haul. This book is about building wealth over the long term. To do that you need the superior

returns of stocks over bonds to accomplish that feat. As shown in **Chapter 3**, 1 dollar invested in small stocks in 1926 grew to $19,000 by 2013. That same dollar in long term bonds grew to only $125 and if in short term bonds/treasury bills only grew to $20. Want further proof? Again look at the Forbes 400 Richest People In America list and you will find zero people on that list who got there by investing in bonds. The vast majority got there by investing in stocks or their own company's stock over the long term and a few got there by investing in real estate.

2) Government bonds have been considered a "safe haven" by investors for nearly 100 years. That now may be changing. The Western World (America, Old Europe and Japan) have been expanding their social welfare benefits (welfare, housing, food stamps, subsidized utility rates, clothing allowances, free cell phones, college financial aid, etc.), safety nets (disability), retirement transfer payments (social security, government worker pensions and retirement healthcare) and medical transfer payment systems (Medicare, Medicaid, ObamaCare, subsidized government worker health insurance) for decades and have recently expanded them at an exponential rate. In America, this massive increase in debt has happened at the Federal, state and local level. The promises politicians have made with these programs are impossible to pay for, so governments run either perpetual and ever increasing deficits and debt (Federal government) and/or balance budgets by accounting gimmicks (state and local governments) by borrowing more and more money via issuance of bonds so they appear to have "balanced budgets", but total debt outstanding continues to soar year after year.

This is obviously unsustainable and the only argument is the exact projected date that each program goes bust, and every time the projected bust dates of these programs are re-calculated, that bust date gets earlier. America and the rest of the Western World will eventually be forced to do what Latin American and other Third World and Second World countries such as Russia and Greece did in recent decades. They will have to default or partially default, meaning not pay back the principal or part of the principal and/or stop making interest payments. This would result in devastating losses to government bond holders. The second option is to simply inflate their way out of the bonds by allowing inflation to wipe out the value of the bonds, so the payments can be still made. Stocks generally rise faster than inflation, but bonds do terrible with high inflation and decline in value.

It is extremely important to note that this is not one of those end of the world gloom and doom books talking of total economic collapse. I do not see that happening at all. As explained in more detail later in the book in **Chapter 92,** it is only the governments who are in trouble. The bulk of corporate America and individuals are doing quite well as far as debt is concerned and in fact better than they have historically on average (see the statistics in **Chapter 92).** It is only the governments as currently run, that have unsustainable economic models and not corporations or individuals and therefore, I believe it is primarily government bond holders who are at tremendous risk over the coming years and to a lesser degree people who rely on transfer payments from the government. See my positive take in Chapter 92 on how I see this situation ultimately being resolved.

3) **Bond prices** went nearly straight up from 1981 until July of 2012 as interest rates went from 14% down to 1.3% for the 10 Year Bond. Bond prices move in the opposite direction of interest rates. The 100 year historical average long term bond yield is about 6%. You need to understand that even a couple of percentage points increase in interest rates to say 3.5% will result in huge losses for bond investors. If interest rates simply rise to the long term average of about 6%, bond investors will suffer devastating losses. This is simple math and it is simple math that you must be fully aware of that millions of bond investors and financial planners are ignoring. I will never try to predict where interest rates will go because it is impossible and I am not saying interest rates are going to go to 6%, but if you invest in bonds you must understand this simple math and the tremendous losses you will incur if interest rates simply return to "normal". These loses would happen even if the governments never actually default on their bonds. Remember, bonds have both **credit risk** (chance of default) **and interest rate risk** (big losses if interest rates rise).

4) In addition to systematically destroying the value of the dollar (wiping out 95% of its value since 1913), the academics/bureaucrats at the Fed have branched out beyond just printing money and controlling/manipulating **short term interest rates**. In recent years

they have branched out into directly manipulating **long term interest rates**/bond prices. Since 2008, the Fed has artificially increased bond prices by printing trillions of dollars to use to buy government bonds to manipulate long term interest rates lower to allow the Federal Government to borrow more and more money as the deficits and debt continue to explode.

In effect, the highly politicized Fed is temporarily bailing out, the out of control spending of the politicians who appoint the academics/bureaucrats at the Fed. This has increased bond prices artificially and caused interest rates to go to extremely low levels (as low as 1.3% on the 10 Year Bond in 2012). This is not sustainable and the Fed has unwittingly painted themselves into a corner. They have only 2 options, one is to stop printing more money to buy more bonds which will cause bond prices to fall and interest rates to rise. The other option is to keep printing money until inflation soars which will cause interest rates to soar and bond prices to fall. No matter what option the Fed picks, bond holders will likely lose.

5) Then there is the snowball effect of rising interest rates. If interest rates rise, the cost to borrow for governments increases, which results in higher deficits, which results in more borrowing, which results in higher interest rates (and plunging bond prices). This vicious circle snowball effect has already happened in most Southern European nations which has caused interest rates in those countries to rise 5 percentage points (500 **basis points**) or more resulting in huge losses for holders of those government bonds and in the case of Greece, also partially defaulting twice on their bonds. Again, I will never attempt to predict interest rates; therefore, I am not predicting if or when this could happen in the USA, but if you invest in bonds, you need to be aware of this possibility.

6) In addition to the aforementioned interest rate and credit risks, Municipal bond holders face additional risks. As stated in the real estate chapter earlier in the book, cities and towns have given unsustainable benefit packages to the public employee unions and especially the swelling ranks of retired public union employees. In many cities you have the obviously unsustainable situation where there is only 1 public union employee still working for every 3 that are retired. Therefore, they have to constantly keep raising local taxes,

fees and fines to put off the day of reckoning. The day of reckoning has already hit a smattering of cities that have been forced to declare bankruptcy including Detroit which is the first major city to do so. For centuries, English based American law always placed the bondholders first in line in bankruptcy proceedings. This precedent may be changing and depending on how the increasingly activist courts rule during these bankruptcy proceedings, it could have a huge effect on all municipal bonds. If bond holders get shafted in those proceedings, investors will steer clear of loaning money (i.e. buying municipal bonds) to cities/states/utilities, which will cause Muni bond interest rates to soar, resulting in big losses to all current municipal bond holders. As I am writing this, they are saying Puerto Rico is on the verge of defaulting on its bonds and declaring bankruptcy.

Bond Rules (if you still insist on investing in bonds) - I know some people will insist on investing in bonds anyway even though, as I point out, they are inferior to stocks over the long haul and as of right now (2013), bonds appear to be an especially bad choice. So if you insist on bonds, here are some general rules to follow:

1) Determine the current **10 Year Bond Yield** and the **S&P 500 Dividend Yield** via internet search. Use the formula:

10 Year Bond Yield - S&P 500 Dividend Yield = ?

Compare result to the Table

10 Yr Bond Yield - S&P 500 Div Yield	Bond Investing Environment
3 or lower	Extremely poor, avoid bonds at all cost
4	Very poor, avoid bonds
4.5	Poor, avoid bonds and if you must, only invest in short term bonds/treasury bills
4.75	Below average for bonds, only invest in short term bonds/treasury bills
5	Average environment, expect average bond returns
5.5	Above average environment for bonds
6	Good environment for bonds
7	Very favorable for long term bonds
8 or higher	Extremely favorable, ideal time to invest in long term bonds and bonds will likely outperform stocks

As of August 2013, the 10 Year Bond is at 2.7% and the S&P 500 dividend yield is at 2.1%

2.7 - 2.1 = 0.6 So based on the above chart, this is a horrible time be a bond investor.

2) A second way to determine whether it is a favorable environment for bonds is to compare the 10 Year Bond Yield to the **Year Over Year Core Consumer Price Index (Core CPI)**. Look up the Core CPI via internet search. Use the formula:

10 year Bond Yield - Year Over Year Core CPI = ?

Compare result to the Table

10 YR Bond Yield - Year Over Year Core CPI	Bond Investing Environment
2.0 or lower	Extremely poor, avoid bonds at all cost
2.5	Very poor, avoid bonds
3.0	Poor, avoid bonds and if you must, only invest in short term bonds/treasury bills
3.5	Below average for bonds, only invest in short term bonds/treasury bills
4	Average environment, expect average bond returns
4.5	Above average environment for bonds
5.0	Good environment for bonds
5.5 or higher	Extremely favorable, ideal time to invest in long term bonds

As of August 2013, the 10 Year Bond Yield was at 2.7% and the Year over Year Core CPI was at 1.7%

2.7 - 1.7 = 1.0 So based on the above chart, this is a horrible time to be a bond investor.

If you decide to invest in corporate bonds, you need to decide whether to go with regular corporate bonds or convertible bonds. Use the formula:

Corporate Yield - Convertible Yield = ?

Compare result to the Table

Corporate Yield - Convertible Yield	Expected Relative Performance of Convertible versus Corporate Bonds
5 or higher	Extremely poor for Convertibles, Corporate bonds will fare better
4	Very poor for Convertibles, Corporate bonds will fare better
3	Poor for Convertibles, Corporate bonds will fare better
2	Average environment, Convertibles will do about as well as Corporate bonds
1	Above average environment for Convertibles, will likely out perform Corporate bonds
0	Good environment for Convertibles, will fare better than Corporate bonds
-1	Very good environment for Convertibles, will fare much better than Corporate bonds
-2 or lower	Extremely favorable for Convertible bonds, will significantly outperform Corporate bonds

As of August 2013, the **Bank of America Merrill Lynch Corporate 7-10 Year Effective Yield** index was 4.32% (look up via internet search)

As of August 2013, the **Value Line Convertible Bond Index Yield** was 3.80% (look up via internet search "Barron's Market Lab")

4.32-3.80 = 0.52. Based on the above chart, it is expected that convertible bonds will outperform corporate bonds in total return, so **IF** you want to be in corporate bonds, go with a convertible bond fund instead of a corporate bond fund.

Hedge Funds - Hedge Funds have exploded in popularity from a couple of thousand in the 1990s to more than 8000 funds today. The reason for the explosion is that they are able to charge extremely high fees and they have special rules granted to them by Congress, that allows them to have lower tax rates, and to have fewer public disclosure requirements, that allows them to operate in relative secrecy compared to the rules that apply to mutual funds. These make it extremely lucrative to be a hedge fund manager, but not necessarily so to be a hedge fund investor. With outrageous management fees of 2-5% every year, plus 20 to 50% of any profits on investments, and zero equivalent give back on investment losses, and very high redemption fees and restrictions on when you can withdraw your money and the massive compensation they reward themselves, thousands and thousands of hedge fund managers have made tens of millions of dollars from running hedge funds, many magnitudes more than they could have ever made from their ability to make it as investors on their own. Just how lucrative is it to be a hedge fund manager? In the early '90s there were less than a handful of them on the Forbes 400 Richest Americans list and now more than 30. Many of the highest paid hedge fund managers rake in several billion dollars per year, while many activists protest the pay of top CEOs who make 10 million per year or less than 1% of what many of the highest paid hedge fund managers make. According to Steven Kaplan, the top 25 hedge fund managers earned more than all 500 of the CEOs in the S&P 500 in 2011. According to Absolute Return + Alpha, even run of the mill hedge fund managers among the 8000 plus hedge funds are raking it in, with the average compensation being close to $700,000 per year in 2011. Hedge Funds (and **Private Equity Funds**) pay only 15% "**capital gains**" tax while everyone else is subjected to much higher "**ordinary income tax rates**".

I can't blame them for becoming hedge fund managers, and looking back and knowing what I know now, I probably should have become a hedge fund manager myself. While hedge fund managers have been doing great, investors in these funds on average haven't made out very well at all the past 5 years relative to the stock market and I would bet a good portion of their investors don't even realize how bad the performance has been, given that hedge funds have special rules exempting them from requirements to report their performance to public entities. Not only do they not publicly report their performance, there are no rules or standards as to how they have to report performance to their own investors, so they can and do use any criteria they wish to measure how they perform. Therefore, they or friends in the industry can go on TV or the internet and claim a performance that cannot be proven or disproved by a would-be investor or reporter. Have a healthy degree of skepticism towards any such hedge fund return claims you hear on TV or read about.

There are independent organizations that track overall hedge fund performance by getting what literature is available from the funds from investors who will send it to them and converting the data to commonly used performance data. In the past 5 straight years the average hedge fund has badly underperformed the stock market. How bad? Real bad. Take a look at this chart:

Year	HFRX Equity Hedge Fund Index Return	S&P 500 Return
2009	18.1%	26.5%
2010	8.9%	15.1%
2011	-19.0%	2.1%
2012	4.8%	16.0%
2013	9.8%	31.9%

Supposedly hedge funds are designed to reduce volatility by their hedging strategies, but what good is reduced volatility if your performance is going to be terrible relative to the market? As you can see from the chart, the performance of the average hedge fund has been abysmal with 5 consecutive years of underperforming the stock market and underperforming by a shocking margin. Hedge fund apologists will say that they are designed to limit losses in down years, but the average fund registered large losses in 2011 in an up/flat market. Meanwhile, the net worth of the hedge fund managers continues to soar and more of them make it on to the Forbes list every year. Needless to say, it has been a great time to be a hedge fund manager but lousy for the average hedge fund investor.

Sure there are some outstanding hedge fund managers, and if you can find them and get into their funds go for it, but they are obviously not the majority or the typical. Additionally, some of whom were considered among the best of the best in the hedge fund industry turned out to not be what people thought they were, and either fell upon hard times or were prosecuted for illegal insider trading or fraud.

One hedge fund was considered the greatest hedge fund of the 1990s, coming close to 40% annual returns in the mid 1990s, using highly leveraged (which I warn against later in the book) arbitrage bets and S&P 500 options bets (which I warn against doing later in this book) and using derivatives (which I warn against later in the book). The fund managers won top economic awards for their methods. Then it suddenly collapsed completely when their award winning method stopped working. An investor who put $1,000,000 in the fund in 1994 had it worth over $4,000,000 in midyear 1998, only to find it worth close to zero just a couple of months later.

Another hedge fund family grew to one of the biggest in the world over nearly 20 years, then the demise only took 18 months. It was considered the best of the best during the 1980s and early 90s and investors studied and reported on their every move, then a bad currency bet (which I warn against later in the book) and shorting (which I warn against later in the book) soaring tech stocks, while simultaneously betting long on sinking value stocks, resulted in big losses and likely contributed to the decision to close the funds.

Bernie Madoff for decades simultaneously operated a successful brokerage business and a hedge fund that promised 20% average annual returns (which I warn against later in the book) and appeared to deliver such returns on paper to investors, including other hedge funds that were investing in his fund which are called **feeder hedge funds**. For decades he was known as the premier money manager on Wall Street and in 1992 the Wall Street Journal called him the "Ace of Wall Street". During one 8 year period Madoff claimed to have had only 3 down months out of 87. In reality his hedge fund was a $50 billion **Ponzi Scheme**. For more than 10 years the **Securities and Exchange Commission (SEC)** was alerted to the fact it was a fraud but they ignored the warnings. As with all Ponzi Schemes, Madoff couldn't get enough new investors to pay off the existing investors, so it collapsed. In 2009 Madoff pleaded guilty and was sentenced to 150 years in prison. Many investors lost their life savings either by investing directly with Madoff or via feeder hedge funds. Total losses were estimated at 18 billion.

Another hedge fund manager ran what was called the most successful hedge fund of the middle '00s with the fund growing to nearly 10 billion in assets and making the manager a multi-billionaire. In a letter to investors, the manager boasted 22% average annual returns. The manager was called one of the new investment superstars on Wall Street. However, it turned out the gains were likely ill-gotten, as the manager was arrested and convicted for running a massive insider trading operation.

Another hedge fund manager was known as one of the most successful hedge fund manager in the world and was dubbed the king of the hedge fund world. The manager's personal net worth skyrocketed and rose to among the richest in America. There were claims the manager made nearly 30% average annual returns for the first half of his career as hedge fund manager. However, it was apparently too good to be true and the manager's firm plead guilty to illegal insider trading and was ordered to shut down its operations to outside investors and had to pay an enormous fine, as punishment for what the government perceived as ill gotten gains. The unsealed indictment stated "Insider trading was substantial, pervasive, and on a scale without known precedent in the hedge fund industry."

Another hedge fund manager made billions by a lucky bet against one industry sector. Money poured into the firm after that success. However, the bets weren't as good after that, with big losses in one of the following years, including losses in precious metals (which I warn against later in the book). As explained earlier, hedge funds take a percentage of profits, but give nothing back on losses, so on the way up the manager took a big chunk of the profits, but on the way down the manager didn't give anything back to investors on losses, which is standard practice in the hedge fund world, so the manager made out far better than the investors did and especially investors who got in later.

There was another hedge fund star often praised in the financial media until the SEC filed securities fraud charges against the manager. Later the manager admitted to taking millions of dollars from the hedge fund to pay his personal taxes and security manipulation among other charges, and the manager was banned from the securities industry for a number of years.

Despite these high profile events and the dismal performance by the average hedge fund over the past 5 years compared to the stock market, investors continue to pour money into hedge funds, and hedge fund managers are constantly on or talked about on business TV shows and are treated with rock star status.

Because of the excessive management fees and 5 years of horrendous relative performance, I cannot recommend putting your money into a hedge fund. Also note they have minimums of $100,000 or $500,000 or $1,000,000 or more, so they are out of reach of most investors anyway. Some wise guys have quipped that hedge funds are for millionaire suckers. You would likely be far better off putting your money into an S&P 500 Index fund that charges a 0.1% per year management fee or an actively managed mutual fund or to manage your own money via individual stocks where you keep all the profits yourself. If you want to get involved with hedge funds and you have the wherewithal to do it, be a hedge fund manager, not a hedge fund investor. As I am writing this, a "highly respected analyst" after making a series of bad predictions about what would happen in the sector they covered since the market bottom in March of 2009, has announced the closure of their financial advisory business and is instead going to open, yes, you guessed it, a hedge fund.

Index Funds - Index funds simply invest in a stock index such as the S&P 500 or the Russell 2000 Small Cap Index. If you decide to not invest in individual stocks and go with a fund instead, you should consider whether to go with an Index Fund or an actively managed stock mutual fund where the fund manager picks stocks and tries to beat the market. Index funds have several advantages. The first is that you will never under perform the market because you are investing in the market. The second is that if you are in an S&P 500 index fund, you will likely do very well over the long term as that index has averaged 10% annual returns since 1926. Small stock indexes have performed even better. The third is that these funds have lower management fees so you keep more of your money. The fourth is that they do very little trading so their end of year **capital gains distributions** that you have to pay taxes on (if not in a sheltered account such as an IRA or 401k or 403b) are minimal compared to an actively managed fund. The 5th advantage is that you don't have to worry about a change in fund manager because it doesn't matter who the manager is, the performance is the same. The only disadvantage is that you will never outperform the market.

Exchange Traded Funds (ETFs) - An ETF is essentially an index fund but they trade like stocks on a stock exchange. The supposed advantage of these over an index fund is that you can trade in and out of them much faster and easily than you can an index fund. In reality that is no advantage, because that means you think you are capable of timing the market, which can never be done with any long term success, so you can wind up losing a lot of money. Another supposed advantage is that you can buy ETFs on **margin** or buy **leveraged** ETFs. Again this is no advantage, as you should never buy any stock or investment on margin, i.e. borrow money to buy stock as explained in detail later in **Chapter 79**. Also, every time you trade these, it is a taxable event so even if you manage on paper to do as well as someone passively sitting for the long term in an index fund, you will end up paying taxes sooner along the way, so you won't keep pace with the index investor as far as long term wealth building. Furthermore, when you buy or sell an ETF, there is a bid/ask spread, so depending on the liquidity of the ETF, you will lose a percentage to the market maker on every trade. The operating costs of ETFs are lower than Index Funds, for example 0.04% versus 0.1%. While that is 2.5 times cheaper, both numbers are negligible so it doesn't matter. Also, this tiny advantage is instantly wiped out by the bid/ask spread and commission you pay when you buy and sell them. Because of these reasons, I conclude there is no reason for a fundamental stock investor to ever be in an exchange traded fund, and if you want to mimic the market you are much better off in an index fund. The ETF industry is exploding with new ETFs being issued every day for everything under the sun including index fund ETFs, actively managed stock fund ETFs, sector ETFs, bond ETFs, country ETFs, currency fund ETFs and commodity ETFs. Whenever something is booming such as the number of hedge funds or ETFs, you have to ask yourself, who is making the money, the sellers of the products or the buyers?

Mutual Funds - Stock Mutual funds are actively managed like hedge funds and they attempt to pick stocks to beat the market and beat index funds. Mutual Funds aren't exempt from a lot of the rules like hedge funds so they must operate more transparently. Everything is exactly known about their performance at all times and the fees they charge and therefore their performance is constantly being monitored by investments services, investment advisors, newspapers and the internet. Hedge funds on the other hand don't have to report their performance like mutual funds and when they do report, they often use different metrics to report their performance, which can mask how they are actually performing and just how much the fees are taking away from the investor. Probably because of this, mutual funds have to be much more competitive than hedge funds, which explains on average their vastly superior performance versus hedge funds the past 5 years. As shown above, hedge funds have performed horribly on average the past 5 years, grossly underperforming the stock market while the average stock mutual fund generally trails the stock market by 1-2 percentage points on average over the long term.

So if they trail the market by 1-2 percentage points on average, why invest in a mutual fund and why not just go with an index fund? That is an excellent question and why you must consider whether to go with an index fund or not. If you are not sure, default to an index fund. The main reason to go with a mutual fund is the hope the manager(s) you pick can beat the market. Due to the cost of actively managing stocks, the mutual fund has a built-in cost disadvantage versus index funds and it shows in the results. By most studies, 69% to 75% of mutual funds or about 3/4's trail their respective index funds over the long term. So to succeed with mutual funds, you have to pick a fund *in advance* that winds up being among the top 25% of funds that beats the market. Additionally, if you are picking a mutual fund for a taxable account, you need to pick a fund that beats the market by more than a couple of percentage points, because mutual funds are trading in and out of stocks and hit investors with a larger capital gains distribution tax at the end of every year. Therefore, even if a mutual fund has the exact same performance as an index fund, you will keep more of it and build wealth faster in an index fund. The bottom line is, IF you can find a stock mutual fund that ends up being in the top 20% of funds, it is worthwhile to do so. If not, go with an index fund. In the next chapter, we will cover some techniques that *may* help you pick a mutual fund that will make it in the top 20% of its category.

Summary - Let's recap here. Before investing in stocks, make sure you meet the criteria in **Chapters 4 and 5** to invest in stock funds and/or individual stocks. If you don't, you should stay away from stocks or you will lose a lot of money. If you don't own a house, you should consider buying one if we are in the correct part of the real estate cycle as outlined in **Chapter 6**. Next, if you have a job that offers a 401k/403b/TSP, put in enough to get all the matching funds as outlined in **Chapter 7**. Next, if you have any money left over focus on paying down credit card debt per **Chapter 8**. Next, fully fund your 401k/403b/TSP per **Chapter 9**. Next fully fund your IRA per **Chapter 10**. Next, if you still have money, open a taxable account and decide whether you want to invest in individual stocks, stock index funds or stock mutual funds.

Chapter 13 How To Pick A Stock Mutual Fund

If you meet the criteria of **Chapter 4** to invest in stock funds and you have a 401k/403b/TSP or an IRA and you don't want to go with individual stocks, you need to pick which fund to put your money in. Within a 401k/403b/TSP your choices are generally limited. As previously stated, you should pick a small cap value fund if available. If not available, pick whatever small cap fund that is available. If no small cap fund is available, pick whatever stock fund is available. Within the categories of funds, you may have a choice between an index fund and an actively managed fund. For example, your employee plan may offer a Russell 2000 small cap fund or a Wilshire 4500 small cap fund and one or more actively managed small cap fund(s). You need to go back to **Chapter 12** and review the advantages and disadvantages of index funds versus actively managed funds and decide whether or not the actively managed funds available to you are likely to beat the index fund. If you are not sure, you can put a portion of the money in one and the rest in the other one or simply default to the index fund.

Some plans offer a wide number of funds to choose from and if you are in an IRA, you have thousands of funds to choose from. In those cases use these guidelines:

1) First off, don't go into any fund that has a **load** (upfront fee) or any exit fee (**redemption fee**) or **12B-1 fee** or any other fee. With thousands of funds to choose from and many good ones among them, there is no point in paying extra money. As I showed earlier in the book, even a 1% difference in total return can make a huge difference over the long term.

2) If you are picking a fund for a taxable account, the advantage of an index fund increases dramatically as explained in the last chapter. Index funds do very little buying and selling, therefore, gains are deferred. If an index fund and an actively managed fund have the exact same percent return, you will build wealth much more rapidly in the index fund. Mutual funds are required to pass on **Capital Gains Distributions** to shareholders. Despite the great sounding name, these distributions are essentially a tax bill if you are in a taxable account.

Even worse, they are typically distributed in December, the worst possible time, meaning you have to pay taxes on these gains in the least amount of time, i.e. the following April 15th. I am not saying you should rule out buying an actively managed fund in a taxable account, but the one you pick has to clearly outperform the index fund to make it worthwhile. Within a tax sheltered account (401k/403b/IRA), the tax advantage of the index fund is eliminated, so if you can find a fund that will just beat the index, it is worthwhile. Keep in mind, though, that 3/4's of mutual funds fail to beat their respective index funds as explained in the previous chapter. This is due to the built-in average 1-2% disadvantage in the cost required to operate an actively managed fund versus a passive index fund.

3) Tend to avoid funds that have a high **turnover** if in a taxable account. Turnover is a measure of what % of stocks in the fund get sold each year. A typical fund has a 150% turnover and a high turnover is over 200%. Funds that have turnovers over 300% are going to slam you with a huge tax bill via Capital Gains Distributions in December that over the long term will cancel out a chunk of any out performance that the fund may have.

4) Tend to avoid funds that have grown too big, especially small cap funds, which is where your focus should be. Simple math shows it is harder for a small cap fund with 3 billion to invest than one with 500 million to invest. This is because mutual funds can only purchase each stock up to 5% of their total assets and they cannot own more than 10% of any company. Therefore, as the fund's assets grow in size, their investment options become progressively reduced in the small cap part of the market. For example, Peter Lynch's out performance of the market decreased in the second half of his career as his Magellan Fund exploded in size. The same has happened to Warren Buffett as his holding company has grown to a gargantuan size; he has underperformed the market over the past 5 years for the first time in his investing career. I would say with everything else being equal, avoid any small cap fund with over 2 billion in assets and favor ones under 1 billion.

5) Never pick one of the top 2% performing funds from last year. To get into the top 2% in any given year means the fund manager got lucky and made a heavy bet on a couple of sectors that happened to get

hot that year. Any fund manager can get lucky every now and then by betting on some sector of the market that suddenly gets hot. Study after study has shown these funds almost always under perform the market the following year. When Peter Lynch had his amazing and unprecedented 13 year run as manager of Fidelity Magellan, no other fund came close to his average annual return over that period, and yet, he was never in the top 2% of funds in any individual year.

6) Focus on funds that have a good performance over a 3-5 year period. You want to see funds that have beaten the market averages over a 3-5 year period. As stated above, never go by just one or even 2 year performance. Any performance longer than 5 years is often irrelevant, because the same fund manager may not even be present.

7) Once you get in a fund, stick with it until it underperforms the market averages for 2 consecutive years. In a taxable account, remember that switching in and out of funds is a taxable event and will result in taxes being paid earlier than later. Any good investor/fund manager can have a bad year, but when they under perform the market 2 years in a row, you should probably find a new fund.

8) Get data on the funds by using resources such as Morningstar, Lipper, Value Line and online sources such as Yahoo. Some of these are available in your local library. Do not focus on their star ratings or other ratings, focus on small cap value funds with good 3-5 year performance (while avoiding any fund in the top 2% in the past year), smaller than 1 billion in assets (especially for small cap funds), low turnover (if in a taxable account) and low operating percentage and no extra loads or fees.

9) In summary, if in a taxable account, seriously consider going with an index fund due to its tax advantages, unless you think you can find a fund that is likely to significantly outperform the market. If in a sheltered account, seriously consider picking an actively managed fund, if you think it can outperform its respective index. Aim for small cap value funds with no load, no exit fees or other fees, assets less than 1 billion, turnover less than 200%, a 3-5 year record of beating the market averages and one that was not in the top 2% performing funds from the previous year. If a fund underperforms its

peer group/respective index 2 years in a row, replace that fund with a new one, otherwise stick with it.

Chapter 14 What About International Funds?

In general, I do not recommend investing in **International Funds**. Many experts will point out that the total capitalization of all stocks in countries outside of the USA is 55% of the world's total and therefore, you should be invested outside the USA. My response is, so what? Over the last 35 years, stocks in the non-USA developed world, as measured by the **Morgan Stanley EAFE index**, have more or less been equal with the S&P 500. However, the EAFE has dramatically underperformed the S&P 500 the past 5 years. So what is the point of investing outside the USA to get about the same returns as investing inside the USA or much worse the past 5 years? I don't see the point. Investing overseas involves not only market risk, but additionally, **political risk** and **currency risk**. For mutual fund companies and financial advisors who refer clients to mutual fund companies and get commissions for doing so, the answer is obvious. With 55% of the world's stock market capitalization located outside the USA, it is an obvious way to greatly increase their profits by selling International Funds in addition to domestic funds, but that doesn't necessarily make it a good idea for you to invest in them.

They will also point out that because International Funds don't **correlate** all the time with the USA stock market (one may be up and one may be down at any given time), your overall portfolio returns will be less volatile with a mixture of USA stock funds and International stock funds. Again my response is, so what? I am interested in wealth building, not lower nor higher nor medium volatility. I don't care about volatility.

Also, keep in mind, a very large percentage of companies that make up the bulk of the USA stock market capitalization get close to half their sales in international markets. Therefore, investing in a lot of USA companies is by proxy investing overseas anyways.

What about **Emerging Market Funds**? Emerging Markets as measured by the **Morgan Stanley EEM index** have outperformed the USA stock market the past 20 years, due to the initial freeing up of the economies of China, Russia, Brazil and India and many others, which resulted in faster GDP growth in those countries than the USA. The big reforms are already now way in the past, and I believe the easy money has already been made in Emerging Stock markets, and the growth rates in those countries will be much slower going forward than the first 2 decades after freeing up their economies. In fact, things may now be reversing and in numerous Emerging Market countries such as Russia, Brazil, Argentina, Chile, Venezuela, Ecuador, Bolivia, Thailand, Turkey, Indonesia and Egypt, things appear to be headed towards less free markets, which will be bad for their economies and stock markets. Consequently, in the past 5 years Emerging Markets have underperformed the USA stock market and there is no guarantee that will turn around. Anyone who was invested in Emerging Markets or other International stock mutual funds the past 5 years would have been better off with all their money in the USA stock market. In summary, I am not against investing in International stock funds including Emerging Market funds, but I don't see the point in taking on additional risk that may or may not result in better returns than just sticking with the USA stock market.

Chapter 15   Checklist For Starting In Individual Stocks Via Fundamental Stock Investing

Remember, what makes this book unique is that it is about overall long term wealth building, not simply about trying to be the best stock picker. To build the maximum wealth you must save, which is outlined in the second half of the book, and invest well, but you also must use every legal means to minimize taxes, which are the number one obstacle to wealth building. Therefore, before you start picking individual stocks, go through the following check list to make sure you are maximizing your wealth building potential:

1) Make sure you meet the criteria of **Chapter 4** to invest in individual stocks. If not, don't do it.

2) Only invest money that you will not need for the next 5 years. Don't invest any money that you will need in the next 5 years; keep that money in cash.

3) Make sure you have your spending under control, and you are saving as much as possible. Saving techniques are outlined in the second half of the book.

4) If you don't already own a house, buy one if we are in the correct part of the real estate cycle to be buying houses. See **Chapter 6** for details.

5) If you have a job that offers a 401k/403b/TSP plan, put in enough to get all the matching funds as outlined in **Chapter 7**.

6) Pay down credit card debt per **Chapter 8**.

7) Fully fund your 401k/403b/TSP per **Chapter 9**.

8) Fully fund your IRA per **Chapter 10**.

9) Make sure you want to do individual stocks. Going with stock mutual funds or index funds is a great way to build wealth and little effort is required. Picking individual stocks can allow you to

outperform the market and reach your wealth goals sooner, but it requires you to pay attention to your stocks' earnings reports and a few extra hours of research a week. You have to learn the system that follows and do the extra work. If you are willing, the rewards will be worth it, but first make sure you are willing to commit to it.

10) Select a **discount brokerage** to use for your stock investing for your IRAs and your taxable account. The primary criteria for picking a discount brokerage is low commissions. Do not pick a brokerage that charges more than $10 per trade. Again, this book is about wealth building and those commission costs are fairly high, especially as a beginning investor early in your career when you have less money. You want the commission to be a tiny percentage of your buys and sells. Look for a basic flat rate with no minimum account balances, no maintenance fees, no added costs per share etc. Forget about any bells and whistles and "trading and charting tools" or "margin"; you won't need any of that stuff as a fundamental stock investor. The brokerage must also be **SIPC Insured** in case they go bust. Also, pick a brokerage that was around before the last bear market hit, so that they have proven they can survive a bear market. Theoretically, you could be with a new discount broker that has the lowest commission rates, but that goes under during the next bear market, and even if they have SPIC insurance, your money will be tied up for 1-3 months, and you won't be able to get at it just as the market is rebounding.

11) Have enough money to start investing in individual stocks. I would say about $2000 is the minimum to invest. You want to at least spread your investments over 5 stocks so that would be about $400 dollars per stock. So, say your brokerage charges you $7 dollars per trade, that would be a commission of under 2% per trade. If you are paying more than 2% every time you buy or sell a stock, that is too much of a percentage to overcome for you to beat the market, and if you can't beat the market, there is no point in doing individual stock investing. Also, owning less than 5 stocks is too risky, as will be explained later in the book, and for some people, too stressful when the inevitable bad stock pick is made. As you build wealth, you should increase the number of stocks you own. How many stocks to own is discussed in further detail in **Chapter 83**.

Chapter 16   Fundamental Stock Investing Philosophy

Fundamental Stock Investing, which is defined as buying stocks as if you were buying a business, is a simple and common sense method that is vastly superior over the long haul, as proven by investing legends Warren Buffett, who became the richest man in the world, and Peter Lynch, who averaged staggering 29.2% annual returns over a 13 year period and beat the S&P 500 by an average of 13.4 percentage points per year during that period. That 29.2% remains unprecedented for any money manager over such a long period of time. Using *Fundamental Stock Investing,* the past 15 years I have averaged 16.1% annual returns versus 3.1% for the S&P 500, also beating the index by 13 percentage points per year. Not only that, because the method generally involves holding stocks for longer time periods, transactions costs are lower, but most importantly, gains are taxed at much lower rates, and the gains are also deferred, all of which results in much higher increases in wealth than the official gains compared to ALL other investing methods. There are many systems you can use to make money in stocks, but when you combine the returns with the huge tax advantages, *Fundamental Stock Investing* becomes the superior method. It is also the simplest and easiest to learn method and the only method that uses common sense. What is unique about this book is that it also explains how you must combine savings with successful stock investing to build significant wealth over the long haul, and it outlines critical techniques to save money later in the book so you have more to invest.

The reason *Fundamental Stock Investing* works so well is that it is the only method that attempts to correlate a company's future profits (over the next 1-3 years) to the current stock price and determines if the stock is cheap, fairly valued or overpriced. In fact, it uses the exact criteria one would use when deciding if you were going to buy a business or not. It is the only method that makes actual business sense. In the short run, anything can and will happen to a company's stock price, but in the long run, a company's stock price correlates exactly with its profits. This difference between a stock's price in the short run and the long run is where you make money by *Fundamental Stock Investing.*

Chapter 17   Fundamental Stock Investing Basics

It is very important that you understand the overall basic principles of *Fundamental Stock Investing* so you understand all the major key points immediately and not get lost in details. In this one short chapter, I will cover all the major points. Then in the following chapters, I will go into further details and nuances to aid your investing ability. I give credit to Peter Lynch for greatly influencing my overall stock investing philosophy; however, I take what I consider a decidedly more practical, direct, simple and efficient approach to *Fundamental Stock Investing* which also utilizes all the tools available on the internet today.

1) First, come up with a list of companies that you want to investigate further to determine if you should consider investing in them. This will be covered more in depth in a later chapter. There are approximately 5000 publicly traded companies on USA stock exchanges. Start paying attention to the world around you, and you will start noticing all kinds of companies making all kinds of products and services. This is one of many ways to find companies to investigate.

2) Once you have your list, go to an online resource to research your company, such as your discount brokerage website, Yahoo Finance, Google Finance, etc. I personally have found that as of 2014, Yahoo Finance is the best.

3) Type in the company's **Ticker Symbol** (for example Johnson & Johnson is JNJ) if you know it or the name of the company.

4) When the company comes up on the screen, first thing you check is **Market Capitalization** or **Market Cap** for short, so you can determine the size of the company. Here are the size categories:

0-50 million **Tiny Micro Cap**
50-100 million **Micro Cap**
100 million to 1 billion **Small Cap**
1 billion to 5 billion **Mid Cap**
5 billion and up **Large Cap**

75

30 billion and up **Blue Chip Large Cap**
100 billion and up **Giant Blue Chip Large Cap**

Remember, in general small companies make big moves and big companies make small moves. All else being equal, focus on smaller companies, but do not ignore big companies just because they are big.

5) Categorize the stock into one of the 5 categories of stocks. Click Profile on Yahoo to aid yourself in this determination. Click on **Analyst Estimates** on Yahoo to determine growth rate.

a) **Slow Growth** (Earnings increasing 0-5% per year)
b) **Medium Growth** (Earnings increasing 5-15% per year)
c) **Fast Growth** (Earnings increasing 15% or greater per year)
d) **Cyclical** (Auto, steel, trucks, truckers, rails, shippers, chemicals, mature high tech companies such as Intel, airlines, heavy equipment, construction companies, metal companies, fertilizer companies, oil/oil service companies, miners, egg and meat producers, home builders, "Money Center" banks, etc.)
e) **Turnaround** (Companies trying to recover after teetering on the brink of bankruptcy or re-emerging from bankruptcy)

6) For growth stocks, determine the **Price To Earnings ratio (P/E)** of the stock. The initial Yahoo screen will list the **Trailing P/E** for the past 12 months. If the trailing P/E is listed N/A, the company is losing money. The **Forward P/E** for the upcoming year is the one to go by. It is listed near the bottom of the opening screen. Note, if there are no analysts following the company (a huge positive), this will be N/A, so you will have to estimate it on your own. (See below on how to estimate earnings).

7) Determine the **Growth Rate** (GR) of the company. Click on Analyst Estimates on Yahoo. Look at the projected estimate for this full year and compare to last year's actual full year and calculate the projected % increase. Also, compare next year's projected estimate to this year's projected estimate to see if that Growth Rate appears to be sustainable. Then, add the current annual dividend % yield, if the stock pays a dividend (on the front screen of the Yahoo page for the stock), to the % Growth Rate, to calculate the **Total Return** (TR).

8) For Growth companies, compare the Forward P/E to the projected Growth Rate (or Total Return, if they pay a dividend). **This is the core and single most important thing in most fundamental stock evaluations and the most important principle in this book.**

a) If the Growth Rate/Total Return equals the Forward P/E, the stock is fairly priced.
b) If the Growth Rate/Total Return is higher than the Forward P/E, you have found yourself a potential bargain.
c) If the Growth Rate/Total Return is lower than the Forward P/E, the stock is overpriced and most likely should be avoided.
d) Remember that a Growth Rate higher than 30-40% is almost always not sustainable for more than a year or two so any stock with a Forward P/E greater than 40 should be avoided no matter how high the Growth Rate. Also remember these rules don't apply to Cyclicals and Turnarounds, only to growth companies.
e) For obvious reasons, a stock with a Growth Rate of 25 and a P/E of 25 is superior to a stock with a Growth Rate of 15 and a P/E of 15. Using the **Rule of 72**, a 25% grower will double earnings (and likely the stock price) in 3 years, while a 15% grower will take 5 years, and a 10% grower will take 7 years. You should become familiar with the Rule of 72.
f) A stock with a Growth Rate of 15 and a P/E of 10 is usually superior to a stock with a Growth Rate of 25 and a P/E of 25, because the former is a bargain to begin with, and because it is so cheap (i.e. lower P/E), there is less risk and because a 15% Growth Rate is easier to sustain than a 25% Growth Rate.

9) Next, check the cash and debt per share. The more cash and the less debt the better. This is extremely critical during recessions, as companies with weak **balance sheets** (i.e. little cash and excessive debt) can go under, and you can lose everything. Also, young fast growing companies that take on too much debt can fall apart and go under. A company that is debt free cannot go under no matter how bad the recession gets.

Click on Key Statistics in Yahoo Finance. There you will find the number of **shares outstanding**. Click on Balance Sheet and find the cash and short term investments and long term investments and add them up which will give you the total "cash" of the company. Find the long term debt. (To keep things simple and not get lost in details, ignore short term debt, unless it is a huge number). Subtract the long term debt from the total cash and divide by the number of shares to give you net debt or net cash per share. If positive, this is very good, as there is more cash than debt. If it is negative, they have more debt than cash.

Now determine if the net debt or net cash is significant or not by comparing the net cash or net debt per share to the price of the stock. For example, if JNJ is selling for 63 and it has net cash per share of 3 dollars, it is good that they have net cash but not a huge plus; they are considered to have a **strong balance sheet**. If you find a company that has 2 dollars per share in cash and they are selling for 10, that is a significant positive as they have a very strong balance sheet. If the stock is selling for 50 and they have 4 dollars per share in debt, it is a slight negative but not a big deal, and they have a good balance sheet. If they are selling for 50 and they have 25 dollars per share in net debt, it is usually a significant negative, and they have a **weak balance sheet**. All else being equal, tend to avoid companies with weak balance sheets, and favor companies with strong balance sheets.

You want to buy growth stocks which are fairly priced or bargains and that have strong balance sheets and hold them until the Growth Rate declines significantly, at which time you sell them.

10) Check the following secondary indicators:

a) Analysts – Click on Analyst Estimates and it will tell you how many analysts are following the stock. The fewer the better. If there are no analysts, there will be no estimates, which is a huge positive.

b) Institutional ownership – The lower the better. The average is about 60%. Click on Key Statistics.

c) Insider ownership – The higher the better. Click on Key Statistics.

d) Insider Buying - Any recent insider buying is a huge positive. Ignore Inside Selling. Click on Insider Transactions.

11) If there are no analyst estimates, you have to estimate earnings on your own. Click on Press Releases. Go to most recent quarterly earnings report and read the press release. The company will tell you how much **Earnings Per Share (EPS)** went up in the last quarter and use that percentage for the Growth Rate. Calculate the Forward P/E by taking the quarterly EPS and multiplying by 4 to get a full year estimate for EPS. Divide the price of the stock by the full year EPS estimate and you got the Forward P/E. If the earnings are seasonal, you need to look at full year earnings. When evaluating earnings, do not include one time charges and gains; you want to use the so called "operating" or "non-GAAP" or "ex items" or "core" earnings, not the GAAP earnings. **GAAP** stands for **Generally Accepted Accounting Principles**.

12) Special notes on Retailers and Restaurants.

a) Look for a favorable Growth Rate to Forward P/E. See step 8 above.
b) Check **Same Store Sales** provided in company press releases under "Press Releases" on Yahoo. If this is negative, avoid the stock even if earnings are increasing, because it means the earnings are coming from new units only, and the existing units are deteriorating. However, Same Store Sales often turn negative during a recession, so you need to compare how their Same Store Sales are, compared to retailers or restaurants in the same category as them.
c) The balance sheet is critical. For young fast growing chains, you want little or no debt. Companies that are expanding too fast by taking on debt, soon crash and burn. For mature companies, large debt can also be dangerous in a recession.
d) How many states are they in? You want a lot of room for expansion. If they are already in 40 states, you can anticipate the Growth Rate slowing soon. If they are in few states, you might be able to anticipate a high Growth Rate for years to come.

12) Cyclicals – These are very tricky, because the usual P/E rules don't apply. The best is to buy them when they are losing money in a recession or big downturn in their particular industry, the stock is way down and the headlines are all doom and gloom for their industry, and it feels like things will never get better. You buy them and wait for business to rebound. You want to sell these well before the boom is

over. They key is the debt/cash per share (see step 9 above). Can they survive the downturn? If debt per share is too heavy, they can go under completely and you lose everything. If they survive due to a strong balance sheet, and weaker competitors go under or are forced to reduce capacity to survive, they will be monster **multi-bagger** winners, after the recession ends in their industry. A multi-bagger is a stock that more than doubles. For example a 3 bagger is a stock that goes up by a factor of 3 and a 10 bagger is a stock that goes up by a factor of 10, etc. So the risk/reward is extremely high, in fact, there is often no in between. Also note the stock will turn up, way before the recession in their industry is over. Conversely, the stock will start to plunge, way before the economy or business in their industry heads south. These are definitely not stocks you can buy and hold forever.

13) Turnarounds – These are high risk/high potential return stocks. You buy these when the stock is beaten way down and the cash/debt per share is survivable and it appears that the business can turn around. You sell them when they actually turnaround or if the turnaround fails and business starts to worsen. You can find multi-bagger winners here and total losses here.

That in a nutshell, is the core of *Fundamental Stock Investing*. Any stock you invest in, you break down by the method above, and you will be able to determine if you should be buying, selling or holding it. Often people greatly overcomplicate things by overanalyzing, by looking at a million other details that will confuse them or cause them to overlook or de-emphasize the critical criteria explained above. Even worse, they will listen to opinions of "experts", who say trite sayings such as "that stock is extended", that will stick in their head and cause them to make the wrong decision.

What follows now will be many chapters that will explain the nuisances that will aid your stock picking and expand upon the basic principles explained above. However, remember the core of it all, on how to evaluate a company, was explained in this chapter.

Chapter 18 Earnings are the key, There Is Nothing Random About It

Earnings, which are also called profits, are what ultimately drives stock prices. Specifically, **Earnings Per Share (EPS)** is what drives stock prices. In the short run, anything can and will happen with stock prices, and short term stock price movements mean nothing to the fundamental stock investor. In the long run, a company's stock price closely follows earnings. There is nothing random about it in the long run. Academics in Ivy laced brick towers of the insulated college campus world talk about the **Random Theory** that proposes that stock movements are random and therefore it is impossible to pick stocks and that you would be just as successful randomly picking stocks by throwing darts at a board. You will see disconnects and even extreme disconnects in the short run that may make investing in individual stocks appear to be random luck, but in the long run, stock prices correlate directly with earnings. If it weren't true, Warren Buffett would never have been able to amass 60 billion dollars. Peter Lynch would not have been able to beat the market by 13 percentage points per year over 13 years. I would not have been able to beat the market by an average of 13 percentage points per year over 15 years, etc. If you buy a stock at a reasonable P/E valuation and earnings double over the next 4 years, there is a very good chance the stock price will approximately double too. If earnings go basically nowhere over those 4 years, it is very likely the stock price will go nowhere too. If earnings fall by 50% over 4 years, then expect the stock price to be cut in half. If earnings turn to losses several years in a row, the company will be bankrupt or nearly bankrupt and the stock near zero. In the real world, there is nothing random about where an individual company's stock price goes in the long term.

There is also the **Efficient Market Theory** that says it is impossible to beat the market, because all information that is currently relevant to a company is already reflected in its current stock price. This is also known as the so called "price is truth" theory. Based on this theory, there is no such thing as an overpriced or under priced stock, so it is futile to try to pick winning stocks. Again, these academics are totally wrong. You will see disconnects and even extreme disconnects in the short run that present tremendous opportunity to fundamental stock investors, and that is where we make our money. If it weren't true, Warren Buffett et al wouldn't have been able to beat the market. Buffett likes to say "I would be a bum in the streets with a tin cup if the markets were efficient" as he told Fortune Magazine in 1995.

To succeed in investing you want to buy stocks at reasonable, or better yet, cheap valuations, in which earnings are going to significantly increase over the next several years. If a company's earnings are going nowhere or going down, there is no reason to expect to make money, no matter how cheap the stock is. Whether you are buying a fast growth stock, or a medium growth stock, or a depressed cyclical in a recession, or a turnaround, you should only do it, if you expect earnings to be significantly higher 1 to 3 years or more from now, than they are now. Also, never pay too much for anything, including stocks. So, forget the Random and Efficient Market theorists, and remember it is earnings, specifically EPS, that are the bottom line in *Fundamental Stock Investing*.

Chapter 19   When Is A Good Time To Start Investing In Stocks?

The best time to start investing in stocks is right now. Do not try to time the market, or try to predict the direction of the market, or the direction of interest rates, or listen to experts' predictions, or try to predict what the Fed will do.

Wealth takes time to build, and the sooner you get started the better. The old adage "it is not timing the market, it is time in the market" is correct. It doesn't matter how old you are, remember the time is going to go by whether you invest or not, so you might at well save, invest and build wealth.

There are numerous mathematical models showing how starting early gives you a huge advantage. The most famous is the model of the person who starts saving and investing $2000 dollars a year at age 20 and invests it in stocks in a sheltered account and earns the 10% average annual returns of stocks since 1926, then stops investing at age 30, but leaves the invested money in stocks in the sheltered account. The model compares this to another person who puts off starting until age 30 and invests $2000 ever year for 35 years and gets the same percent annual returns. Despite only investing $20,000 versus $70,000, the person who started early ends up with almost twice as much money and is a millionaire by age 65. You can't get around this fact, so don't put off starting, no matter how small the amount of money you are starting with or how old you are now. Of course, I failed to follow this advice and didn't start investing until age 28 and didn't start with individual stocks until I was 30.

Here is another real life example. The decade of 2000-2010 was called **The Lost Decade For Stock Investors**. That is because the Dow went from 12,000 in March of 2000 to 7,000 in 2003 to 14,000 in 2007 back to 6500 in March of 2009 to 12,000 in early 2011. So in the end, the "Market" went nowhere and had 2 out of the 5 Stock Market Collapses since 1926, happen within the same decade. Despite this, many of my friends that were using *Fundamental Stock Investing* and following many of my stock picks, saw their net worth double or more due to good stock picking and the fact they were continually adding new money/savings to stocks. I nearly quadrupled my total invested in stocks during this terrible period for stock investing.

One of the keys to building wealth is to not only start early, but to be saving and constantly putting more money into stocks every year, especially when stocks are down. This is when wealth really starts accumulating, by starting early and by continuously adding to your investments.

Chapter 20   I Am Over 50, Is It Too Late To Start Investing?

Let's suppose you are already age 50 and have never saved and invested in your life; is it too late to start? Hell no! The average 50 year old today has a life expectancy of about 80. That means they got 30 years to go. Those 30 years are going to go by whether you save and invest or not. Significant wealth can be built in 15 years using the methods outlined in this book. Again, never forget, the time is going to go by whether you save and invest or not, so you might as well start now.

Chapter 21 I Am Afraid To Start Now Because The Stock Market Might Crash

Some people are afraid to start investing, because they saw some "expert" on TV who sounded very convincing, who said the stock market is going to crash. At some point after you start investing, the stock market will in fact crash. You can count on that happening. When it happens, nobody can predict, so don't waste your time trying to guess or listening to "experts' predictions". More will come later in the book on the folly of listening to stock market "experts". Let's review the history:

There have been 205 stock market declines of 5% or more since 1926. There have been 42 stock market "corrections" (defined as a 10% decline in the S&P 500) since 1926. There have been 14 Bear Markets (defined as a 20% or greater decline in the S&P 500) since 1926. There have been 5 "Stock Market Collapses" (defined as a 40% or greater decline in the S&P 500) since 1926.

As you can see these stock market decline events happen routinely and will continue to happen routinely; it is just part of stock investing. When the next decline happens and how bad it will be, no one can predict. For 100% of these declines, stocks have always come back and ultimately gone higher. When you start investing, a Correction will almost certainly happen within the first 3 years, a Bear Market will happen within 8 years or so, and a Market Collapse will happen sometime within 20 years. Count on it. Once you understand this, accept this and expect this; there is nothing to fear.

I believe the appropriate attitude to have based on the stock market history the past 90 years, is not to fear being in stocks when a decline hits, but to fear being out of stocks when a rally happens. Based on the history, every time the market has declined, it has not only come back, but has eventually gone onto new highs. However for most stock market rallies, if you miss them, you will never be able to get into the market at those cheaper prices ever again. Look at stock market declines as an opportunity to buy more at cheaper prices.

Of course if you panic and abandon stocks during these scary declines, you will get killed investing in stocks. If you don't have the stomach to ride these declines out (and buy more when stocks are way down), you won't make it in stock investing. Every one of these Bear Markets and Stock Market Collapses have been scary, and they are assigned scary reasons for the decline (after the fact), and when they are happening, everything will be doom and gloom with no end in sight, and every time you will hear "experts" saying "this time it is different and it won't ever come back" and they will sound convincing. But before you invest, you must ask yourself if you will be able to handle it emotionally when it actually is happening to you?

When the inevitable stock market collapse comes, about half of all "retail investors" (aka the little guy) get permanently scared out of stocks. A friend of mine went into stocks for the first time in his life after age 50 in 2006 and had the misfortune of a 3-4% drop on his first day. Even worse, he had the misfortune of getting into stocks just 18 months before the 2008/2009 stock market collapse, which was one of the five worst collapses in the past 100 years. However, he did not panic, and never sold, and hung in there, and has more than doubled his initial money, despite getting into stocks at the worst possible time. Even better, he added significant new money after the collapse.

Chapter 22   What If The Market Environment Is Too Uncertain To Invest In?

I will let you in on an important secret. The market is ALWAYS uncertain 100% of the time. Since the founding of stock investing and trading in this country in 1792, the investing environment has always been uncertain. You will always hear people saying "things are too uncertain right now with all the things going on." There has never even been a 5 minute period where things were certain. One of the great advantages of *Fundamental Stock Investing,* is you can and must ignore "everything that is going on", and focus strictly on your individual companies' fundamentals (in relation to their current stock price), and ignore everything else going on in the world.

Since 1926, we have had a depression, a World War, 15 recessions, a 10 year period of the worst of all economic worlds - stagflation (lousy growth AND high inflation simultaneously), 5 additional major American wars, 20 minor wars/military actions, have seen interest rates hit over 20%, seen interest rates collapse to zero, seen runaway inflation, seen deflation, seen unemployment above 7.5% at some point during 9 consecutive decades and unemployment above 9% in 4 decades, oil embargos, gas lines/shortages, the onset of AIDS, the Y2K scare, the collapse of Lehman Brothers and Bear Stearns, the "Second Ice Age" scare in the mid 1970s, the Global Warming scare, the Running Out of Oil scare (every five years), the Population Bomb scare, dire predictions of every kind, oil soar to $150 dollars a barrel only to collapse down to $29 dollars a barrel less than 2 years later, the Subprime Mortgage Crisis, massive labor strikes, the Savings & Loan Crisis, Presidents shot, the European Debt Crisis, race riots, nuclear power accidents, terrorist attacks, devastating earthquakes and hurricanes and tsunamis, the Asian Financial Crisis, 19 government shutdowns since 1976, all major Latin America nations default on their debt within the same year, Russia default on its debt, Greece default on its debt twice, a 45 year Cold War with the very real threat of nuclear annihilation, 9 nations attain nuclear bombs, endless Middle Eastern wars, NYC go bankrupt, massive trade deficits, massive budget deficits and massive national debt, the collapse of the Soviet Union and all its satellite countries, etc. We have seen wave after wave of politicized appointments of academic bureaucrats appointed to the

Fed, and you never know what they are going to do next (other than systematically wipe out the value of the dollar). That is a mind boggling amount of uncertainty and things to worry about, and yet, 1 dollar invested in the stock market in 1926 is now worth $4,000, and 1 dollar invested in small stocks is now worth $19,000.

Forget about uncertainty and laugh the next time you hear someone say "the investing environment is too uncertain right now", and focus strictly on the fundamentals of the stocks you own and are considering buying. In fact, you should enjoy the luxury of *Fundamental Stock Investing* in that you can ignore all the bad things that are happening, and focus strictly on the fundamentals of the stocks you own or are considering buying.

Chapter 23   Ignore The Experts

To make it in investing, it is critically important that you ignore all "experts" on stock market predictions, economic predictions and interest rate predictions and predictions about what the Fed might do. As pointed out earlier in the book, the Forbes 400 is completely dominated by people who got there by investing in stock in their own company or other companies for the long term. There are zero people in there who claim to be market timers. These people never tried to time the market or predict the direction of the economy or interest rates and neither should you.

Like a broken clock is right twice a day, market timers occasionally get lucky and predict a market top, but never correctly predict the market bottom that follows, so it did them no good, and never correctly predict another market top the rest of their lives. There are perennial doom and gloom "Bears" who every year predict a stock market crash and eventually some year they are correct, but what good did it do them when they missed all the much bigger rallies that took place in the between years? They take credit for predicting the crash but fail to mention that they were wrong the 4 straight years before that.

Then there are the market timers who change their predictions so often, it appears they timed the market. However, if they really could predict the market, they would be in the Forbes 400 and not having to be selling advice to other people. One of the most famous, was someone who was credited by the financial press for calling the 1987 stock market crash. The person gained instantaneous overnight fame, and some people foolishly listened on the edge of their seats every time the person spoke for the next 5 years. The person never made another correct call again, and in the spring of 2003, famously predicted the stock market would go sideways for years to come, just days before a massive 4 plus year stock market rally began that saw the Dow nearly double.

You also need to ignore "experts" with their buy and sell recommendations that sound so convincing with all their "calls", and while they can be entertaining, you will loose your shirt actually following their stock advice. You need to be your own person, and do your own fundamental research, and make all your own decisions on an individual stock by stock basis, and ignore what everyone else is saying about stocks, the stock market, interest rates, the economy and the Fed.

Chapter 24   Ignore All The Silly Stock Market Sayings That Have No Meaning

Wall Street is full of clever and convincing sounding, but silly sayings, that are non-factual and non-quantifiable and therefore, are useless to the fundamental stock investor. It is important to ignore them, because they are slick and sound convincing and may cause you to make a wrong decision on a stock. Stick to factual information such as "This is a small cap retailer growing earnings at 20% per year and only selling at 15 times next year's earnings (Forward P/E); they have 3 dollars per share in net cash for a stock selling at 11. Insiders are buying and they are buying back their own stock and have removed 15% of shares outstanding in the past 3 years. Only 1 analyst follows the stock, and institutions only own 25% of shares. One of the senior managers was buying stock (insider buying) last month at a price of 13. They still have 1/3 of the country to expand into, and same store sales are up 4%." That is the type of language you want to be speaking in. Ignore trite platitudes such as:

"That stock is overextended."
"The stock is oversold."
"The stock is due for a pullback."
"Don't get greedy."
"That stock is a value trap."
"Bulls make money."
"Bears make money."
"Pigs get slaughtered."
"The stock is forming a top."
"The stock market needs to pause to digest the recent gains."
"This stock is now rolling over."
"This is a 'risk on' stock market."
"The stock is bottoming."
"The stock chart is broken."
"Buy only The Best-Of-The-Breed companies."
"I really like the technicals on that stock."
"This pull-back in stocks is the pause that refreshes."
"This is a stock you can buy and put away and hold forever."
"We are in a confirmed uptrend."
"The market is due for a pull-back."

"The age of stock picking is over."
"The stock market rally is getting tired."
"I am cautiously optimistic."
"The Dow Transport Average is breaking down."
"That stock is forming a reverse head and shoulders pattern."
"A correction would be healthy for the market."
"The stock market is in rally mode."
"This is a stock picker's market."
"This earnings season is going to be the most important one in years."
(Actually, they are all equally important.)
"The stock market is overbought."
"This company is monetizing their sales."
"That stock has a faulty base."
"The stock market is getting frothy."
"That stock represents solid value."
"There is just too much uncertainty right now."
"I am constructive on this stock."
"The market sentiment is too negative right now."
"The market needs to consolidate recent gains."
"The stock is stuck in a trading range."
"I don't like that way that stock is acting."
"Stocks are melting up."
"A correction is in order."
"The stock is forming a solid base with a perfect handle."
"Don't buy this stock heading into the print (earnings report)."
"This is a 'risk off' stock market."
"Buy on the rumor, sell on the news."
"Stay in the market until the Fed takes away the punch bowl."
"Only invest in the true leaders."
"Don't fight the tape."
"It's all in the (conference) call."
"The options market indicates this stock could go up."
"The stock market is climbing a wall of worry."
"Stocks are grinding higher."
"That stock is a good short squeeze candidate."
"Gaps get filled."
"Stock price is truth."
"Stocks are melting down."
"The market has to pull back before it can go higher."
"Don't fight the Fed."

"Buy a stock just as it is breaking out from a sound base pattern."
"The trend is your friend."

This is just a partial list and there are many more and new ones will come into vogue. They are all slick sounding but they are trite and have no useful meaning. Some people become well versed in these expressions and start throwing them around themselves and mistakenly think they now understand the stock market but in fact they know less than nothing, because they don't realize these mean nothing and the fundamentals are what really matter. Stick to actual facts about the companies you own or are considering buying and ignore all these useless sayings. You can be certain Carlos Slim and Warren Buffett never used phrases like these while investing their way to the richest men in the world and neither should you, other than to chuckle when you hear them said by others.

Chapter 25 More Details On Stock Investing: Analyzing Growth Stock's Growth Rate In Relation to P/E

Growth stock are defined as stocks that are steadily increasing earnings many years in a row and are not as affected by economic cycles as happens to cyclical stocks whose earnings soar during economic booms and then collapse and turn to losses during recessions. There are 3 general categories of growth stocks:

Slow Growth - Earnings increase 0-5% a year.
Medium Growth - Earnings increase 5-15% a year.
Fast Growth - Earnings increase more than 15% a year.

When considering buying growth companies, the general rule of thumb is that the % earnings Growth Rate (GR) should equal or exceed the price to earnings ratio (P/E) of the company. If the GR equals the Forward P/E, the stock is fairly priced. If the GR exceeds the Forward P/E, you have a bargain. If the GR is lower than the Forward P/E, the stock is overpriced. This is the single most important thing to use when evaluating growth stocks.

If the stock pays a dividend, you should factor the dividend in by adding the % annual dividend yield to the GR to get the Total Return (TR) and then compare it to the Forward P/E. Therefore, as you can see, when a stock pays a dividend, it is a small additional positive.

Example 1: Proctor & Gamble (PG) is selling at 85 and it is expected to earn 4.28 per share next year compared to 4.05 this year and its current annual dividend yield is 2.8%. Your GR is (4.28-4.05)/4.05 x 100 = 5.7%. Adding the GR to the annual dividend yield gives you a TR of 5.7 + 2.8 = 9. The Forward P/E is 85/4.28 = 20. So the TR is 9 and the Forward P/E is 20, so the stock is significantly overpriced and should be avoided. Obviously PG is a great company and is doing well by increasing earnings and paying a dividend that gives a TR of 9, but the problem is the stock is way too expensive selling at 20 times next year's earnings. If you are going to pay 20 times earnings, you want to see at GR/TR of 20 or higher to put the odds in your favor. This does not mean the stock will go down or up necessarily, but as a fundamental stock investor, the odds are stacked against you, and you should look for better opportunities elsewhere. As pointed out in an earlier chapter, you can get the data online for these evaluations from your discount broker's website or Yahoo Finance or Google Finance or other similar websites. I prefer Yahoo.

Example 2: Tandy Leather Factory (TLF) is selling for 8.3 and is expected to earn 0.80 next year versus 0.69 this year and doesn't pay a regular dividend. The GR is $(0.80-0.69)/0.69 \times 100 = 16\%$. The Forward P/E is $8.3/0.80 = 10$. So the GR is 16 and P/E is only 10, so this is the type of stock you want to buy to put odds of success in your favor.

Example 3: Sonic (SONC) is selling for 20 and is expected to earn 0.84 next year versus 0.72 this year. The GR is $(0.84-0.72)/0.72 \times 100 = 17\%$ and P/E is $20/0.84 = 24$. So GR is 17 and P/E is 24. That is a nice GR but the P/E of 24 makes it too expensive at the current stock price. This is a stock you would want to buy if the stock pulls back to a Forward P/E of 17 or lower.

Those simple calculations are the toughest ones you will ever have to make as a fundamental stock investor, and obviously anyone can do them with a 5 dollar calculator.

The GR or TR (for dividend paying stocks) versus P/E is the single most important consideration. If the P/E is greater than the GR or TR, then avoid that stock unless and until the stock pulls back such that the GR or TR at least equals the P/E.

Other notes for growth stocks:

- Use the Forward P/E when evaluating growth stocks, meaning current price divided by next year's estimated earning per share (EPS).

- When evaluating EPS, always use the EPS from "Continuing Operations" or "Non-GAAP" or "ex-items" or "core earnings" which factor out one time events that impact GAAP earnings. You want to look at core earnings for the business. Earnings estimates on Yahoo do this for you with some exceptions (about 3% of the time they don't do this for some reason and instead list GAAP estimates). In the company's press release, they usually give you both GAAP and non GAAP numbers. Always use non-GAAP numbers (sometimes called "ex-items" or core earnings). For Real Estate Investment Trust (REITs) stocks, they call it Funds From Operations (FFO).

- NEVER buy a stock selling at a Forward P/E of more than 40 times earnings no matter how high the Growth Rate. Think about it. Would you buy a business that you have to pay 40 times the profit it will make next year? That means it would take 40 years at constant earnings to get your money back.

Great fortunes were lost and many investors wiped out when the **Tech Bubble** burst in 2000-2002 Stock Market Collapse. A generation of investors got scared out of stocks and never came back. The S&P 500 lost more than 40% and the NASDAQ lost about 80%. A lot of retail AND "professional" investors thought they knew what they were doing when stocks went straight up in the late '90s but they really didn't know anything. Stocks with P/Es of 100 or greater were commonplace. Stocks with NO earnings selling at outrageous valuations were everywhere. Even great companies stocks were slaughtered with staggering losses such as Microsoft (lost 73% of its value), Cisco (88%), Dell (83%), Oracle (84%), Yahoo (98%) and Intel (82%). What was wrong with these companies? Absolutely nothing; all were great companies that were doing fantastic and continued to grow earnings, even after the Tech Bubble burst, but at 50 to 100 times earnings or more, they were wildly overpriced, and fundamental investors like myself never owned such stocks, because we knew the stocks would eventually implode, it was just a question as to when. Therefore, as an investor I came out of the Tech Bubble collapse totally unscathed, because I never owned stocks selling for more than 40 times forward earnings.

In this current market (mid to late 2013), I see similar stocks but not widespread like back in 1999/2000. Today we have Netflix at 390 (95 times forward earnings), Pandora at 33 (130 times forward earnings), Amazon at 406 (155 times forward earnings), Tesla at 195 (130 times forward earnings), Zillow at 103 (206 times forward earnings), Salesforce.com at 60 (115 times forward earnings), Linkedin at 260 (120 times forward earnings), Yelp at 83 (435 times forward earnings!!), Barracuda Networks (CUDA) at 40 (1000 times forward earnings !!!) and Twitter at 75 with a market cap of 45 billion and with no P/E, they are losing money. To make money on these stocks you must rely on the **Greater Fool Theory**, meaning when you foolishly buy stocks selling at 50, 100, 200, 300 and 1000 times forward earnings, the only way you can make money is if even greater fools come in after you and buy the stocks. Regardless of how these companies' actual businesses perform going forward, you can count on most of these stocks losing at least 50% of their value over the next 5 years, but you won't be able to predict when it actually happens.

- Remember that growth rates of more than 30% per year are not sustainable over the long term. There are rare exceptions to this, but for the vast majority don't expect any number over 30% to be sustainable over many years.

- Favor smaller growth companies over larger growth companies. In general, small stocks make big moves and large stock make small moves. Also by the simple laws of averages, small stocks normally have more room to grow than large stocks and in theory, have more potential for sustaining a higher growth rate over the long term. For example, in 2011 when Apple was selling for 700 and with a market cap of 600 billion and was growing earnings at 30% a year, it was clearly unsustainable, while a company with a market cap of 300 million, has a much better chance of sustaining high earnings growth.

- Focus on Fast Growth companies that can have sustained growth rates of 15 to 30% over several years that are fairly priced or cheap, meaning the Forward P/E is equal to or less than the GR. This is where your biggest winners are in the world of growth stock investing. When there is a Correction/Bear Market/Stock Market Collapse you have a great opportunity to load up on these fast growers at cheap prices. After you buy a Fast Growth company, you want to hold it until its growth rate falls below 15%, then you sell it.

- Remember the rule of 72. If you take the number 72 and divide it by the GR, that tells you how long it will take the company to double its earnings (and presumably the stock price eventually, provided you didn't pay too much for it to begin with). A 25% grower is going to double in about 3 years, a 20% grower in about 4 years, a 15% grower in about 5 years and a 10% grower in 7 years. Obviously, you want to favor faster growers. So a 20% grower selling at a P/E of 20 is superior to a 10% grower selling at a P/E of 10.

- For older more established growth companies, which are more likely to be in the Slow Growth or Medium Growth category, look at the typical P/E for that industry to evaluate whether a stock is cheap or not. You can even look at individual companies over a period of years to find the normal P/E range for that company, and you can make money simply by buying the stock when it is at the low end of its P/E range and sell when at the high end of its P/E range.

Here are some typical P/E ranges for older more established Slow Growth and Medium Growth companies. For example, Proctor & Gamble is a large, mature slow/medium growth company and falls into the Consumer Non-Durables category, therefore, it typically trades based on the table below at 12-18 times earnings. Therefore, at 20 times earnings, it is obviously not likely to be a good investment over the intermediate term. Do not use these ranges below for younger Fast Growth companies with plenty of room for expansion, instead, compare their current GR to their Forward P/E:

Restaurant 11-19
Retail 10-18
Regional and Small Banks 8-14
Measuring/Scientific Equipment 10-18
Cable/Satellite/TV/content providers 12-20
Telecom 13-17
Drug 12-20
Generic Drugs 8-15
Software 11-17
Mature High Tech 10-16
Consumer Non-Durables 12-18

- **Sales** are also important. In addition to earnings growth, you obviously also want to see sales, also known as **revenue,** increasing. You will often see larger mature slow growth companies do a **restructuring**, in which they cut costs by closing or selling underperforming divisions, lay-off employees and cut overhead costs. This often gives a short term to intermediate term (i.e. 1-2 year) boost to EPS and to the stock price. However, companies can only cut so much, so after the restructuring and the initial 1-2 year benefit to EPS (and to the stock price), they will have to increase sales to continue to increase profits (and the stock price). Therefore, you want to see sales/revenue always increasing in growth companies. Note that during a recession or weak economy you will see small sales declines in many growth companies. These sales declines in growth companies are much smaller than the typical collapse in sales you will see in cyclical companies.

Chapter 26   More Details On Stock Investing: Analyzing The Balance Sheet

Avoid companies with high debt loads (i.e. poor Balance Sheets). Bad things can happen to companies with high debt loads. If a recession hits they can be in big trouble and go under. If interest rates rise, their borrowing costs rise, so their earnings decline. If a good acquisition candidate comes up, they won't be able to finance it due to their high debt load. They are also less likely to be acquired. They don't have the flexibility to buy back their own stock after a big stock market decline. Everything is less favorable when investing in companies with a large debt load, and all of their business decisions have less margin for error.

Favor companies with strong Balance Sheets, i.e. more cash than debt or relatively low debt loads. Good things tend to happen to companies with lots of cash. They can use that cash to buy back shares of their own stock, which make their shares more valuable. They can pay and increase dividend payments. They can buy out competitors. They can be bought out at a higher price by another company or **Private Equity** firms seeking to get a hold of their cash. A company with more cash then debt CANNOT go bankrupt. They can ride out recessions better than other companies. They can invest more on new product or service development. If there is a big stock market decline, they can take advantage of that tremendous opportunity by buying back their own stock. If they have poor management, the management will eventually be fired and replaced and the cash can ride them through this tough period, and the new management has a chance to turn the company around.

Always examine the Balance Sheet by calculating the net cash (or net debt position) for every company you are considering investing in. For example, from the latest quarterly report press release from PG (easily obtained on Yahoo Finance, click Press Releases or click balance sheet). Ignore short term debt. Add up cash, which is "cash and cash equivalents" + short term investments + long term investments. For PG that is $6.0 + 0 + 0 = 6.0$ billion. Their long term debt is 19.1 billion. Their net debt is $19.1 - 6.0 = 13.1$ billion. Determine shares outstanding by clicking Key Statistics and they have

2.74 billion shares. So net debt per share is 13.1/2.74 = 5 dollars per share in net debt. The stock is selling for 85, so although they have more debt than cash which is a negative, but 5 compared to 85 is practically negligible, so their balance sheet is good and not a significant factor, so their GR/TR compared to P/E is the primary consideration.

For argument's sake, say a company has net debt per share of 25 for an 80 dollar stock that would be significant and a negative, but not a troubling negative. If it had 50 dollars per share in net debt and selling at 80 that would be a troubling debt load and in most cases the stock should be avoided. On the other hand, if they had 3 dollars per share in net cash for an 80 dollar stock, it would be a positive, but a negligible positive. If they had 20 dollars per share in net cash for an 80 dollar stock, that would be a significant positive. Remember, you are always comparing the relative size of net cash or net debt per share compared to the current price of the stock. Therefore, a net cash per share of 1 dollar for a stock selling at 3 is a huge positive and a net debt per share of 6 for a stock selling at 8 would be a staggering debt load and the stock should be avoided.

For small young growth companies, you want strong balance sheets with little or no debt. A couple of missteps and such companies with lots of debt can quickly get in big trouble and the stock will plunge. This is a very common occurrence for young, small growth companies, such as restaurants or retailers, that try to expand too fast and finance the expansion by taking on debt.

Also note, that for old line industrial companies (e.g. Boeing, Ford, Caterpillar, US Steel, etc.), you also have to add in their pension liabilities to their debt totals, when making these calculations. These are listed in their balance sheets in their quarterly and annual reports, as a separate line item in their liabilities. On Yahoo Finance they are listed as "other liabilities".

Chapter 27   More Details On Stock Investing: More On Investing In Retailers and Restaurants

Retailers and restaurants are always a place a fundamental stock investor needs to investigate, because there have probably been more 10 baggers in this area than in any other part of the stock market. This is due to the homogeneity of the USA in that if a retailer or restaurant is successful in one part of the country, it is usually successful everywhere in the country. So obviously, it is best to find a good one when it is still only in a few states and has lots of room for expansion.

When evaluating restaurants and retailers, pay close attention to **same store sales (SSS)**. Same store sales are a measure of how existing units are doing and excludes new units that have been open for less than one year. You want to see same store sales increasing. Note however, that during a recession, same store sales can decline even for a healthy company. So, you have to compare same store sales in comparison to other companies in their industry. For example, if a retail or restaurant stock you have owned has increased same store sales a few years in a row and then we have a recession and same store sales are down, but most restaurants and retailers have down same store sales that is not cause for selling based on that alone. Again, just as with EPS, you want to evaluate same store sales in absolute terms, i.e. were they good or not and ignore whatever "analyst expectations" were for same store sales.

Why are same store sales so important and why do you want to see them generally increasing? They are the measure of the core business of the retailer or restaurant. You can have a case where a young start-up retailer/restaurant has soaring profits due to massive new store openings in which people go in to check out the new place, but simultaneously, the same store sales are declining, because people are not returning after their initial visit. In this case, the core of the company is actually falling apart, and even though earnings are temporarily soaring due to new units, soon earnings will plunge and you can lose a ton of money on a stock like that. I know, because I made that mistake once on the Lone Star Steakhouse chain and took a big loss.

When evaluating restaurants and retailers, look for ones that have plenty of room for expansion. This is easy; go to Yahoo Finance and click Company Profile. It will tell you how many units they have in how many states. You can also go to the company's press releases where it will provide such information, or go to the company website and click **Investor Relations** and then click **Annual Report**. If you find a company that has low debt or no debt, increasing same store sales, earnings growing at 15-30% per year, increasing the number of units open every year, and they are in less than 30 states, and the stock is reasonably priced (i.e. Forward P/E is less than 40 AND equal to or less than the GR), you have a potential huge Fast Growth company winner. This is because America is a very homogeneous country, and what works in one state is going to work in all 50 states. This is where I have had many of my biggest winners.

If the restaurant or retailer is already in 40-50 states, they obviously have less room for expansion, and these former Fast Growth stocks are now going to fall into the Medium or Slow Growth stock category. You can still make money off them as I pointed out earlier from the table in **Chapter 25;** mature retailers trade between 10 and 18 times earnings and restaurants between 11 and 19 times earnings, so as long as earnings are increasing, debt is under control and same store sales are increasing, buy them when they are cheap (at the low end of their normal P/E range), and sell them when they get expensive (at the high end of their normal P/E range). Also note, some can successfully expand overseas or into a second new concept type of retailer/restaurant to reinvigorate EPS growth, even after they have filled all 50 states.

Chapter 28   More Details On Stock Investing: How To Make Money In Cyclical Stocks

Buy cyclical stocks when business is terrible and the stock is way down from its all time high. Huge money can be made in cyclical stocks when business is bad and the stock is way down from its all time high provided it has a strong enough balance sheet to survive the downturn. Whenever the economy heads south and goes into a recession, it is a good time to be looking to be buying cyclical stocks. Typically, cyclical stocks start falling well before the economy starts heading into recession, and cyclical stocks start rising well before the end of a recession, and well before business starts actually improving. This makes cyclical stock investing a little tricky. Therefore, you would never buy and hold forever a cyclical stock (or any stock for that matter), because they are generally mediocre investments over the long term. If you buy and sell the cycles properly, a cyclical stock would be held for 1-3 years and longer in rare circumstances.

Classic cyclical companies are companies that are very sensitive to the overall health of the economy such as autos, auto parts, steel, mining, chemicals, commercial fertilizer manufacturers, airlines, airplane manufacturers, home builders, truckers, rails, rail car builders, construction companies, "Money Center" banks, oil/oil service, hotels, etc. Defense stocks are also cyclical, but their fortunes are not necessarily tied to the economy but to political cycles. Large established technology companies are also cyclicals, but they often have their own cycles independent of the economy, and their cycles tend to be shorter than the overall economy. Meat/poultry companies are also cyclicals, but their cycles are not tied to the economy; they are tied to grain production and capacity and supply/demand changes.

Here are some general rules to follow when buying cyclicals:

1) Be aware that cyclical investing is high risk/high reward. If you get it right and buy at the bottom of the cycle, you are looking at doubling and tripling or more of your money. If you get it wrong and buy at the peak of the cycle for that industry, you can relatively quickly lose 50-90% of your money and be in a stock that may take years to come back.

2) The P/E rules of growth stock investing do not apply to cyclicals.

3) The stock should be way down from its previous cycle all time high. The stock should be down at least 50 to 90%. The more down the better.

4) Business should be lousy. However, it must be lousy for the entire industry and not lousy just because one particular company is doing lousy. For example, when looking at a home building stock, all the home building companies should be doing lousy, not just the one company you are looking at. Again the P/E is meaningless, because at cycle bottom, there is no P/E, because it is infinity or extremely high, because it is either losing money or making negligible amounts of money.

5) The lousier the business for the industry the better, because the rebound will be even stronger due to pent up demand. The longer the downturn, the longer and bigger the following boom is likely to be. For example, during the 2008/2009 recession, things were so bad for autos that it was an auto depression. Things were so bad both Chrysler and GM de facto went bankrupt and were bailed out by the taxpayers. This ensured a big rebound. Ford (F) went from 2 to 18 (a nine bagger), Toyota (TM) from 60 to 130, Honda (HMC) from 21 to 45, Nissan (NSANY) from 5 to 23 (nearly a 5 bagger) and Tata (TTM) from 3 to 36 (a 12 bagger). I loaded up on all of these stocks and caught a good portion of their runs and made good money.

6) The balance sheet of the cyclical stock must be strong enough to survive a protracted downturn. If you buy a depressed cyclical with a weak balance sheet and the downturn lasts longer than expected, they could go bankrupt and you will lose 100% of your investment. Always calculate the net debt/net cash per share for a cyclical and compare to the stock price. A cyclical that is debt free or that has more cash than debt cannot go bankrupt, at least in the intermediate term, and they are excellent candidates to buy in a cyclically depressed industry, if you can find them. However, most cyclical industries are highly capital intensive, so it takes huge sums of money to keep manufacturing facilities up to date, which often requires taking on debt, so most cyclical companies have more debt than cash. This

makes cyclical investing challenging, but very rewarding if you get it right. It also explains why these tend to not be great investments over the long term. Look for companies whose net debt per share is less than 50% of the stock price. For example, if you are looking at a depressed cyclical selling at 9 dollars per share, you would like to see net debt below 5 dollars per share. Also, you want to see net debt per share relative to its stock price lower than competitors in its industry, i.e. you want to buy the stock with the strongest balance sheet in the industry. If things get worse, you want your company to be the last company standing in a weak industry in a bad recession. You want to seek out cyclicals with the strongest balance sheet in their industry. Also, closely monitor the balance sheet each quarterly report. It is normal for the balance sheet of a cyclical to worsen during an industry downturn; however, if the balance sheet is rapidly deteriorating, the company could be in trouble, and you should not buy, and you should sell, if you already own it.

7) Cyclical investing requires patience. You can meet all of the criteria above, and business may stay lousy or worsen for 1-2 more years, and the stock could go nowhere or continue to decline. As long as the balance sheet is strong enough to survive, you want to stick with the stock, and buy more if the stock continues to decline significantly and wait for the inevitable turnaround. I made the mistake of running out of patience on fertilizer stocks in the early '00s. I bought them correctly during the 2001 recession when the stocks were way down and losing money or barley profitable. However, when the recession ended, these businesses didn't recover immediately, and I foolishly ran out of patience and sold for a tiny gain. I forgot the lesson that the longer the downturn in an industry the better, because the ultimate recovery will be longer and stronger. When the recovery finally came for the fertilizer business in 2004, it was the greatest boom in the history of the fertilizer industry, stocks such as Agrium (AGU) soared from 12 to 107 (a 9 bagger), CF Industries (CF) from 12 to 166 (a 14 bagger), Potash (POT) from 4 to 76 (a 19 bagger) and Mosaic (MOS) from 15 to 153 (a 10 bagger). I missed most of these gains. Remember, the longer and deeper the downturn, the bigger the rebound for the surviving companies.

8) Remember that cyclical stocks often start turning up well before any sign of business improvement even begins. Often you can't wait to

buy a cyclical stock when business starts to improve. If you do that, you will miss a huge chunk of the eventual rebound. Also, you will see false starts, where the cyclical stocks start to take off, only to fall right back to the bottom before they really get going. This gives you a chance to buy more.

9) As always, ignore what everyone else is saying about cyclicals or any stock for that matter. Often the best time to buy cyclicals is when every one hates them and/or ignores them and/or says there is no turnaround in sight and/or every headline for that industry is terrible and/or every analyst has a sell rating on them.

10) Money Center Banks and Investment Bankers are cyclicals, but a special set of rules apply to them. See **Chapter 31** for how to buy and sell them.

Here are some general rules on when to sell cyclicals:

1) Sell cyclicals when the economy/industry has rebounded and has been profitable and booming for a few years. By this time the stocks have gone way up, and if you got in at or near the bottom of the cycle, you will have made a ton of money. Once a cyclical has recovered for a few years, it will be profitable again and will actually have a P/E again that is actually meaningful. Again, the growth stock rules for P/E do not apply because they are not growth stocks. The P/E of a cyclical is usually relatively low even during a recovery/boom. Due to the cyclical nature of these companies, they are considered less valuable, because their industries are usually capital intensive, and people know they will eventually be falling on hard times again. During boom times, for example, auto stocks typically trade between 5 and 10 times peak earnings. Here are some typical P/Es of cyclicals during booms for their respective industries:

Auto 5-10
Foreign Auto 6-12
Auto Parts 6-12
Steel 4-9
Iron Ore Miner 6-13
Copper Miner 5-14
Coal Miner 10-20

Gold Miner 10-17
Heavy Equipment 9-15
Heavy Equipment (retailers/rental) 6-12
Fertilizer 5-11
Meat/Poultry/Egg Producers 6-12
Paper/Pulp/Lumber 6-12
Home Builder 7-12
Construction Materials 6-12
Consumer Durables (tires, appliances, etc.) 6-12
Truckers/Truck Manufacturers 7-15
Rail 10-17
REIT 6-12
Hotel 10-16
Oil/Gas Producers 8-14
Oil Service/Oil Drillers 7-13
Oil Refiners 4-9
Chemicals 8-16
Disk Drive 6-14
Semi/Semi Equipment/Semi Test 10-15
Mature Technology/Software 8-15
Aerospace 11-17
Defense 8-14
Industrial 10-17
Money Center Banks 8-14
Investment Bankers 8-12
Insurance 6-11

After a cyclical has returned to profitability and has had a couple of years of profitability and the stock has gone up a lot, sell it if it goes beyond the top of the above P/E ranges in the table above.

2) Sell cyclicals when profits have increased 3-4 or more years in a row. The odds of it continuing, get lower each year.

3) Sell cyclicals when you hear about more than 1 company in the industry not increasing capacity by adding more shifts, but actually building new manufacturing facilities, especially after the industry has been booming for a few years.

4) Sell cyclicals that have gone up a lot over a few years and whose stock suddenly goes into a Climax Run. See **Chapter 44** on how a Climax Run works and how to sell into a Climax run.

5) Sell cyclicals when business actually starts to deteriorate, i.e. sales and profits start going down. By this time you are usually at least a little late, because cyclical stocks usually peak well before there is even a hint of a downturn in the industry.

6) Sell cyclicals that you have bought, whose stock price have gone up a lot in price (as investors try to anticipate an improving industry/economy), but where there has been not only no improvement in the industry, but the industry is worsening and losses are actually worsening.

7) Sell cyclicals that have been profitable and booming for a few years in a row, and everyone it talking about them and how great they are doing, and all the "experts" are recommending them.

Ignore the stock price movements in cyclicals the day they report quarterly earnings. You will notice that often when a cyclical's business is rebounding and improving and they report greatly improved earnings, the stock will open higher, then reverse and close down 1-4% that day. Conversely, when a cyclical's business is depressed, and they report another lousy quarter, the stock will initially fall, then reverse and close up 1-4% for that day. These are some of the games the hedge funds and fast money types play with stocks, and as with all short term stock movements, they are meaningless and should be ignored. I only point it out, so you will not be surprised and be less annoyed by these silly games when they happen.

Tend to avoid cyclical stocks that do massive Secondary Offerings, i.e. selling more stock to raise money for the company. These offerings dilute your shares, if you already own the stock, and when earnings rebound, the denominator in Earnings Per Share (EPS) gets bigger, so the EPS is smaller than it would have been, and it is EPS that ultimately drives stock prices in the long run. Sometimes cyclicals are forced to do secondary offerings, just to have cash to survive, or else they will run out of cash. So, you need to evaluate what the rest of the industry is doing for comparison. If the whole industry is forced to do secondary offerings it is ok, but if it is just one company, then avoid that one company.

Chapter 29   More Details On Stock Investing: More Information On Cyclical Auto Stock Investing

Another way to find out if it is a good idea to buy or sell the highly cyclical auto stocks is to track how much pent up demand there is. Peter Lynch was one of the pioneers at using this technique, and I utilize his method as an additional aid for evaluating auto stocks. You can do this, as I have done it, by tracking yearly US auto sales (obtained via simple internet search) and yearly estimates for the current year and next year (via simple internet search). Then you put the data in a table, as I have below, and you compare it to the long term trend demand. The long term trend demand is based on what a typical average year might be. You, the investor, has to come up with this trend demand estimate on your own, based on looking at the long term sales numbers. My guess at this right now is 15.0 million units per year. Then you evaluate the pent up demand by subtracting actual sales from your estimated trend demand (see table below).

If there is pent up demand, it is generally a good time to buy auto stocks, especially if it will take more than a couple of years of good sales to soak up the pent up demand. We had an auto depression in this country in 2008 and 2009 with demand well below trend. During this time, strapped consumers put off buying new cars and the average age of cars on the road soared to nearly 12 years old, the oldest in US history. Obviously, those cars won't last forever, so there should be several good years of auto sales. You should continue to update and track this table as time goes on, as another clue as to when to buy and sell auto stocks.

U.S. Auto and Truck Industry Sales, Actual Versus Trend (millions)

Year	Actual	Trend (my estimate)	Units Above/(Below) Trend	Units of Pent-up Demand	Buy Auto Stocks?
1980	11.5	12.8	(1.3)	1.3	-
1981	10.8	13.0	(2.2)	3.5	Yes buy
1982	10.5	13.2	(2.7)	6.2	Y!
1983	12.3	13.4	(1.1)	7.3	Y!!
1984	14.4	13.6	0.8	6.4	Y!
1985	15.7	13.8	1.9	4.5	Y
1986	16.3	14.0	2.3	2.2	Y
1987	15.2	14.2	1.0	1.2	Y
1988	15.8	14.4	1.4	(0.2)	Sell
1989	14.8	14.6	0.2	(0.4)	No
1990	14.2	14.7	(0.5)	0.1	N
1991	12.5	14.6	(2.1)	2.2	Y buy
1992	13.3	14.4	(1.1)	3.2	Y
1993	13.9	14.4	(0.5)	3.7	Y
1994	15.0	14.4	0.6	3.1	Y
1995	14.7	14.6	0.1	3.0	Y
1996	15.1	14.9	0.2	2.8	Y
1997	15.0	15.4	(0.4)	3.2	Y
1998	15.6	15.3	0.3	2.9	Y
1999	17.0	16.1	0.9	2.0	Y
2000	17.4	16.3	1.1	0.9	sell
2001	17.0	16.5	0.5	0.4	N
2002	16.8	16.6	0.2	0.2	N
2003	16.6	16.6	0	0.2	N
2004	16.8	16.6	0.2	0	N
2005	16.9	16.6	0.3	(0.3)	N
2006	16.5	16.7	(0.2)	(0.1)	N
2007	16.1	16.7	(0.6)	0.7	N
2008	13.2	15	(1.8)	2.4	Y buy
2009	10.4	15	(4.6)	7.0	Y!
2010	11.8	15	(3.2)	10.2	Y!!

Year	Actual	Trend (my estimate)	Units Above/(Below) Trend	Units of Pent-up Demand	Buy Auto Stocks?
2011	12.8	15	(2.2)	12.4	Y !!!
2012	14.5	15	(0.5)	12.9	Y!!!!
2013	15.6	15	0.6	12.3	Y!!!
2014	16.4e	15	1.4	10.9	Y!!
2015					
2016					

e - estimate

Chapter 30   More Details On Stock Investing: How To Make Money In Turnarounds

Turnarounds can be hugely profitable multi-baggers, if the company actually turns around. A **Turnaround** candidate is an established and formally solidly profitable company, that has had missteps, and has fallen on hard times, and has fallen behind its competitors. These are not the same as cyclicals that go up and down regularly with the economy. These are companies that were either growth companies or cyclicals, and their management wrecked the company by expanding too fast or taking on too much debt or fell behind at innovating or did too many dilutive acquisitions, etc. and are on the brink of bankruptcy or are trying to emerge from bankruptcy. The absolute key for turnarounds is a survivable balance sheet.

Here are the general rules for buying and selling turnarounds:

1) Turnarounds are very high risk/reward stocks. You can make a ton of money, if you are right, and if you are wrong, you can lose everything.

2) Don't ever buy a company that has never been profitable, that is not a turnaround; that is called a money sink. For a company to be a turnaround, it must have once been a successful profitable company.

3) Look for turnarounds whose stock is way down, 50 to 90% or more. Remember, Wall Street always overdoes everything on the upside and downside. Don't even consider looking at a turnaround company, until the stock has taken a severe and protracted beating, and has been in decline for 6 months to a year or longer. Never buy right after the initial big fall, because often there is more downside to come.

4) The balance sheet is everything in a turnaround. The balance sheet of the turnaround stock must be strong enough to survive until the company can turn itself around. If you buy a turnaround with too weak of a balance sheet, they could go bankrupt and you will lose 100% of your investment. Always calculate the net debt/net cash per share for a turnaround and compare to the stock price. A turnaround that is debt free or that has more cash than debt cannot go bankrupt, at

least in the intermediate term, and they have a good chance to turn themselves around. Look for companies whose debt per share is less than 50% of the stock price. For example, if you are looking at a depressed turnaround selling at 2 dollars per share, you would like to see net debt below 1 dollars per share. In rare cases, you can buy a turnaround with a higher debt level, but in that case, the debt must be declining each quarter, and the company must be at least breaking even or nearly breaking even in profits. Also, closely monitor the balance sheet each quarter. If the balance sheet is rapidly deteriorating, avoid or get out of the stock. You want to see the company improving, i.e. losses narrowing or actually turning to profit, and the balance sheet at least stabilizing, if not improving. If the quarterly results are still worsening, you want to avoid the stock or get out.

5) Be aware, the possible turnaround company will never mention the word bankruptcy in their quarterly press releases. If business is really bad and worsening, and the balance sheet is worsening, they won't tell you, "Hey everyone, if this keeps up for a couple more quarters, we are going to one day, without warning, suddenly announce that we have filed for bankruptcy, and when that happens, the stock will instantly go to near zero, and you will lose everything." They won't say that; they will just suddenly file for bankruptcy protection, and if you are in the stock when that happens, you lose everything. So you need to get out of the stock, if the losses are worsening and/or the balance sheet is worsening.

6) As always, ignore what "experts" are saying; you have to look at the numbers yourself and make your own determination. A lot of so called "experts" just go by emotion or "gut feeling" or by what they heard other "experts" are saying or the herd is saying. Never go by "gut feeling" when investing; look at the actual numbers, which takes less than 5 minutes each quarterly earnings report.

7) Once a turnaround stock has successfully turned around and is profitable again and the balance sheet is decent again, then as an investor, you need to reclassify it from the turnaround category to a growth company or cyclical company, as applicable, and buy or sell based on those rules.

Six Flags Amusement Park (SIX) was a successful turnaround investment for me. Due to taking on too much debt, expanding too fast and the recession, the company went bankrupt in 2009. It re-emerged from bankruptcy with much lower debt at lower interest rates and came public again in an IPO in May of 2010 at a price of 10. It became instantly profitable, and not only that, they were soon buying back shares and instituting a dividend. Although the stock was hated by Wall Street, it became obvious to me that it was no longer in any danger of bankruptcy. Not only were they profitable ex items, profits were soaring from 1.31 ex items in 2010 to 1.76 in 2011 to 2.16 ex items in 2012. They were constantly raising the dividend and buying back shares. The shares responded rising to 40 by mid 2013, and I was able to get a good portion of that rise.

Sirius XM Radio (SIRI) came public in the 1990s and rose to 61 during the Internet Bubble of the late 1990s, even though the company was losing money. The company got slammed by the auto depression of 2008-2009 with big losses, and the stock was driven all the way down to 75 cents. They survived, and in 2010, they basically broke even. By 2011, they were now profitable, and cash was increasing, and debt was declining, and it was clear they were not going to go bankrupt. Debt per share had fallen to 0.6, and I bought the stock at about 1.7. The turnaround continued, and they increased profits in 2012 and 2013, and the stock was rewarded by rising to 4 by late 2013.

Rite Aid (RAD) is the 3rd largest pharmacy retailer in the nation. After decades of successful growth and expansion, they paid way too much and took on way too much debt in the disastrously dilutive acquisitions of Thrifty Payless and Brooks Pharmacy, and this nearly ran the company into the ground, and the stock plunged from 48 down to 25 cents. In **Chapter 39,** I warn about the dangers of dilutive acquisitions. Years and years of losses followed, and although I followed the stock, the losses were too great and the debt too high to consider buying the stock. However, by 2012 they had reduced debt 4 years in a row and had closed over 1000 poorly performing stores, and in Q3 they finally and suddenly reported their first quarterly profit in 6 years. I bought the stock at 1.2 shortly after that earnings report. Since then, the turnaround has continued with debt still declining, and profits increasing and same store sales turning positive in 2013. The stock rose to 6 in late 2013 making it a 5 bagger for me.

Commonwealth REIT was a turnaround that did not work out for me, as the company failed to actually turnaround, and I lost money as explained in more detail in **Chapter 56**.

Chapter 31   More Details On Stock Investing: Evaluating Bank Stocks

There are nearly 7000 banks in the United States compared to just a handful in most other countries. Nearly 300 of these banks are publicly traded stock companies, and the majority of them are not covered by any analysts, making this fertile ground for investing.

There are 3 categories of banks, the handful of so called **Money Center Banks**, the 12-15 **Regional Banks** and the largest 10 of these are sometimes called **Super Regional Banks**. The rest of the thousands of banks are called **Small Local** or **Community Banks**. Do not confuse these Regional Banks with the Fed's Regional Banks. Also note, there are **Investment Banking** stocks such as Goldman Sachs (GS) and Morgan Stanley (MS) and scores of much smaller investment bankers. The Money Center Banks also have their own Investment Banking divisions. All of these plus insurance companies (discussed in the next chapter), fall under the broader category called **Financials**.

Money Center Banks and Investment Bankers are actually cyclicals, because they are much more affected by the economy than Regional Banks and Small Local Banks. Regional and Small Local Banks tend to behave more like Medium Growth and Slow Growth Stocks than Cyclicals. Money Center Banks are giant banks that have operations throughout the country and also have significant international operations. They also have money management and investment banker operations, trading/investing and other businesses. The former CEO of Wells Fargo was on TV the other day saying his company "has 90 different businesses". The Money Center Banks currently are JP Morgan Chase (JPM), Bank of America (BAC), Wells Fargo (WFC) and Citigroup (C), and they boom and bust along with economy, and therefore, are considered cyclicals. Citigroup, for example, has alternated between booms and teetering on the verge of bankruptcy at least 4 times since 1970.

<u>Money Center Banks</u> - You can make a ton of money on Money Center banks by buying them during recessions and selling them during booms, and I have benefited from doing this several times. Of

course, you can also lose everything if you own a Money Center Bank during a recession, and it is too weak to survive until the recovery comes, as I did with the doomed Washington Mutual. When recessions hit, their profits typically plunge and so do the stocks. You don't want to be in a Money Center Bank (or Investment Banker) headed into the next recession or next "banking crisis", such as the 1983, 1989 and 2008 banking crises. On the other hand, like all cyclicals, a tremendous amount of money can be made on them coming out of recessions, and you will find multi-baggers here.

You want to buy Money Center Banks (and Investment Bankers) at the depths of recession when business is horrible and after the stock has lost 50 to 90% of it value. Of course, you MUST first determine if the bank/investment banker can actually survive the downturn, because if it doesn't and goes bankrupt, you will lose everything. That is what happened to me with Washington Mutual. The key measure in cyclical bottoms is the **Equity to Assets Ratio**. A typical Equity to Assets ratio is 6. Anything above 6 means the bank is strong and will likely survive. The higher the better. Any number above 8 means the bank is extremely strong. In a bad recession, you will see numbers below 6. Avoid any bank with an Equity to Assets ratio less than 5; the risk is too high, that the bank could go under completely. When a Money Center Bank issues its quarterly earnings statement, the release is usually many pages long. They rarely mention the Equity to Assets ratio in their write-up, so instead, you have to scan through table after table until you find the Equity to Assets ratio. Sometimes, they don't even provide the ratio, so you have to find total assets and total equity and calculate the ratio yourself by dividing total equity by total assets and multiplying by 100. Once you buy a beaten down Money Center Bank/Investment Banker during the next recession/"banking crisis" you want to carefully monitor Equity to Assets ratio every quarter, until the economy improves and the bank's earnings start improving.

Once the recession/banking crisis is over, you want to use 5 different criteria to evaluate the Money Center Bank. They are P/E, Book Value, Non-Performing Assets (NPA), Equity to Assets ratio and % Dividend Yield.

Here is a table that provides approximate guidelines to buy and sell:

Money Center Bank Criteria	Buy	Sell
P/E	< 8	>14
Book Value	< 1.25	> 2.5
NPA	< 2%	> 4%
Equity to Assets Ratio	> 7%	< 6%
% Dividend Yield	The higher the better	N/A

With Money Center Banks and Investment Bankers, you have to be more careful than with Regional and Small Local Banks, due to the cyclical nature, which gives them a much higher inherent risk. For Investment Bankers, after they are a couple of years out of recession, their normal P/E range is 8-12. After they have recovered for 2 or more years and the Forward P/E goes above 12, it is best to sell them. For Money Center Banks that are more than a couple years after the bottom, carefully monitor the above criteria in the table, and if any of the sell criteria are met, it is best to sell. If not, continue to hold them/add to your position (i.e. buy more).

Regional and Small Local Banks - These banks are typically not as cyclical as the money center banks/investment bankers and behave more like Medium Growth and Slow Growth Stocks. Most remain profitable even during recessions, although their earnings will decline somewhat. So, you basically look for banks that are increasing earnings AND meet all the criteria below:

Regional and Small Local Bank Criteria	Buy	Sell
P/E	< 8	>14
Book Value	< 1.25	> 2.5
NPA	< 2%	> 4%
Assets to Equity Ratio	> 7%	< 6%
% Dividend Yield	The higher the better	N/A

Keep in mind that Regional and Small Local banks are lower risk/reward than Money Center Banks/Investment Bankers and Small

Local Banks are usually under followed by Wall Street, and there are so many of them (nearly 300); if you look hard enough, you can find some nice bargains.

Chapter 32   More Details On Stock Investing: Evaluating Insurance Stocks

Property Insurance companies - Property Insurance companies are cyclical in nature, but their cycles are tied to natural disasters, which are of course completely random. However, do not attempt to buy and sell insurance companies based on disasters. The reason is that they also have reinsurance to back claims and also, when there is a disaster, they are then able to put in big rate increases that ultimately increase profits. Therefore, don't try to predict the cycles, simply buy and sell them on superior earnings versus their competitors and price, i.e. P/E. You want to seek out insurance companies that are increasing sales and earnings faster than competitors, and buy them when they are cheap i.e. selling at 6-8 times earnings or lower, and sell them when they are expensive, selling at 10-12 times earnings. Book value can also be useful as a secondary way to assess an insurance company, where you want to consider buying when book value is below 1.3, and selling when book value is above 2.5.

Life Insurance companies - Life Insurance companies are cyclical in nature, but their cycles are tied to the overall economy. They take money from people who buy life insurance, and then they invest the money, and then pay claims when people die. When the investment climate worsens, so do their profits, and when it improves, so do their profits. You want to seek out insurance companies that are increasing sales and earnings faster than competitors, and buy them when they are cheap i.e. selling at 6-8 times earnings or lower, and sell them when they are expensive, selling at 10-12 times earnings. Book value can also be useful as a secondary way to assess a life insurance company, where you want to consider buying when book value is below 1.3, and sell when book value is above 2.5.

Chapter 33 More Details On Stock Investing: Analyzing Stock Buy Backs

Favor companies that are buying back their own stock. First off, you need to know there are 2 types of **stock buy backs**. One is what I call a **real stock buy back,** and the other is what I call a **phony stock buy back.**

A real buy back is when you see the actual share count of the company going down each year. In the quarterly report at the bottom of the earnings table, you will see average shares outstanding for this year's quarter compared to the same quarter last year. You also want it to be a stock that is "cheap", and by cheap the GR should be higher than the Forward P/E. If these are both true, this is a company that cares a lot about their shareholders, and when the share count is reduced, it causes the denominator in the EPS to get smaller, so EPS goes up, and remember, in the long run, EPS is what drives stock prices. This is an extremely wise use of cash by the company, even better than paying a regular ongoing quarterly dividend and much better than paying a one time special dividend, which does absolutely nothing for the stock in the long run.

Hotel operator REIT Ashford Hospitality Trust (AHT) saw its stock crash down to less than 1 in 2009 on fears that they would go bankrupt. However, all during that time they were reporting positive FFO, meaning ex one time charges; they were still profitable. Not only that, without once ever even announcing that they were doing a stock buy back; they simply started buying back the ridiculously cheap stock at a furious rate. From 2008 to 2010, they reduced shares outstanding by 54% from 111 million to 51 million. Meanwhile EPS (FFO) soared 66% from 1.12 to 1.86. Obviously they couldn't have had the cash to do this, if they were supposedly on the verge of bankruptcy. I loaded up on the stock. Not only did the shares become more valuable because there were fewer of them, this caused EPS (FFO) to surge dramatically because the denominator in EPS i.e. shares got much smaller. The stock was an 18 bagger going from less than 1 to 14.5, and I made a good portion of that gain.

Satellite TV operator Direct TV (DTV) had always been a relatively cheap stock. Taking advantage of this, the company used its ever increasing profits to buy back billions and billions of dollars of stock at cheap prices, which caused their EPS to grow even faster. This went on for years and years, and between 2006 and 2013, they bought back 56% of their shares. This added to already increasing profits, so it supercharged their EPS, which increased by a factor of 5 from 1.13 to 5.40, and consequently the stock soared and was a 5 bagger going from 13 to 66. I loaded up on the stock, so it was one of my biggest holdings, and I made a big profit on the stock.

Do not favor companies, that are doing what I call a "**phony stock buy back**". A phony buy back can come in 4 different ways, and some shareholder unfriendly companies do all 4 types of phony stock buy backs.

The first type of phony stock buy back is when a company is buying back significant stock but simultaneously rewarding management with free stock options so fast that the buy back just matches the options they are giving to themselves so the shares outstanding never go down and in some bad cases actually increases. This is why you need to see the actual share count going down and not simply trust the company when they say "we are buying back our shares". This is a disaster on multiple fronts. It is a waste of cash which belongs to the owners i.e. the shareholders. It distorts management's priorities because they are getting rich off these free options and shareholders get nothing. By announcing the buy back, they are pretending to help shareholders but in reality they are being like politicians who pretend to be helping people but in reality are just helping themselves via the massive issue of free options to themselves. High Tech companies are the biggest offenders of this type of phony buy back claiming they have to give away all these free options "to hire and retain the best and brightest". While that may or may not be true, regardless it is one of the many reasons Tech stocks always make up less than 20% of my stock portfolio. More on that in **Chapter 51**.

The second type of phony buy back is when a company does a buy back when the stock is overpriced. For example a company that is growing earnings at 7% per year and selling at Forward P/E of 20 is an overpriced stock. Buying back that stock is an expensive waste of shareholders dollars that could be better spent on dividends, buying out a competitor at a cheap price, investing in R&D or simply saving it for a rainy day. Cisco was the most notorious for this type of phony buy back. During the 1990s and early 2000s, they wasted billions and billions of dollars of company cash buying back wildly overpriced stock that was selling at 30 to 100 times earnings. When the stock finally collapsed from near 90 down to 10, all those billions had been wasted on grossly overpriced stock that ended up crashing. They should have saved all that cash and then bought back stock after the stock crashed down to 10 times earnings in 2002.

The third type of phony buy back is when a company announces a buy back, then never actually follows through on the buy back and the shares outstanding don't decrease. They are basically lying like a politician. Another version is when the buy back is so small it is negligible. Any buy back that is less than 4% of outstanding shares is a phony buy back. When a buy back is announced by a company the first thing you do is to calculate the % buy back by taking the dollar amount they announce and dividing it by the Market Cap of the company and multiply by 100.

The fourth type of phony buy back is when a company announces the buy back just a few days before it drops a bomb of a bad quarterly earnings report on shareholders. In general beware of any stock buy back announced in the last few days before earnings are reported because it is usually just a BS smoke screen to try to distract from and mute the effect of the coming bad news.

Another type of stock buy back is called a **Dutch Auction** share buy back. The difference between a conventional buy back and a Dutch Auction buy back is the Dutch Auction is done all at once as opposed to spread out over months or years like a regular buy back. A Dutch Auction can be real or a phony one, and you need to evaluate it based on the same criteria as a conventional buy back. Since they were made legal in 1981, they have been very rare. The couple that I remember were "phony" Dutch Auctions, in which the stocks were overvalued at the time of the buy back (even though the CEOs claimed their stocks were undervalued), and to make matters worse, the companies used debt to do the buy back.

Chapter 34   More Details On Stock Investing: Secondary Offerings

The opposite of buying back stock is when a company dilutes their shares via a "**Secondary Officering**." A secondary offering dilutes existing shares by putting more shares out on the market, and if earnings remain constant, EPS goes down, because shares are the denominator in EPS, and there are more shares outstanding. Remember, it is ultimately EPS that drives the stock prices over the long run. Sometimes this makes sense if the stock is very expensive, because they can make a lot of money selling the expensive stock to foolish buyers and use it to pay down debt and expand. Then again, you shouldn't be buying expensive stocks to begin with.

Not all secondary offerings are dilutive; sometimes they do a secondary offering to make it easier for insiders or large investors to sell their shares in an organized fashion. In this case, no new shares are added and the company gets no cash; it is just simply shares changing hands. In fact, this often presents a buying opportunity (provided the stock meets all other criteria), because the market almost always treats it like it is a dilutive offering, and they sell-off the stock temporarily. So when a company does a secondary offering, read the details of the press release to determine if it is a dilutive offering (bad) or just insider shareholders or investors selling shares (a non-event).

Chapter 35   More Details On Stock Investing: Insider Buying And Selling

Favor companies with **Insider Buying**. Click Insider Transactions on Yahoo and you will see insiders who are buying and selling shares. Ignore purchases that are "non-open market", because that is just them giving themselves free options. Focus on "direct purchases". Almost always, the only reason an insider is making a direct purchase of stock with their own money is that they know the stock is undervalued and/or the future prospects are good.

Ignore **Insider Selling**. There are numerous reasons for insider selling, primarily the insider is diversifying their investment portfolio on the advice of their financial planner. They also could be using the money to buy a new home or vacation home or paying for a child's college education or be selling due to divorce or some other personal payment. Never sell a stock due to insider selling. Remember insider selling is normal and natural as it outnumbers insider buying by a factor of about 10 to 1.

Many investors wrongly assume insider selling is as important as insider buying, but that is not the case; insider buying is important, and positive and insider selling is meaningless.

Chapter 36   More Details On Stock Investing: Institutional Ownership

Favor companies with low **institutional ownership**. On Yahoo, click Key Statistics to find out the % institutional ownership. The average is about 60%. Low institutional ownership means Wall Street has not "discovered" the stock yet or most of Wall Street does not know about the stock yet. Provided the other fundamental factors such as GR in comparison to P/E and the balance sheet are good, this can be a big plus. You want to get into good stocks before mainstream Wall Street does. You don't want to be following the herd; you want to be out in front of the herd. On the other hand, you don't want to avoid a stock just because institutional ownership is high, but it is a negative to factor into the big picture.

Chapter 37   More Details On Stock Investing: Number Of Analysts Following A Stock

Favor companies with few analysts following the stock. On Yahoo click Earnings Estimates to find out how many analysts follow a stock. Typical is about 7 analysts for a mid cap stock, 10-15 for a large cap stock, 3-4 for a small cap stock and 0 for micro cap stocks. Fewer analysts means Wall Street has not "discovered" the stock yet or most of Wall Street does not know about the stock yet. This gives you an edge, because you can know more about a stock with zero or few analysts than the Street knows about the stock. Provided the other fundamental factors such as GR in comparison to P/E and the balance sheet are good, this can be a big plus. You want to get into good stocks before mainstream Wall Street does. You don't want to be following the herd; you want to be out in front of the herd. On the other hand you don't want to avoid a stock just because analyst following is high, but it is a negative to factor into the big picture.

Chapter 38   More Details On Stock Investing: Insider Ownership

Favor companies with high **insider ownership**. You want management to have a significant personal stake in the company and its stock. This makes them **shareholder friendly** and care about the stock price. Conversely, with low insider ownership, the management doesn't care about the stock price, and they focus more on just enriching themselves with high salaries and stock options, which they immediately cash in the instant they can, and setting up themselves with outrageous "**Golden Parachute**" retirement packages, they will reap even if they run the company into the ground and get booted out. In these cases, management's concerns are not aligned with the shareholders, and these are the people who give CEO's a bad name.

Also, you will see companies with low insider ownership constantly making dilutive acquisitions (more on that in the next chapter) to increase the size of the company but not increasing Earnings Per Share (EPS), which is what ultimately drives stock prices. These managers then use the increased size of the company to justify giving themselves huge salary and bonus increases and even more (dilutive) options payments, which they immediately cash in as soon as possible and set up even bigger Golden Parachute packages.

What is a good level of insider ownership? For micro caps, it is good if at least 20%, for small caps at least 10%, for mid caps at least 4%, and for large caps, it is good if most insiders each own several millions of dollars in company stock.

There is one important caveat to the more is better insider ownership. If insiders own 40-50% or more of the stock, there is a risk they can take the stock private at a crappy price, and no one can stop them. For example, say you discover a small cap company growing earnings at 15% a year but selling at a P/E of only 10, and the stock sells for 18 and also has 3 dollars per share net cash. Great situation and you buy this stock on the expectation it will grow earnings solidly for 3 years or more, and eventually Wall Street will get onto the story and drive the stock price and P/E up to say 17 or so. Therefore, 3 years from now the stock would rise from 18 to the mid 40s. What can happen is management can get impatient waiting for the stock to be fairly priced, and they realize how cheap it is and buy the company out now (i.e. take it **Private**) at 21. Typical investors would cheer and say "wow a 16% profit", but as a fundamental stock investor, you will realize you lost out on a chance to double or triple your money. I am not saying to never buy stocks with greater than 50% insider ownership, but realize there is the risk that it can be taken out at a crappy price.

Chapter 39   More Details On Stock Investing: Carefully Evaluate Acquisition Announcements

Favor companies that make accretive acquisitions. Avoid companies that make dilutive acquisitions. **Accretive** means the company they are buying is going to add to EPS (ignore one time acquisition costs). **Dilutive** means it is going to lower EPS. Remember it is EPS that ultimately drives stock prices.

Whenever a company makes an acquisition, you need to read their press release. They will talk about all these wonderful things that will happen. **Synergies** is their favorite, because it can't be quantified and it sounds good. Ignore all that stuff and fluff, and go right to the key sentence in the press release. The key sentence will usually be buried near the end of the press release and will say something such as "the acquisition is expected to be dilutive to EPS for ? years and then accretive thereafter" or "the acquisition is expected to be accretive after ? years". Also, they sometimes will tell you how much it will affect earnings which is very important, such as, "it is expected to add 0.13 to EPS after acquisition costs next year". Occasionally, the acquisition is so small that they will say it will have a negligible effect on earnings, in which case the acquisition is a non event, as far as you are concerned. Other times, they won't address whether or not it will be accretive or dilutive to earnings, which usually means it is dilutive, meaning bad for you the shareholder. In those cases, compare the size of the acquiring company to the company being bought to get a feel for the size of the acquisition and compare the P/E of the two companies. You want to see the company being bought to have a lower P/E, which will definitely make it accretive.

For an acquisition to be good news, you want it to be accretive "next year". Any acquisition that won't be accretive until the second and especially the third year is bad news, because it means they paid way too much for the company. It is especially bad if it is a major acquisition, because it means you are looking at lower earnings the next 2 to 3 years, and it is EPS that ultimately drives stock price over the long run. Obviously, you want to avoid companies that make dilutive acquisitions, especially if it will be dilutive for more than 1 year, and if significantly dilutive. Music to the ears of the shareholder is when the company says those beautiful words "the acquisition will be immediately accretive to earnings".

Chapter 40   More Details On Stock Investing: What If There Are No Analyst Estimates?

What if there are no analyst estimates? Some small companies have no analysts following the stock, so when for example you go to Yahoo Finance, there will be no earnings estimates. This actually is a good thing, but it will require you to do a little more work when evaluating the stock. It is a good thing, because that means no analysts follow the stock, so the stock is basically undiscovered by Wall Street, so if the company has good fundamentals and is fairly or cheaply priced, you can get in way ahead of the Wall Street herd. It requires more work, because you have to come up with earnings estimates yourself.

Click on Press Releases in Yahoo. Go to most recent quarterly earnings report and read the press release. The company will tell you how much earnings per share (EPS) went up in the last quarter and use that percentage for the Growth Rate. Calculate the Forward P/E by taking the quarterly EPS and multiplying by 4 to get a full year EPS estimate. Divide the price of the stock by the full year EPS estimate and you got the Forward P/E. If the earnings are seasonal, you need to look at full year earnings by finding out what typically happens in each quarter of the year by reading old press releases or the annual report, which are all available at each company's website. On Yahoo click Profile and then click the company's website, then click investor relations, then click press releases and/or annual report. When evaluating earnings, do not include one time charges and gains; you want to use the so called "operating" or "non-GAAP" or "ex items" earnings or FFO for REITs, not the GAAP earnings.

135

Chapter 41 More Details On Stock Investing: Book Value

In general, **Book Value** is a useless measure and should be ignored. In most cases, it is not even remotely close to estimating the value of a business for a variety of reasons and can dangerously undervalue or overvalue a stock. The one key exception is the Book Value of financial stocks, which is important, such as banks and insurance companies (as discussed in **Chapters 31 and 32**) and often for real estate companies such as hotels. For 99% of stocks, Book Value means nothing.

Chapter 42 More Details On Stock Investing: Cash Flow And Return On Equity And EBITDA

Ignore Return On Equity (ROI), cash flow and free cash flow and discounted free cash flow and free cash yield. In the olden days, these measures were important, because most companies used to present only GAAP earnings. Now about 98% of companies give you both GAAP and non-GAAP earnings and non-GAAP EPS. The non-GAAP EPS or ex items or core earnings or FFO for REITS, factor out one time events and charges and gains and especially non cash write-downs or revaluation of assets, one time cost of acquisitions, etc., so you know exactly how the core business is performing.

Back in the olden days, most companies would only give you GAAP earnings, which often gave you a distorted view of how the company was actually doing. Because of that, you had to rely on cash flow and free cash flow and ROI and discounted free cash flow to find out how the company was actually doing. Warren Buffett used these techniques and still does, because that is what he is used to doing. You no longer need to do that anymore. You need to focus on sales and earnings and particularly non-GAAP EPS and the balance sheet and P/E. Once you start getting into additional stuff such as cash flow, free cash flow and discounted free cash flow, you are digging too deep, and you will get distracted from the really important stuff and lose sight of the big picture.

Also ignore Earnings Before Interest, Taxes, Depreciation and Amortization (EBITDA). Often debt ridden companies who are losing money or are barely profitable or who are reporting declining EPS due to a massively dilutive acquisition, will emphasize their EBITA to make things look better than they really are. However, in the real world, companies have to actually pay interest on their debt and have to actually pay taxes. Often when a company gives you their EBITDA, it is just a smoke screen to cover up real losses or poor earnings. For example, Comcast (CMCSA) stock was selling for about 28 in 2001, and 6 years later in 2007, it was selling at 20 despite reporting "great EBITDA" numbers all those years. So why did the stock go nowhere but down? Because their EPS was down in the dumps, due to their massive interest payments on debt to pay for the build out of their cable/fiber optics systems and to pay for all their acquisitions. When they finally started reporting real and growing EPS is when I bought the stock, and it took off to 50 by mid 2013. Ignore EBITDA.

Chapter 43 More Details On Stock Investing: Dividends

Consider dividends an extra positive benefit to a stock. NEVER buy a stock strictly for the dividend. As explained earlier, add the % dividend yield to the EPS Growth Rate (GR) to get the total return (TR) and compare to Forward P/E when evaluating a growth stock that pays a dividend. Dividends for Medium and Slow Growth stocks make a difference, because the GR is not as big compared to the % dividend yield, so the dividend does make a significant contribution. It is much less important for Fast Growth stocks, which is why most don't even bother to pay a dividend, and they are also using excess cash to expand their business.

Most of the S&P 500 falls into the Slow Growth Stock category with some in the Medium Growth Stock category, so the dividend is important for most of those stocks. Since 1960, the % dividend yield on the S&P 500 has ranged from 1.1%, when most stocks were wildly overpriced in 1999, to 5.6% in the mid '70's and early '80's, when most stocks were extremely cheap. Typical is about 2-3%. See the table in **Chapter 82** which shows the range of the S&P 500 dividend yield over the years. When the S&P 500 gains 10% on average over the long haul, a rough guide is about 7-8% of that is due to earnings growth, and 2-3% of that is due to dividend payouts, so you can see the importance of dividends for Slow Growth and Medium Growth stocks.

Be wary of very high dividends yielding in excess of 5%. Unless it is a Real Estate Investment Trust (REIT) or utility, the dividend may be too great for the company to maintain. If you look at the dividend per share, and it is greater than 40% of EPS (also known as the **dividend payout ratio**) or if earnings are declining, the dividend may not be maintained, and the company may have to cut it. This is yet another reason you never buy a stock strictly because of the dividend.

Also many cyclical stocks are forced to cut or eliminate the dividend during down cycles to preserve cash. Never count on a cyclical stock maintaining their dividend during a downturn. When a cyclical's stock price starts falling as investors try to foresee the next recession, you will find very high percent dividend yields on these stocks, and people foolishly buy the stocks for those dividends, but they are illusory, because they will soon be cut or eliminated when the economy heads south.

If you are factoring in the dividend for a growth stock, look at the company's history of paying dividends and even better, increasing dividends. You can see this in the company's annual report. You want to see a company that has paid a dividend many years in a row right through recessions and that has never cut the dividend, and even better, has increased it every year for several years in a row. You would be shocked how many companies have raised their dividends every year for 20 or 30 years or more in a row.

One time special dividends are a nice perk, but they do nothing for a stock in the long or even intermediate term, so they are not a big deal for the fundamental stock investor and can often be seen as a waste of cash. You would much rather see them do something that matters in the long run, such as a permanent increase in the quarterly dividend or buying back stock if the stock is relatively cheap. One exception is the few companies that pay a special one time dividend every or nearly every year. Truck manufacturer Paccar (PCAR) is an example of that.

You absolutely MUST reinvest the cash you get from dividends because it is a critical part of your overall wealth building strategy. As you can see above, a good chunk of the long term gains in the S&P 500 are due to dividends. When sufficient dividend cash accumulates in your account, you can buy a new stock or add to a stock you already own. However, do not use **Automatic Dividend Reinvestment Plans** for your individual dividend paying stocks. Some large cap stocks have these programs that automatically buy more stock in their company when they pay you a dividend. More often than not, it is not the best place for you to put this new money, so you don't want it automatically going into that stock; you want to decide which stock you put the new money into. Also, if in a taxable account, it will greatly complicate you taxes when you sell that stock.

Chapter 44   More Details On Stock Investing: Don't Sell A Fast Growth Stock Just Because The Stock Has Become Expensive

Don't necessarily sell a Fast Growth stock (a company growing earnings 15-30% or greater per year) that has gotten expensive. This is a mistake I made earlier in my investing career. This may sound contradictory to what I said earlier, but this is an important caveat to Fast Growth stock investing. Never buy into or add more money to a growth stock that is expensive (i.e. the Forward P/E is over 40 or P/E significantly higher than the GR). However, once you buy a Fast Growth stock that is fairly or cheaply priced, stick with that stock as long as the fundamentals remain good, even if the stock goes up so much it becomes expensive or even very expensive. As long as earnings growth is still solid (at least 15% or greater), the balance sheet is still strong, and same store sales (if applicable) are positive, stick with that stock. The reason is that everything on Wall Street is overdone, and you want to use that to your advantage.

You may have found a great Fast Growth stock, bought it at a fair or cheap price, owned it for a few years, and now it is getting discovered by the herd of Wall Street. They can drive such stocks up to ridiculous levels, and you want to take advantage of that by staying in the stock. Don't sell until the fundamentals actually fall apart, e.g. earnings growth slows dramatically to less than 15%, or they take on too much debt or if applicable, same store sales (SSS) turn negative, while most of their competitors' SSS are still positive, or they have run out of expansion room by being in all 50 states, etc. Again, don't take a new position in an expensive Fast Growth stock or add to you position in an expensive Fast Growth stock, but if you bought it cheap or at a fair price and it has gone up a lot and is now expensive, don't sell until the fundamentals actually start falling apart.

Sell a Fast Growth stock that has gone up a lot for a long time (i.e. over a year) and that has become expensive and has gone into what is called a **Climax Run**. For example, suppose you bought a Fast Growth stock with a GR of 20% and a Forward P/E of 15, and you have owned it for 3 years, and the GR is still 20%, but the stock has gone up so much its Forward P/E is now 44. As stated earlier, don't buy or add to stocks you already own that are expensive, but also don't sell them if the fundamentals remain strong, with one exception. That exception is when a stock goes into a Climax Run. A Climax Run is when a stock that has already gone up a lot for a long time (i.e. over a year) suddenly starts going straight up on no news (4% or more for 2-4 days in a row on massive volume (2-10 times normal daily volume)). Often during one or more of these days, the stock will "**gap up**" at the open, meaning the first trade will be much higher than the previous day's close. For example, a stock that closed at 64 opens at 66 with no trades between 64.01 and 65.99. You should sell on day 2 of the Climax Run. Yes, you may miss out on the final 10-20% if the Climax Run lasts 4 days, but when the run ends, the stock typically collapses and continues to plunge over the next few months, and you often see 20% declines in a couple of days and 50% declines over a few weeks. A Climax Run is the only time you want to sell an expensive Fast Growth stock, even if the fundamentals are intact.

As stated earlier, for Slow Growth stocks (increasing earnings 0-5% per year) or Medium Growth stocks (increasing earning 5-15% per year), you want to sell them when they get expensive. The table in **Chapter 25** shows typical P/E ranges for mature Slow Growth and Medium Growth stocks in various industries. You want to sell these when the Forward P/E is above the top of the range. For example, for a Medium Growth retailer, you want to sell it when its Forward P/E goes above 18. Remember, that table does not apply to Fast Growth stocks.

Chapter 45   More Details On Stock Investing: Where Do I Get New Stock Ideas?

Where can one get new stock ideas? You can and should get them from literally everywhere. Any stock you hear about whether you hear about it on TV or in newspapers or on the internet or from friends, family or co-workers, you can quickly research it in less than 5 minutes online these days, using the methods of this book and dismiss most of the ideas. Every now and then after you research them, you will find something worth buying. There are other methods that you should also use. Once you look up a stock, you can click "Competitors" on Yahoo or some other financial website and research them. You may find a competitor that is a much better investment. For every 50 companies you look into, you may find 5 or so worth investing in. The more companies you research, the more you will find worth investing in. After a big stock market sell-off, you will find even more worth investing in, and after a big rally, you will find fewer.

Become more aware of the world around you. Think about every product or service you use or you see or you are aware of and investigate them. First, find out if they are a public company, i.e. they trade on a stock exchange. If they are, then investigate them using the methods of this book. Train your family members and friends to do the same and alert you about new products and services, and then you can look into them.

For new restaurants and retailers, I live in the Northeast which is generally a more expensive place to start a business, so with the exception of Dunkin Doughnuts (DNKN), we were one of the last places to get every new retail or restaurant concept. If you live in the South or Middle America, you will get most of the new chains first, so take advantage of this.

You can use a more systematic approach and take a look at say 30 different industry groups, (e.g. retailers, restaurants, autos, chemicals, mining, etc.) and research each group and try to find the most attractive stocks in each industry.

One method I also use is the newspaper Investors Business Daily (IBD) every day, which lists the companies that reported earnings the day before. The Wall Street Journal also lists earnings reports from the previous day. There may also be online sources that provide them. I quickly screen this data by ignoring those with declining earnings. Then, eliminate those with declining sales. Then I quickly multiply the quarterly EPS by 4 in my head to get approximate annual EPS, then quickly calculate the P/E in my head and eliminate any with a P/E greater than 40 or greater than their GR. This quick screen takes me about 3-15 minutes a day depending on how many companies reported the day before. For every 200 reports, the screening eliminates on average about 190 companies and that leaves about 10. Then I go on Yahoo Finance and dig deeper into those 10 using the methods of this book. By the end, I usually come up with 0-4 new ideas worth investing each day and I write them down on a sheet of paper. When I have money to invest (from new income/dividends/savings or from selling something else), I go to this sheet, which typically has about 30-50 new ideas since the last quarter ended and decide which to buy, or instead, to buy more of something I already own, depending on which appears to be the best opportunity. Never forget that sometimes the best stock to buy is one you already own. You can develop your own screening system using a completely different method. Also, your discount broker's website may have screening capability. Note that even though I have studied it thoroughly and am an expert on it, I never use IBD's CANSLIM investing system. More on that later in the book.

When a recession hits, I then dive into researching all the big cyclical industries and go on Yahoo and look at all the established cyclical names, whose stocks have been beaten way down and are now loosing money or barely profitable. A recession is a golden opportunity to load up on cyclical stocks.

After a big stock market sell-off, it is a great time to go look at all the Fast Growth stocks that were too expensive the last time you looked at them and are now beaten down to more attractive valuations or to buy more of the Fast Growth Stocks that you already own.

Chapter 46   More Details On Stock Investing: Don't Buy Cheap Stocks With Deteriorating Fundamentals

Don't buy cheap stocks with deteriorating fundamentals. An investing strategy based simply on buying stocks with low P/Es is doomed to fail. You always have to compare GR/TR to the P/E for growth stocks to determine whether or not to buy a stock. If a company's earnings are declining, then there is no GR/TR; the fundamentals are declining. No matter how low the P/E is, don't buy stocks with earnings that are declining. Remember, it is EPS that drives stock prices over the intermediate and long term, and if EPS is declining, expect the stock price to eventually be lower, no matter how low the P/E goes. Many stocks have low P/E's for very good reasons, the most common being earnings are going nowhere or are going down. On the hand, if the P/E is low and earnings are actually growing and the GR is higher than the P/E, you have a bargain on your hands.

Also, as previously warned, don't fall for labels or silly trite sayings or convincing sounding sayings. For example, you may hear an "expert" saying XYZ stock is a "Value Trap" and ABC stock "represents solid value". Those terms sound convincing but have no meaning and are not quantifiable. Stick to facts, and do your own research on XYZ stock and ABC stock, which will take less than 5 minutes, and find out what their earnings are actually doing, and compare to the Forward P/E, and decide on your own, whether the stock is worth buying or not. Don't go by silly labels; stick to facts.

Chapter 47   More Details On Stock Investing: Don't Buy A Stock That Has Never Been Profitable

Never buy a stock that has never been profitable. This rule does not apply to turnarounds or cyclicals, where often you will be buying them when they are not profitable (i.e. losing money) or barely making money. However, they have been profitable in the past. What I am talking about is companies that have come public in an IPO, and now and even years later, are still losing money.

Usually there is a hope or promise of some new product or drug they are developing. Maybe they are selling products or services at a loss and surviving by burning through the cash they got from their IPO, with the hope they eventually turn profitable. Never buy a stock like this; they are way too risky. The drug may not get approved; in that case, you will lose everything. The new product may sound great and innovative, but when it comes out, the public may be awed by it but decide to not actually buy it, and you will lose everything. The company with great sales but losing money, may never make money, and you will lose everything.

It is best you wait until the new drug is approved, or the new product or service actually is selling, and the company is making a profit. Always wait at least until they are actually making a profit, then evaluate the stock by comparing the GR to the Forward P/E. If the new drug or product or service turns out to be as wonderful as promised, you will miss the initial big move in the stock, but if it is a truly great drug/product/service, earnings will grow solidly for years, and you will get opportunities to buy the stock at a fair price, even if you have to wait for the next Bear Market or Stock Market Collapse.

Chapter 48 More Details On Stock Investing: Ignore Short Sellers

Ignore short sellers. If you click Key Statistics on Yahoo Finance, you will see the % of shares that are being shorted. **Shorting** a stock is a speculative bet that a stock will go down, and short sellers profit if a stock goes down. The typical stock has a percent short interest of about 5%. Anything above 10% is a significant short position, and above 20% is called a "**heavily shorted stock**." In general, you should ignore the percent short position and focus on all the fundamentals of the company with respect to price. Hedge funds make up the majority of the volume of shorting, and as shown earlier in the book, these hedge funds on average have had a dismal record in the stock market in the past 5 years. They are even worse at shorting stocks than they are investing in long positions in stocks. You don't want to get scared out of a stock with great fundamentals just because the stock is heavily shorted.

Some short sellers use all kinds of techniques in their desperation to drive down the stock price. They launch "**short attacks**" in which they alone or in a **coordinated short attack** with other short sellers, pick a target day in which they endlessly sell short 100 share lots, taking advantage of the SEC's repeal of the "**down tick rule**" (more on that later). These "short attacks" can drive down a stock 3-8% in one day on no news. This is designed to trigger **stop loss orders** (more on this later) and shake out scared weak holders, who think "someone must know something", and create even more selling. They also try to get the stock to break Technical Analyst's "trend lines" and "moving averages" so those people will also sell and create even more selling. These short attacks can be unnerving and annoying, but as long as the fundamentals of the company are sound, these short attacks should be ignored.

Some short sellers are constantly on stock **Message Boards** ranting about how the company is terrible, and the stock is going to go down, and that you should get out before it is too late. They operate under multiple aliases to make it look like there are 10 people ranting, when in reality, it is just one. Some post a new rant every 5 minutes. That is why you should completely avoid stock message boards.

Some short sellers are so devious, they will put out long winded so called "research reports" on well known websites, focusing on tiny details on the company, and making them sound significant, and in many cases, they accuse the company of illegal accounting practices, fraud, deception, etc., and in some cases, they make up outright lies. They usually put the reports out anonymously or under a pseudonym, so they can't ever be prosecuted for their illegal stock manipulation, and they simultaneously launch a "short attack", taking advantage of the SEC's repeal of the down tick rule. More sophisticated short sellers even try to sabotage a company, by constantly contacting government agencies, such as the SEC, and telling them to investigate the company for fraud or other malfeasance, with the hope the SEC will investigate, and when that news comes out that an investigation is underway, the stock plunges, and the short seller profits, even in the many cases where the SEC ultimately finds nothing wrong. Even worse, the SEC aids these nefarious short sellers by their policy of never announcing that their investigation has ended and that they found nothing. Most of the time, it is announced the SEC is investigating, and then you never hear anything ever again, so a negative cloud hangs over the stock for months and even years, so the SEC is unwittingly aiding and abetting the shorts who are manipulating the stock. Furthermore, the SEC never investigates nor prosecutes these short sellers for fraud or stock manipulation, even though it is rampant. All of this stuff is designed to scare you out of the stock, so the short seller can profit.

Some short sellers also routinely use the illegal practice of **Naked Shorting**. Naked Shorting is shorting a stock, without first borrowing the shares as required by the law; this allows for having an unlimited number of shares available to sell short, which can drive stocks down even faster. Despite it being illegal, the SEC looks the other way and never enforces the law, other than a brief period in the fall of 2008, and then they only enforced the law for 19 "important" financial stocks and only for a few months.

Some people see a high short position and automatically avoid the stock. This can be a mistake. Many of my very biggest winners over the years were in stocks that were heavily shorted the whole time.

Jos A. Bank (JOSB) is a perfect example. This stock was a 57 bagger (meaning it went up 57 times in value) over an 11 year period from 2000 and 2011 rising from 1 (split adjusted) to 57. All during that time, there was a huge short position from 20% to over 50% in which some hedge funds lost hundreds of millions of dollars (of other people's money). The shorts tried everything those 11 years. There were 50 short seller rants a day on message boards, every day for 11 straight years. There were one day coordinated short attacks at least once a month, in which the stock was driven down 5% or more in one day on no news. There were constant "research reports" saying the whole business was fraudulent. There were hedge fund short sellers getting articles published in Baron's Magazine claiming the company was misleading about their same store sales. There were short sellers putting out "research reports" on internet sites saying that there was malfeasance involving their inventories. A noted friend of short sellers would go on TV as a "reporter" and speak of accounting irregularities in the way they calculated their margins. The short sellers threw everything they had at the company and more for 11 years, but they always failed. In reality, the company was a small little retail company selling men's suits in a few stores, that grew into a big company with hundreds of stores, by careful and controlled expansion across the country over those 11 years, while they were debt free or nearly debt free the whole time, and they had steady and solid earnings growth of 15% to 30% for year after year, as they expanded across the entire USA, and all this time the stock was always cheap, selling at a P/E below its GR. Same store sales increased year after year. The short sellers couldn't have picked a worse stock to short, and all the scare tactics were for not, and I held in there, and this was a huge winner for me.

Ebix is another example. The stock was an 87 bagger between 2003 and 2011, rising from a split adjusted 0.33 to 29. All during this time, the short position was between 20 and 60%, during which time, some hedge funds lost hundred of millions of dollars (of other people's money). There were short attacks seemingly almost every other week, driving the stock down from 5-8% in one day, over and over again. But each time it would rebound and go much, much higher, as the company increased earnings massively through a series of accretive acquisitions, without taking on significant debt. The shorts constantly put out "research reports", attacking everything they could about the firm, claiming excessive debt (even though it was actually minimal), accounting fraud, not including certain debt on financial reports, embezzlement by the CEO, "shady dealings", you name it. The stock would get knocked for a loop after each of these "research reports", only to rebound much higher. I sold in 2011 and made one of the largest profits of my investing career. I sold because earnings growth started to dramatically decrease. Since I sold, the short attacks have continued relentlessly to this day (early 2014) and after years of trying, the short sellers eventually even talked the SEC into launching an investigation of the company, which again knocked the stock for a loop. Nine months later, as of now (early 2014), the SEC has been unable to find anything so far. Eventually, they may find something wrong in their books, but it hasn't happened yet. If you got scared out by the short sellers between 2003 and 2011, you missed out on an 87 bagger.

On the other hand, don't buy a stock just because it has a high short position in the hope that a "**short squeeze**" takes place. A short squeeze is when a heavily shorted stock starts to rise, causing margin calls for short sellers, forcing them to "**cover their short**", which is effectively buying, which causes the stock to rise more, which triggers more margin calls, etc. and the stock soars. Always go by the fundamentals, and if the fundamentals are lousy, don't buy the stock, or if the fundamentals are good but the stock is too expensive, don't buy the stock. If they are good, and the stock is fairly or cheaply priced, buy the stock. Ignore what short sellers are doing and saying.

There is one exception where you cannot ignore a high short percentage. Companies that have very high debt (which you should be avoiding anyway) sometimes have **covenants** in their loans from banks that say the loan is **callable** if their **debt to equity** ratio rises above some particular percentage. Some short sellers will launch a vicious coordinated short attack against such companies, so that it drives the stock price so low, that the debt to equity is much worse, so it violates their loan covenant for debt to equity, which can prompt the bank to "call" their loan (demand re-payment immediately), and drive the company into bankruptcy, and destroy an otherwise viable business, and throw thousands of people out of work. Yes, some short sellers can get that vicious, and they could care less about the jobs and lives they wreck, as long as they make a quick profit. They represent the underbelly of capitalism.

Chapter 49   More Details On Stock Investing: Always Evaluate Earnings Reports In Absolute Terms, Not With Respect To "Analysts Expectations"

Always evaluate quarterly earnings reports in absolute terms, not with respect to "**analysts expectations**". When a company reports earnings, you need to look at actually how the company's business is doing and completely ignore what analysts were expecting. For example, you want to know that EPS was up 18% and not care whether it "missed analyst expectations by 1 cent" or "beat analyst expectations by 2 cents". What is important is their actual earnings, and if they give an EPS forecast for the next quarter and/or year what that forecast actually is, not whether "their forecast is light" or "forecast is above analyst expectations" or "in-line with analyst expectations". For example, if a company says Q1 earnings were up 15%, and their full year forecast is for a 13% rise in earnings, you would expect the stock to be selling at a Forward P/E of about 14, if it is fairly priced. If it is, that is good, and you want to buy that stock, or at least hold it if you already own it and consider buying more. If it is selling at a Forward P/E of 12 or lower, you got a bargain. If it is selling at Forward P/E of 17, you don't want to be adding more and just hold if you already own it. If a company was growing earnings at 20 to 25%, and now the GR has slowed to 12% and the Forward P/E is 42, you want to be selling even if it "beat by 2 cents". This is how you evaluate earnings reports, and you need to completely ignore analyst expectations. If you buy and sell stocks based on "misses" or "beats", you will make no money in the stock market.

Keep in mind, when stocks "beat", they will go up in the short run, and if they "miss", they will go down in the short run, but that should have no bearing on your decision making.

Of course, there will be situations when the earnings and forecast are terrible, and they also miss expectations, and you want to be selling. The same with great earnings and forecast that also happen to beat, you want to be buying if the price is attractive.

Ignoring whether earnings "beat" or "missed" is one of the single most important things you must do to succeed as an investor. You will never make money buying or selling stocks based on whether or not a company's quarterly earnings meet or beat earnings expectations. Even more futile is trying to make investment decisions based on trying to predict whether or not a company will beat or miss earnings expectations. Instead, what you need to do is always evaluate earnings in absolute terms, i.e. were the earnings good or bad based on where the stock is currently priced.

Another example is if a growth company reports EPS of 0.44 versus 0.32 last year, that means earnings increased 37%. Those are excellent earnings. It doesn't matter whether the average analyst estimate was for 0.42 or 0.46, the earnings were fantastic. However, you will note if the estimates were for 0.46, the Talking Heads on TV will say the company "missed earnings" or "had a miss" and the stock will get hammered in the short run. If the estimates were for 0.42, then the Talking Heads will say "it was a beat" and the stock will temporarily shoot up.

Fundamental stock investors don't care about and should completely ignore short term stock price movements and consider those moves minor annoyances. Instead, if earnings were up 37%, and the stock is selling at anything less than 40 times earnings, you want to stick with that stock, no matter what the estimates were. If earnings were up 37%, and the stock is selling at only 20 times forward earnings or less, you want to be seriously considering buying more, regardless of whether earnings "missed" or "beat". On the other hand, say earnings were up 12%, and the Forward P/E is 20, you don't want to be buying this stock; it is overpriced and again, that is regardless of whether earnings "missed" or "beat".

You need to forever get out of the silly "beat" or "miss" game and evaluate earnings in absolute terms, i.e. are the earnings and earnings guidance good or bad with respect to the current stock price. The same applies to same store sales; if they are up it is good, if they are down it is bad (unless all similar retailers/restaurants are also down due to a weak economy). Ignore whether same store sales beat or missed analyst estimates.

Also note, you DO want to pay attention to the company's forecasts and follow-up to see if their forecasts are reliable. You will see some companies that try to be as accurate as possible with their forecasts. Other companies will deliberately **lowball** their forecasts so they can always appear to "beat". After you own and/or follow stocks for a while, you will know how credible each company tends to be with their forecasts. Many companies, especially cyclical companies, don't provide any forecast. Cyclical companies don't because their business is to too variable to provide an accurate forecast.

A very small percentage of companies provide a forecast, but not in the press release; they annoyingly only give it in the Conference Call that follows the press release, forcing you to listen to the Conference Call or a replay of the Conference Call or waiting for a news source to post it in an article on the internet after the call. Normally, there is no reason to ever listen to a Conference Call (despite what the "experts" claim), because all the information that you need is in the press release, and the Conference Call is a lot of formality and talk and just going over the info in the press release and going into useless details, that will dilute the importance of the really important numbers. Cisco (CSCO), Western Digital (WDC) and Web.com (WWWW) are examples of the rare and annoying cases where EPS guidance is provided, but only given in the Conference Call, and not in the press release.

Chapter 50   More Details On Stock Investing: What About IPOs?

Do not buy **Initial Public Offering (IPO)** stocks. IPOs are almost always overpriced and often wildly overpriced. As famed investor Jimmy Rogers often quips, "Why do you think they are selling them?" Also only institutions and other connected people such as corrupt politicians can get in on them at the open; everyone else is stuck buying in the **Aftermarket**. Many soar on the first day but many do not. Buying in the Aftermarket is pure gambling. Many are not even profitable when they go public. Also information about them is sketchy and not presented in a clear manner. Avoid them. Almost all of them undergo a significant decline sometime in the first 6 months after the initial rise and euphoria from the IPO. After the decline, and after they have had 2 or more quarterly earnings reports, is the time to investigate whether on not they are worth buying. The quarterly reports are very clear, but before the IPO actually happens, information is sparse, hard to get a hold of, unclear and often deliberately unclear. Sometimes the public gets one set of information about the IPO, and certain favored insiders (illegally) get a more accurate set of information.

Chapter 51   More Details On Stock Investing: Tread Lightly In High Tech

Tread lightly In **High Technology (High Tech)** stocks. There is a very important rule to remember whenever investing in or considering investing in technology stocks, and you must NEVER forget this rule, no matter how good the company appears to be or how good its reputation is or how well they have done in the past.

The fortunes of High Tech companies can turn on a dime without warning.

Never forget that and if you do, be prepared for the consequences. How a company is doing changes much faster in High Tech than in any other industry. Because of this, you want to keep High Tech stocks always below 20% of your total stock portfolio. The 2 richest pure investors ever - Warren Buffett and Carlos Slim, owned no tech stocks for most of their investing careers.

The typical life cycle of a High Tech company goes something like this. A new tech company with an exciting hot new technology emerges. The stock initially soars, but almost immediately, draws in a flood of competitors, whom immediately start hiring the best and brightest engineers and scientists. The company that initially brought the new technology to market is quickly overtaken by one or more of the new competitors, and the initial company's fortunes turn negative on a dime and the stock plunges. It often is bought out at a pittance by one of the new rivals or goes under completely, and the initial investors and those who bought at the top during all the excitement of the hot new industry lose nearly everything. Soon, there are ten or more competing companies locked in a fight to the death over who can make the product better and cheaper. This is great for consumers, but terrible for most investors in these hot industries. This results in an endless price war, and soon most of the companies are losing money or just getting by and their stocks plunge. Often you see companies like this growing earnings from 30 to 100%, only to suddenly, and without warning, announce one quarter that earnings growth has completely ceased, and in fact, will fall. As I stated repeatedly throughout this book, growth rates of more than 30% are rarely sustainable more than a couple of years. Often these stocks are selling at about 40 to 150 times earnings and then completely collapse, leaving investors with near total losses. Among the 10 or more companies, 1-3 will eventually survive and dominate the new industry. Investors in the other 7 plus companies get killed. Which of the companies that eventually ends up being one of the 1-3 survivors is impossible to predict in advance. Even if you think you are an expert on that type of technology, or if you are actually an expert or even work in the industry, you are still not going to have good odds of picking which of the few companies that eventually win. The 1-3 companies that do survive are likely to be massive stock winners (10 to 100 baggers) and will be the talk of Wall Street and constantly in the headlines, but again picking the 1-3 out of the 10 or more is fraught with massive risk and leaves many investors with big losses along the way. Eventually, the 1-3 survivors' businesses become **commoditized**, meaning the differences between their competing products becomes so small that consumers eventually just buy based primarily on price, and margins and profits shrink, and industry becomes just another mature cyclical industry with booms and busts, and they lose their high flying P/E, and the stocks lose one half or more of their value, and from then on, trade as mature Tech companies with a P/E range of 8-15.

This is why Warren Buffett almost never invests in High Tech, and Peter Lynch treaded very lightly in High Tech. When looking for long term winners, as explained above, the High Tech arena is fraught with danger. I am not saying to avoid High Tech completely, because money can and should be made in any industry. However, my portfolio over the years typically has only 10 to 20% of my stocks in High Tech.

Another reason to not favor High Tech is they tend to excessively dilute shareholders by giving excessive stock options to management and key personnel. They say they need to do this to retain the best and brightest, but even if that is true, it is an expensive built in cost of doing business that makes them less attractive investments. Often they mask this cost by doing a "phony stock buy back" in which they buy back just enough shares to match the amount of shares they are issuing as options, so in the end the share count stays the same, but it is a very high fixed cost of doing business.

Chapter 52 More Details On Stock Investing: Beware Of Concentrated Suppliers

Beware of concentrated suppliers. A **concentrated supplier** is a company that sells most of their product to 1-3 end product manufacturers. These are extremely dangerous stocks no matter how well they appear to be doing at the time. This is because they are typically in highly competitive High Tech industries, but they can also be in other industries. The typically much larger and more powerful end product manufacturer can switch suppliers at any time without warning, resulting in a devastating loss of business for the concentrated supplier, or they can squeeze the concentrated supplier by forcing them to reduce prices (which kills the supplier's margins/profits) under the threat of switching to a new supplier.

For these types of "middle man" companies, it is important that you find out if a big percentage of their sales go to just a few customers which makes them a concentrated supplier. An example of this was the fate of the suppliers to end product manufacturer Apple (AAPL), during its big run from 2004 through 2012, when its stock went from 17 to 700. Some hedge funds would have their minions buy every new Apple product the day it came out and rip it apart to find out who made the components, figuring they would make even more money by buying the stocks of the suppliers. The strategy failed, as none of the suppliers' stocks made even a fraction of the move in Apple. They would have been better off just buying Apple stock as I did, although I missed a good chunk of Apple's run. The suppliers didn't make out so well, because Apple would constantly change suppliers, play suppliers off against each other in a never ending price war, and constantly squeeze the margins/profits on the suppliers, and most were reduced to commodity players.

Chapter 53 More Details On Stock Investing: What About A Company That Is "Restructuring"?

You will often see larger mature Slow Growth companies do a **restructuring**, in which they cut costs by closing or selling underperforming divisions, lay-off employees and cut overhead costs. This often gives a short term to intermediate term (i.e. 1-2 year) boost to EPS and to the stock price. However, companies can only cut costs so much, therefore, after the restructuring and the initial 1-2 year benefit to EPS (and to the stock price), they will have to increase sales to continue to increase profits (and the stock price).

Chapter 54 More Details On Stock Investing: Analyst's Upgrades/Downgrades Of Stocks

As stated repeatedly throughout this book, you must be your own person and ignore the "experts", and that includes **Stock Analysts**. Stock analysts are constantly "upgrading" and "downgrading" stocks between buy, sell and hold/neutral, and even strong buy and strong sell, and when they want to get fancy to "conviction buy" or "focus stock of the week". Completely ignore these "**calls**". These "calls" are almost universally too late or outright wrong. You would lose a ton of money, if you ever started paying attention to and acting based on these calls.

Keep in mind, the analysts have all kinds of motivations when making these calls, and none of them are put out to help you. Often they just got all their firm's client investors into a stock, then afterwards they put out the buy recommendation. Some will put out a buy, because all the other analysts have a buy; this is how the herd mentality works on Wall Street. Some will do the opposite of what everyone else is doing, just to try to be a maverick or contrarian. Some will put out a sell, because they are mad at someone in **Investor's Relations** at a company for not giving them "enough information" to give them an edge. Some do it because they are trying to outdo some other analyst they are locked in a grudge match competition. Some always have a positive rating on a stock, just because their company has an investment banking relationship with the company they are rating. Some do it because the stock has gone way up, and they missed out on it and put out a sell, hoping it will pull back so they can get in and then give it a buy rating. Some put out a buy, because it has gone up a lot, and it feels safe now to put out a buy. Some put out a sell after a stock has gone down a lot, because they now feel safe putting out the sell. Some put out a buy, because their clients are trapped in a company which is falling apart, and they hope a "dead cat" bounce will happen in the stock, so they can get their clients out with a little less damage.

One manager of a large mutual fund was going on TV saying to buy certain stocks, while they were actually selling them, so it would be easier for them to get out of those positions. After being caught, the manager left the fund and went on to be, you guessed it, a hedge fund manager. Although he had nothing to do with this event, the event had an indirect effect of permanently silencing Peter Lynch from ever talking about individual stocks.

In fact, as I am writing this, Goldman Sachs (GS) is upgrading Priceline (PCLN) at 1160 to "Conviction Buy". Goldman hated it when it was at 538 when I bought it, now they are giving it their highest possible recommendation AFTER it had already gone up 116%, but this is how Wall Street works. Needless to say, you should ignore all analyst recommendations, even though they often do move stocks in the short run (i.e. a day or two). What happens in the short run is meaningless to the fundamental stock investor.

Chapter 55 More Details On Stock Investing: What About So-Called Channel Checkers?

Don't believe so-called Channel Checkers. **Channel Checking,** in theory, is a practice in which an investor tries to get an edge on other investors between quarterly earnings reports for company XYZ, by trying to find out how company XYZ sales are faring, so that they will know in advance of the next quarterly report what to expect for earnings, while the rest of the investing world has to wait for company XYZ to actually report earnings. This allows the channel checker to know to buy or sell in advance of the earnings report.

In reality, in this global economy, it is impossible to actually do channel checking that will give anyone any meaningful data. In theory, you channel check by contacting retailers that sell the end product and ask them how XYZ's product is selling. In reality, these retailers not only don't have the information compiled until the end of the quarter themselves, and it is a violation of company policy to give out such information, and the retailer has nothing to gain from compiling this info and giving it to a hedge fund intern. Not only that, there are way too many retailers to contact, and many companies sell their products all over the world. Not only that, even if you did actually get all the sales data, you wouldn't get the company's cost of sales, therefore, you won't know what their margins are, so you won't know if profits will be good or not. Even if they got some of the information, how do they know if it is accurate and in context and proportional and meaningful? Another technique is to contact suppliers to the end product manufacturer XYZ. This is even more improbable, because it is illegal for publicly traded suppliers to provide information material to their business to some hedge fund minion, and again, what does the supplier get out of doing this - nothing.

In summary, channel checking is basically impossible to do, and even if attempted, the data is likely to be distorted or faulty. I am the worst nightmare for these "experts" who go on TV and say "our channel checking shows XYZ's sales are up [or down] more than expected", because I remember what they said when the actual earnings comes out. They are wrong as often as they are right, and the only thing

162

certain is, if they are long the stock, they will say their channel checking shows sales are strong, and if they are short the stock, they will say their channel checking shows sales are weak. Some channel checking claims are even more outrageous. I once heard of a hedge fund claiming to be using a helicopter to count the cars in shopping mall parking lots to figure out same store sales in advance. Don't be fooled by someone claiming to do channel checking; it is always self-serving based on their current position in the stock.

Chapter 56   More Details On Stock Investing: Write Down The Reason You Bought A Stock

When you buy a stock, write down a paragraph summarizing why you are buying the stock when you buy it and store it in your files. Write the name of the stock, ticker symbol, the current stock price, the size of the company, and the industry. Write the main reason you are buying, such as earnings are growing at 17% and the Forward P/E is only 12; combined with the 2% dividend yield, the total return is 19%. List the pros and cons, such as balance sheet, insider ownership, insider buying if any, stock buy backs, institutional holders and analysts following the stock, etc.

The paragraph should be short. Don't get caught up in minutia and irrelevant information, and don't use any useless wall street clichés and sayings; stick to basic facts. Don't base it on anything anyone else said about it, even if it is Warren Buffett. At least 4 times a year, such as when the company reports quarterly earnings, review the earnings report, and review what you wrote, and see if the reason you bought it is still valid. Update the paragraph to reflect any changes in the situation, such as a lower or higher growth rate, P/E falling due to increased earnings and/or lower stock price or rising due to increased stock price and/or lower earnings. This will aid you in letting you know whether you should hold, buy more, or to sell a stock. Below is a list of samples of the stories I wrote up when I bought some stocks in the past, and I have also provided a follow-up showing what actually happened. You can use a similar format or come up with your own format.

To show you an example of writing up a summary for a stock, here is a handful of the stocks I owned, and the updated write-up I had on them on Jan 1, 2009, and what happened with those stocks:

Web.Com (WWWW) – Micro cap provides online marketing and website management for over 70000 small businesses and entities. Pros: Earnings will be up 20% and P/E is a crazy low 3. Company is debt free and has 1 dollar per share in cash. Insiders own 6% of stock. No analysts follow the stock. They recently bought out their chief competitor. Company has solidly increased earnings 7 years in a row.

Cons: The recession could hurt earnings. Institutions own 86% of stock. Shorts control 20% of the stock and will of course be spreading lies about the company and will try to manipulate the stock down. Price is 3.6.

Follow-up: Earnings did come through and the stock more than doubled by mid-year to 7.5. Earnings continued to soar, but the short sellers were able to beat it back to 3.2 by mid 2010, but earnings kept coming through, and the stock was crazy cheap, and it rocketed to 15 by mid year 2011. Earnings kept powering forward, but the short sellers were able to beat it back down to 7 by the end of 2011. Then they made another great acquisition, and earnings soared again, and the stock rose to 19 in 2012 and to 33 by mid 2013. This became a 10 bagger for me.

Wyndham Hotels (WYN) – Mid cap cyclical owns 7000 hotels under the names Super 8, Day's Inn, Ramada Inn, Howard Johnson, Travel Lodge, Knight's Inn, Microtel, Wyndham and many others and was spun off from Cendant in '06 at a price of 33. Pros: Company says they will earn $2 per share in '09, so stock is selling at an outrageously cheap 3 times earnings. Cash has increased several years in a row, and they now have over 3 billion in cash and investments and have nearly as much cash as debt. Insiders are buying. They are buying back their own stock. They pay a dividend yielding 2.5%. The stock appears incredibly undervalued, as each hotel is valued at only 150K based on the stock price. When was the last time you bought an entire hotel for 150K? Stock is down 80% from its highs. Cons: Recessions are horrible for hotels, and earnings will likely plunge and could even turn into losses. Like all hotels, they have large debt, so they cannot survive an indefinite recession. Insiders own little stock, and institutions own 90% of stock. Experts feel company could go under completely. Price is 6.5.

Follow-up: Even though earnings were strong, and the balance sheet was strong, despite the recession, "experts" convinced many people that it would go bankrupt, and those fears drove the stock down 50% to 3. If I were using most other stock investing methods, I would have been using stop loss orders set at 10% below the purchase price and would have been stopped out multiple times and taken losses. Instead, I doubled up my position, because I knew it had a good balance sheet and it was profitable. I asked myself, "What am I missing?" and came up with nothing. Now at 3, each hotel was being valued at 75K, which is beyond silly. Eventually people figured it out, and the stock exploded to 20 by year end. Afterwards, the story kept getting better and better, with solid earnings increases of 15-30% year after year. By 2013, the stock was at 70. I made 10-20 times my money on this one.

Ebix (EBIX) – Small cap Internet software maker for overseas insurance companies, primarily in India. Earnings will be up 20-25% and P/E is 7. Company has low net debt of less than 2 dollars per share, despite many recent acquisitions. No analysts follow the company. Insiders own 32% of shares. Company has increased annual earnings 10 years in a row. Company once sold for 500 dollars a share during the late '90s Internet bubble when it was losing money! Cons: Quarterly profits are solid, but erratic, and the company provides no forward guidance that is of any use. Shorts control 30% of stock, and of course, are spreading lies about the company and trying to manipulate the stock down. Price is 23. [note: In Jan 2010, the stock split 3 for 1, so this price of 23 is equivalent to 7.6 now.]

Follow-up: Earnings continued to rise solidly for 2 more years on a string of successful acquisitions. A series of coordinated short attacks beat out scared/weak shareholders, and the stock fell from 23 to 18 by mid year, despite solid earnings. Then the stock exploded up to 66 by October. Then a series of coordinated short attacks and bogus "research reports" posted anonymously on websites, knocked the stock back down to 42 by early 2010. Then as earnings were still solid, the stock soared again up to 75 (25 split adjusted). Shorts attacked again drove it back to 60 (20 split adjusted), but it roared back up to 87 (29 split adjusted) in mid 2011. Earnings growth then slowed dramatically, and I sold in 2011 at about 75 (25 split adjusted). If I were using most other stock investing methods, I would have been stopped out multiple times and taken losses. This was about a 30 bagger for me over the nearly 10 years I owned it.

Cliff's Iron Ore (CLF) – Mid cap cyclical mines iron ore and coke for steel companies. Pros: Despite recession they could earn 5 dollars per share in '09, so they are selling at only 5 times earnings, and earnings should soar coming out of recession. They have more cash than debt, so will survive the recession. They pay a dividend yielding 1.4%.

Stock is down more than 80%. Cons: The recession could deepen and earnings turn into sharp losses. They have debt, so they can't ride out recession forever. Insiders own little stock and institutions own 80% of stock. Price is 25.

Follow-up: As the market bottomed in March 9th of 2009, this stock got hammered all the way down to 12. Fortunately I didn't panic and stayed with the stock. If I were using most other stock investing methods, I would have been stopped out multiple times and taken losses. By year end, the stock soared to 53. The stock sold off to 46 by mid 2011, but earnings kept coming through, so I stuck with it and it rose to 100 by mid 2011. Then fundamentals started falling apart (i.e. earnings started to decline) later in the year, and I ended up selling at 80.

Ashford Hospitality Trust (AHT) – Small cap REIT owns and manages 110 hotel properties, primarily Marriott and Hiltons in 26 states and in Canada. Pros: Earnings are solid, though declining somewhat in the recession, and P/E is an outrageously cheap, 1 times earnings, and REITS typically trade between 6 and 12 times earnings. With a P/E of 1, this is like buying an apartment building for 500K, that has a positive cash flow of 500K per year from day 1. The company has eliminated its dividend to use for early debt retirement. Insiders own 5% of stock. Stock is selling at only 10% of book value. Cons: The hotel industry is being slammed by recession, so a heavy debt company such as this could go under completely in a protracted recession, and you would lose everything. They pay no dividend, a huge negative for a REIT. Institutions own 95% of stock and shorts are betting they go under. Nearly 15 analysts follow the company, extremely high for a small cap and they all universally hate the company with sell recommendations. Price is 1.1.

Follow-up: Despite the recession, they remained solidly profitable with positive Funds From Operations (FFO). Not only that, they began to buy back stock at a furious rate, the best thing in the world to do when the stock is selling at a P/E of 1!! Later profits began to increase, and EPS soared as they ended up buying back more than 50% of their shares over the next 2-3 years. The stock initially fell to 0.84 in March, and all the shorts were saying it was going under and to get out before it is too late, but to me it was obvious they were wrong and I kept buying more. If I were using most other stock investing methods, I would have been stopped out multiple times and taken losses. FFO were profitable and to prove it they were buying back shares. You don't do that if you are on the verge of bankruptcy; you wouldn't have the cash to do it. The stock soared to 3.5 by year end, to 7 in 2010 and to 9.5 by 2011. Then earnings stopped increasing and started to decline so I sold in mid 2011 at 8.5.

Air Methods (AIRM) – Small cap operates fleet of 240 helicopters that does emergent transports of patients to hospitals. Pros: Turnaround stock with earnings expected to rebound 20-30% and P/E is 8. They have paid down debt and increased cash the past few years and now have a manageable 4 dollars per share in net debt. Company has plenty of room for expansion. Insiders own 26% of shares. Cons: They had a lot of excuses (weather, higher than normal maintenance, non payment problems, high fuel prices) for poor earnings in '08, and they could have the same excuses this year. Company's earnings are wildly erratic and unpredictable and very seasonal, fuel dependent and weather dependent. Their services are so expensive, that they have huge non-payment problems. Institutions own 74% of shares. Price is 15. [note: In Jan 2013 the stock split 3 for 1, so this price of 15 is equivalent to 5 now.]

Follow-up: The earnings did actually rebound in 2009, and the stock rose to 35 later that year (11.6 split adjusted). The earnings were even better in 2011 and 2012 on a couple of very accretive acquisitions, and the stock rose to 147 (49 split adjusted) by 2013. Then they reported a horrible quarter, in which they suddenly lost money. I sold at 120 (40 split adjusted). That turned out to be a bad move on my part, because it turned out to be just one bad quarter, and earnings and the stock continued to soar after I sold. I have found however, when a company has a really bad quarter, 3/4 of the time it is the beginning of a trend and you should sell. This turned out to be one of those 1/4 times where it was just one bad quarter.

Keep in mind, that the above stocks were big winners, but when you own stocks selling at crazy low Forward P/Es of 3, 3, 7, 5, 1 and 8, and the companies are actually increasing earnings, it is tough to lose. Then again, people were panicking in early 2009, as happens in every Bear Market/Stock market collapse. This was the 5th Stock Market

Collapse (defined as a 40% or greater loss in the S&P 500) since 1926, and people were just mindlessly throwing their stocks away, by selling at crazy cheap prices and with huge losses. If you are one to panic like them, you should not go anywhere near stocks. I remained fully invested in stocks (I had 70-80 stocks most of the year.), and for the full year in 2009, I was up 59.6% versus 26.5% for the S&P 500.

Here are a handful of the stocks I owned and their updated write-up on Jan 1, 2012 and what happened with those stocks:

Whirlpool (WHR) - Mid cap cyclical appliance manufacturer under the brand names Whirlpool, Kenmore, Maytag, Kitchen Aid, Roper and many others. Pros: Earnings should be flat but close to all time record levels, and P/E is an insanely cheap 4. The stock typically trades between 7 and 14 times earnings. It pays a dividend yielding 4.3%. The 4 analysts who follow the stock expect earnings to inexplicably collapse down 40% in 2012, despite no such guidance from the company, no expectation of recession or any other reason, and they are almost certainly wrong. Insiders were buying heavily in November. Although they have significant net debt, debt has decreased 2 years in a row. Stock is selling at the same price it was in 1987, and last year's earnings were 7 times higher than in 1987. Cons: I could be wrong, and earnings could be about to suddenly and mysteriously collapse by 40% as the analysts predict. They have big debt with 21 dollars per share net debt. Institutions own 99% of shares and shorts control 14% of shares and are spreading lies and rumors and are trying to manipulate the stock down. Price is 47.

Follow-up: The earnings never collapsed down and in fact rose substantially since then, due to the housing recovery. With the stock selling at a dirt cheap P/E of 4, it had no place to go but up. The stock took off to 80 by April, then a panicked short seller put out a bogus "research report" on a well known internet site, saying something to the effect that the company was fraudulently overstating their earnings, and the stock got knocked back to 55 by mid year. As earnings continued to be solid, I loaded up on the stock during that sell-off, making it one of my largest holdings. The earnings continued to come through, and by mid year 2013, the stock was at 150 and still not yet at the high end of their historical P/E range of 7-14, and the company was forecasting continued good earnings increases, so I continued to hold the stock.

Hartford Financial Services Group (HIG) – Large cap insurance and financial services provider, operates nationwide and was founded in 1810. Pros: Company says earnings should rebound strongly from last year's storm related depressed levels and should be up over 50%, and P/E is an insanely cheap 4, and it typically trades between 6 and 12 times earnings. It trades at only 1/3 of book value. It pays a dividend currently yielding 2.5%. Stock is down 85% from 2008 levels. Cons: They may fail to deliver on their earnings promise. Earnings are erratic, seasonal and wildly unpredictable. They massively diluted their shares in the wake of the Credit Bubble. Institutions own 89% of stock, and nearly 20 analysts follow the company. Price is 16.

Follow-up: Earnings did in fact rebound and continue to increase. The stock rose to 21 early in 2012, only to fall right back to 16 by mid year. With earnings coming on strong and the stock down in the dumps, that is a buy, and I greatly increased my position in the stock to one of my biggest positions. The stock rose to 24 by year end, and with strong earnings and the company forecasting better earnings, I continue to hold, with the stock rising to 35 in mid 2013.

Lincoln National (LNC) – Large cap sells Life Insurance. Pros: Earnings should be over 4 dollars per share, and P/E is an insanely cheap 4. Stock sells at less than 1/2 of book value. They are buying back their own stock. They pay a dividend currently yielding 1.7%. The stock is selling at 60% below 2008 levels, and stock is selling at the same price it was 17 years ago, and earnings are have tripled since then. Cons: Nearly 20 analysts follow the stock. Institutions own 82% of stock. Price is 19.

Follow-up: Earnings not only came through, they increased, and with the stock selling at 4 times earnings when insurance stocks typically trade at 6-12, this was a good situation. I had owned the stock since 2009, but the stock severely tested one's patience. By the end of 2012, the stock was selling at the same price it was in 2009. Fortunately as a fundamental stock investor, I was patient and kept adding more and more to my position all that time, building it to one of my biggest holdings. Finally on Jan 1, 2013, the stock finally started getting properly valued and rocketed up to over 50 by mid 2013. With earnings still increasing, and the stock still well below the top of the typical P/E range for its industry, I continued to hold. This again shows the folly of the so called "Efficient Market" theory. If the market was efficient, it would have sold at 50 all that time.

Commonwealth REIT (CWH) – Mid cap REIT owns and manages 480 office and industrial properties in 33 states. Pros: This is a turnaround, as earnings will be flat or down slightly, and P/E is an insanely cheap 4, and REITS typically trade between 6 and 12 times earnings. It pays a massive dividend, currently yielding 11.9%, and the dividend appears to be secure. Stock sells at 1/3 of book value. Cons: Earnings have been drifting downward for 8 straight years for a total decline of 31%. Occupancy rates are weak and have declined for 8 straight years and are at 87.0%. Insiders only own 1% of stock. They are doing a gimmicky spin-off of some of their properties in an IPO. Price is 16.

Follow-up: This did not work out. What happened is there was no turnaround, and earnings continued to drift lower and lower each year, meaning the fundamentals were deteriorating, and you should sell a stock, no matter how cheap it is, if the earnings are deteriorating. Not only that, the dividend was not safe, as I wrongly thought it was, and it was cut. I sold at 15 for a loss.

Tata Motors (TTM) - Large cap Indian cyclical manufactures low end autos, light trucks and commercial vehicles, plus the Jaguar Land Rover, and sells them worldwide, and is one of the largest auto companies in the world. Pros: Earnings should be lousy in the first half due to the weak Indian economy and should rebound in the second half, and P/E is only 6. They have a strong balance sheet, with almost as much cash as debt. They sell the cheapest vehicles in the world, with high gas mileage, which should ensure huge growth in the Third World for decades to come. They pay a dividend currently yielding 2.5%. No analysts follow the stock. Cons: Vehicle sales are rising in India, but outside competition is flooding in, keeping a lid on profits. Their Nano failed to break into the American market. Although their low end cars are cheap and fuel efficient, they are generally of cheap quality. Foreign stocks carry significant currency risks. Price is 16.

Follow-up: Almost immediately, the stock started soaring in 2012, nearly doubling to 30. Then, even as all their rivals were increasing earnings, their earnings started to unexpectedly decline so I sold mid year at a price of 27.

Citigroup (C) - Large cap Blue Chip Money Center bank is the 3rd largest bank in America. Pros: Earnings are expected to be up 11% and P/E is a crazy cheap 5. Non performing loans have declined to 3.2%. Stock sells at less than 1/2 of book value. They have paid back all government loans, and the government has sold all the shares they owned, as part of the taxpayer rescue. Insiders own 4% of stock, impressive for a huge company. Institutions only own 56% of stock. It pays a negligible dividend. Cons: They may not be able to sustain or increase profitability due to excessive regulation and non stop frivolous lawsuits and interference with their business by the government. Non performing loans are still at a dangerous level; if the economy goes South, they could go under. They face waves of extortion lawsuit payoffs from politicians across the country and waves of bogus lawsuits. More than 25 analysts follow the company. They have a lousy cyclical boom-bust history in which they nearly collapsed multiple times (early '80s, early '90s and late '00s), and each time shareholders lost 97-99% of their money. Price is 26.

Follow-up: The stock quickly rose to 38 by spring. Then the earnings started to actually decline. I sold at 33 and switched the money to rival JP Morgan Chase (JPM), which I already owned, and increased my stake buying more JPM (coincidently) at 33. The earnings continued to grow at JPM, and the stock rose to 57 in mid 2013, so I continued to hold the JPM stock.

For all my stocks (I owned between 90 and 100 stocks most of the year.) in 2012, I was up 19.4% versus 15.9% for the S&P 500.

Chapter 57   More Details On Stock Investing: The Effect Of Mainstream Media News On Your Investing Ability

Stop consuming Mainstream Media news on TV, on the Internet, on radio, in magazines and in newspapers. Mainstream Media news is overwhelmingly negative, agenda ridden and biased masquerading, as news and most importantly the information provided will do nothing to improve your life or your ability to become a better investor. It is anti-capitalism, which is what the purpose of stocks are for, for companies to raise capital to invest and expand to produce all the goods and services we consume and enjoy, and if you are reading this book, to invest in.

If you are anti-capitalism, then you have to ask yourself, what are you doing in stocks? And if you believe in capitalism, why are you using Mainstream Media news sources, which are universally anti-capitalism? Note that even though their reporting is anti-capitalism, they hypocritically profit from capitalism.

If you listen to the Mainstream Media news, you will become negative, jaded and cynical and you will be constantly thinking the world is coming to an end, and you will be scared out of stocks. You may even start thinking of yourself as some type of victim or may start wasting emotional energy on envying the so called One Percenters or other successful people, which is a loser's mentality that will get you nowhere in life or investing - even if you are an actual victim of some sort.

Never underestimate the power of positive thinking. You need to be positive and to visualize yourself succeeding as an investor and building wealth. You need to be positive about your own future and avoid negative people and negative ideas and the negative Mainstream Media. Negative people never accomplish anything, and negative people will hold you back, and you should put Mainstream Media in that same negative category.

Stop accessing Mainstream Media news on TV, Radio, the Internet, magazines and newspapers. Spend this time on something useful, such as doing fundamental research on new stock ideas and keeping up with the fundamentals of the companies you own, and spending more time on positive activities, such as exercising or getting outdoors, spending more time with loved ones, etc. At first it will be tough to wean yourself off this bad habit of following Mainstream Media news, but once you do, you will wonder why you wasted all the hours on it and all the negative emotions elicited from doing it. I waited until I was age 30 before I started to wean myself off of Mainstream Media news, and it was tough at first, but looking back, was one of the best things I could have done to improve my investing ability and the overall quality of my life.

Chapter 58 More Details On Stock Investing: Only Watch Financial Shows For Entertainment, Not For Advice Or Education

Don't watch financial shows either. They spend most of their time on silly stuff that will never help you as an investor. Talking about what the Fed might do, talking about what the politicians might do, endlessly trying to forecast the direction of the economy, endlessly trying to predict the direction of interest rates, stocks prices, gold prices and oil prices. They spend the rest of their time interviewing "experts" pushing their own self-serving agendas.

If an expert is fully invested in stocks, they will tell you all these convincing points as to why the market will go up. If they are short the market or in cash, they will tell you how dangerous the market is and due for a crash and sound equally convincing. If they are long XYZ stock, they will tell you how great the company is. If they are short XYZ stock, they will tell you how bad the company is. Never forget that they will all sound convincing. They will non-stop use the endless, worthless and meaningless Wall Street clichés and terms that I warned you to ignore, which are listed in **Chapter 24**.

You will hear the perpetual bears who, like a broken clock, are occasionally right, but if you are not paying close attention, you will forget about all the huge gains they missed. You also have perpetual bulls, who are always saying the market is going to go up. In the long run, they are probably correct, but you already knew that, so their forecasts are useless to you. You will see loud guys say how great XYZ stock or stock sector of the market is and what a great CEO they have, only to reverse the other way the following week and both times sound incredibly convincing and changing their view so rapidly, that there will always exist a past video clip that "was a great call". They will tell you they are looking out for the little guy and trying to help the little guy understand the markets, when in reality they are just self promoting themselves or talking up or down a stock for their own self interest or to increase their fame and following. Of course, if you tried to follow their advice you could end up on the poor farm.

You will see fast money types talking about how they have over 200 different markets they can trade in and using meaningless terms such "price is truth" and "value trap" and "pigs get slaughtered" and moving in and out of positions. Meanwhile, Warren Buffett does none of that and inexorably grows richer and richer. None of them are looking out for you, and none of them can help you. You must be your own person. If you can't watch these shows for anything other than light entertainment, which I sometimes do, then you should avoid them, because they may cause you to do something stupid with your investing.

Chapter 59   More Details On Stock Investing: What About Fraud?

What about fraud? Yes, fraud does happen, and yes, I have been taken by fraud in stock investing. I will give you the good news and the bad news about fraud. The good news is it is actually very rare PROVIDED you avoid the cesspool of penny stocks and avoid small foreign stocks that are relatively new and not well known but trade on a USA stock exchange. There are about 5000 stocks listed on the major US Stock Exchanges. In addition there are thousands of penny stocks trading on smaller exchanges or what is called the **Pink Sheets**. Among non-penny stocks, I would estimate at any given time less than 10 or less than 0.2% of companies of publicly traded companies are engaged in fraud. Therefore, the odds of getting taken are pretty low. Also, fraud has always been there, but as far as I can tell, has not gotten any worse or any better.

Now the bad news. The government (SEC, etc.) won't save you from them. In all major fraud cases, the stock collapses, and the investors lose almost everything BEFORE the government gets involved. They are always too little, too late. Also, the hedge funds/shorts won't help you. Short sellers are often accusing the companies whose stock they are shorting of fraud of some sort. They sometimes openly claim their accounting is fraudulent or a pyramid scheme or doing something illegal or unethical or other nefarious behavior. Sometimes short sellers and/or their minions spread bogus rumors day and night on the message boards, or they write anonymous "research articles" on internet web sites. If you add it all up, at any given time, literally 100's of perfectly legitimate and ethical companies are being accused of fraud by short sellers on TV or at presentations or on message boards or on so called research websites. Unfortunately they are the boy who cried wolf, for every 1000 companies they openly or covertly accuse of committing fraud, maybe 5-10 are actually committing fraud. Also, more than half the companies short sellers are shorting and claiming to be frauds, are not only legitimate, but growing businesses run by honest, hard working people getting tarred by these lowlifes; some are often excellent investments, as pointed out earlier in the book.

So, what are the warnings signs? To be perfectly honest, there aren't any that I can think of. There is no common theme that stands out. Of course, penny stock land is rife with fraud and often are new, small foreign stocks with their operations entirely overseas, but with stocks trading on US exchanges. For non-penny stock companies with USA operations, fraud is rare but it exists, and there is no common theme or red flag. It is certainly not the short sellers, because they accuse hundreds of companies of fraud every day. Certainly not the SEC, they are always way too late.

The people who run fraudulent companies are really good at what they do. For example, Bernie Ebbers quit his job as junior high gym teacher and basketball coach and joined a tiny long distance telephone company and soon used his charisma to talk his way into the CEO job. He then fraudulently inflated the earnings numbers, which drove up his stock price, so his market cap rose, then he would buy out smaller but legitimate companies with his artificially inflated stock. He did this over and over, buying out dozens of companies and ultimately taking over MCI Communications and changing the name to WorldCom. The numbers were spectacular and his scam lasted over 15 years before it collapsed, when he was unable to take over Sprint. He reported billions in profits, when in fact, the company was losing billions. I got taken on this one losing about 85% of my initial investment. Ebbers was tried and convicted and sentenced to 25 years in prison. WorldCom eventually admitted to more than 10 billion in accounting misstatements. Think of all the people this former milkman/bouncer/gym teacher fooled over 15 years, and you will understand why I say it is really difficult to find red flags for fraud. Think about that and the 1000 companies accused everyday by short sellers as frauds and 99.9% are innocent, and you realize how hard it is to know if a company is fraudulent.

Enron was a huge company that committed fraud for over 15 years before their house of cards collapsed. It was called "one of the largest energy companies in the nation", but it really wasn't even an energy company; it was primarily trading energy futures, and it was hiding losses and hiding debt, and yet, it fooled everyone for nearly 20 years. Luckily I avoided that one, because it was selling at 70 times (what turned out to be fake) earnings, and I never buy wildly overpriced stocks such as that.

I was invested in a small software company which had 20 million in cash and solid earnings. Unfortunately, they were lying about the earnings, but the cash from their IPO was real, and one day the CEO took the 20 million and fled to the Grand Cayman Islands, where he avoided prosecution and is living it up and I lost my entire investment.

Another was a penny stock (I warned above to stay out of penny stocks, as they are rife with fraud, and I didn't follow my own advice.) that was selling apparel in Canada. (I warn above to avoid companies that are listed on a US exchange but their operations are overseas, as too many have turned out to be frauds). Great earnings and strong balance sheet and cheap stock but one problem. The company didn't even exist; it was all made up and I got taken.

Another was HQ Sustainable Industries, which was supposedly a food processing company that was selling farm raised tilapia fish. Again this was a young, small US listed stock that was operating overseas in China. Avoid young, small US listed stocks, that have their operations completely overseas. Luckily I sold this, because the (fake) earnings were weakening and took a smaller loss. Others weren't so lucky, and one day the NASDAQ just shut the company down, and the stock never traded again, and people lost all their money.

All I can say is that fraud can be big or small and they are very clever, and the only time the shorts figure out fraud is totally by accident, because they are constantly accusing a thousand companies of "irregular accounting practices" and fraud, and the government (i.e. SEC) will never figure it out until it is way too late. The politicians are useless or worse than useless. After Enron and WorldCom, the politicians passed yet another law, this one called Sarbanes-Oxley, that greatly increased the cost of business for companies, but has done nothing to prevent fraud and wouldn't have prevented the Enron or WorldCom frauds, so it was worse than useless.

Your only protection is to avoid penny stocks where fraud is rampant, and to avoid young, small US listed stocks with operations entirely overseas. Other than that, diversify your holdings enough, such that if you are ever taken by a fraudulent stock, your diversification will protect you.

Chapter 60   More Details On Stock Investing: Expect To Make Lots Of Mistakes

Expect to make lots of mistakes. Every successful investor makes lots of mistakes and I certainly have myself. I have made mistakes in both real estate, in addition to lots of mistakes in stock investing and wealth building in general.

In real estate, I bought 2 condominiums that weren't anywhere near water (which I warn against in **Chapter 6**), but I was saved by buying both at the right time in the cycle, even if it was purely by accident. I sold those condos and moved up to a bigger house at the wrong time in the real estate cycle and ended up selling the house at a loss, although I was saved by simultaneously buying a much bigger house at the absolute best time in the next real estate cycle.

As far as wealth building goes, I foolishly waited until I was 28 before I started investing and didn't start investing in individual stocks until I was 30. As I stated earlier, starting early gives one a huge advantage.

I also foolishly failed to follow some of the money saving techniques that I outline in the second half of the book

As far as stock investing, I didn't stick fully with my *Fundamental Stock Investing* system my first few years, and flirted with other systems and it held back my returns, but I was still able to beat the market as a whole. The next 15 years, I really stuck with my system and did very well and beat the market by a substantial margin (16.1% average annual returns versus 3.1% for the S&P 500) during that time. However, I was still wrong about 30% of the time, i.e. 30% of the stocks I bought I ended up selling at a loss. As pointed out above, I also got taken by a few fraudulent companies during that time and suffered total or near total losses on some stocks. Despite waiting until age 28 and only starting with $8,000 and then making all these mistakes, I still was able to retire at age 42. I was able to do this without ever taking a penny from giving advice to other people, despite the fact that I helped a lot of people build wealth. All this goes to show, you can make a lot of mistakes as I have and yet still manage to build wealth over time.

As stated earlier in the book, if you use *Fundamental Stock Investing* and you are wrong about 50% of the time, you will do ok in stocks, better than not investing at all. If you are right 60% of the time, you will do quite well. If you are right 70% of the time, you are going to beat the pants off of the market and build significant wealth. So you can and will make mistakes, however, you have to be decisive and sell when a stock's fundamentals fall apart (not to be confused with something silly such as selling when a stock "missed analysts expectations" or got downgraded by some firm, or selling a stock that has been going down for no apparent reason). By fundamentals falling apart, I mean it is clear earnings are going to be LOWER for the foreseeable future, or an expensive growth stock's earnings growth is slowing dramatically, or if a turnaround, is not actually turning around, and earnings/losses/debt are getting worse, or a cyclical's industry has peaked and earnings are starting to go down, or a depressed cyclical's debt load is rising to a dangerous level and there is no industry turnaround in sight, etc. You need to be decisive and sell in these situations and not ride them down "hoping" things will turnaround.

You also can't dwell on mistakes or get too emotional or down. When a stock falls apart on me, I usually am mad until I wake up the next day, but when I wake up the next day, I am always completely over it and have moved on and it doesn't bother me one bit. Some people who are perfectionists won't make it in stocks, because they are too troubled by the mistakes. They have trouble admitting mistakes, and they feel a sense of failure or shame or it hurts their pride. It is one of the few endeavors where the most successful people still make lots of mistakes. You've got to be able to rebound and be tenacious to make it in stock investing. You protect yourself by diversification over many stocks, so you will never be wiped out or badly hurt by any one mistake.

Chapter 61   More Details On Stock Investing: Do Not Try To Time The Market Because The Bulk Of Stock Market Gains Happen In Just A Few Days Per Year

Do not try to time the stock market. The bulk of stock market gains happen in just a few days per year. If I have still not convinced you yet of the folly of stock market timing, this should convince you. In any given year, almost all of the gains happen in about 10 individual days. No one ever sees these days coming or predicts them. I have been investing for 24 years and never once did any expert, the day before, correctly say, "Tomorrow is going to be a huge up day." Never, not once did anyone see any of them coming!

After they happen, the talking heads scramble to try to give a reason as to why it was a big up day. Often, they just simply happen, and there is really no reason, which is why they can never be predicted in advance. If you are trying to time the market going in and out, you will never catch these fantastic one day gains that make up the bulk of all stock market gains. I have caught every one of them, because I am fully invested at all times. It is a great feeling to be fully in the market when these unexpected rallies happen.

As stated previously, as a fundamental stock investor, you should be much more afraid of missing a big stock market rally than getting caught in a big decline. T. Rowe Price did a study of the market for the 15 year period from 12/31/97 to 12/31/12, and if you tried to time the market and missed just the 10 best days (spread over 15 years!!), you would have ended up trailing the market by nearly 5 percentage points per year, which is a massive underperformance. If you missed the best individual 20 days over that 15 year period, you would have trailed the market by a staggering 8 percentage points per year. And by the way, this has been the case throughout stock market history. If you are going to fear anything, your biggest fear is to be caught out of the market when these huge one day rallies happen.

Chapter 62 More Details On Stock Investing: Ignore All Opinions And Stick Exclusively To Fundamental Facts

Ignore all opinions on stocks and get your factual fundamental information from the company itself via company press releases, the company annual reports or information from the company that are posted on your Discount Broker's Website or Yahoo Finance or Google Finance or other similar sources. Forget opinions from people on message boards, "research reports" on stock market websites, the internet, TV, newspapers, stock newsletters, stock gurus etc. Opinions, predictions and forecasts have nothing to do with *Fundamental Stock Investing.*

Chapter 63   More Details On Stock Investing: Short Term Stock Movements Mean Nothing

Short term stock movements mean nothing in *Fundamental Stock Investing*. The stock I bought went up, so I am right? Not necessarily. The stock I bought went down, so I was wrong? Again, short term movements in stock price mean nothing. What a stock does in the short term is meaningless. Stocks bounce all over the place in the short term with no apparent reason. Always ignore short term stock movements. However, in the intermediate term and especially in the long term, stock price closely follows EPS. So if a stock you buy immediately starts going up, it doesn't necessarily mean you are right, it means nothing. On the other hand, if the growth stock you bought was fairly priced based when comparing GR to P/E, and earnings 3 years from now are significantly higher than now, then you were in fact "right", and the stock will likely be much higher in price.

Chapter 64 More Details On Stock Investing: The Dollar Price A Stock Is Selling For Is Irrelevant Unless Compared To P/E

The dollar price a stock is selling at is completely irrelevant unless compared to earnings via calculating the P/E. This should be obvious, but just to make sure no one misunderstands, I will reiterate this point. Whether a stock is selling at 1.05 or 23 or 88 or 112 or 1254 tells you absolutely nothing about whether a stock is cheap or expensive. For example, the stock selling at 1.05 could be losing money, so therefore, the stock is extremely expensive. The stock selling at 1254 could have EPS next year of $155.10 per share, meaning the Forward P/E of the stock is only 8, so the stock is actually very cheap.

Chapter 65   More Details On Stock Investing: Spin-Offs

A **Spin-Off** is similar to an IPO, but instead of it being a new company, it is an existing conglomerate or company with more than one division that is "spinning-off" one of its divisions to be a stand alone company, trading as its own stock under a new ticker symbol. Unlike IPOs, spin-offs are almost always profitable and almost always spun-off at a reasonable price and with a reasonable or good balance sheet. Also, even if it is a large company, it will have few or no analysts initially following the stock. Therefore, you can often find some good bargain stocks in spin-offs, so you should always investigate them. Unfortunately, like an IPO, you won't have much useful information to go by when it is first spun-off, so you have to wait a quarter or two, so you have 1 or 2 quarterly earnings reports to fundamentally analyze the stock.

Chapter 66   More Details On Stock Investing: Avoid Penny Stocks Like The Plague

In general, avoid **Penny Stocks** like the plague. A penny stock is a stock selling at less than 1 dollar per share. The vast majority of penny stocks are either companies that are losing money and have no hope of ever making money, or even worse, companies that no longer actually exist as real companies but the stock still trades. Also, there are a significant number of penny stocks, that are not only companies that no longer exist, but never existed, and were strictly created for the purpose of defrauding foolish investors out of their money.

If I have not yet convinced you to avoid penny stocks, I will continue onward. Trading in penny stocks is dominated by con artists, fraudsters, stock manipulators, day traders, scam artists, liars, carpetbaggers, organized crime and other assorted bottom feeders. Most penny stock companies do not file any financial information that is of any use, and in many cases, is deliberately misleading or fraudulent. Furthermore, there are entire companies created for the purpose of scamming you in "pump and dump" schemes. These are called **Boiler Rooms**. They buy stock in fake penny stocks, then promote these to unsuspecting investors, who buy the stock and drive up the price, then the scam artists sell and you lose everything. If I have not steered you clear of the cesspool of penny stocks yet, I will add the SEC and other government agencies almost never catch any of the people running scams associated with profiteering from penny stocks, because they are too busy monitoring illegal trading in real companies and doing a lousy job at that.

Any real company with any hope of returning to profitability that finds its stock beaten down into the morass of penny stock land for more than a month or so, usually quickly does a reverse split of say 1:10 or 1:25 to get its stock trading well above 10 again to get it out of the cesspool. So, it would be the rarest of rare cases that you discover a penny stock that is actually a real company selling a real product or service that actually has real accounting and is actually profitable or has a hope of returning to profitability one day and for some bizarre reason has decided to not do a reverse split. One of the stocks I got taken in for fraud was a penny stock, and I foolishly fell for the scam. Avoid penny stocks!

Chapter 67   More Details On Stock Investing: Stock Splits

Stock splits are meaningless events at best, and gimmicky at worst, and therefore, are a complete non-event for fundamental stock investors. A stock split is when a company doubles (2 for 1) or triples (3 for 1) the number of shares outstanding, which immediately reduces the price of the stock by a factor of 2 or 3 respectively. In the end, the value of the company and the value of the stock you own is exactly the same. For example, say you own 10 shares of IBM, and the stock is selling at 200, so you own $2000 dollars in IBM stock. They decide to do a 4 for 1 stock split. After the stock split, you will own 40 shares, and the stock will be selling for 50, and you will still own $2000 dollars in IBM stock.

In the olden days (1970s and earlier), stock splits actually had a purpose, because the system was rigged so that you had to buy stock in 100 share lots or pay exorbitant commissions. Therefore, a company stock split would allow smaller investors back then to be able to buy shares. Nowadays, you can buy any amount of stock you like, including as little as 1 share, and pay the same commission, so stock splits have no meaning anymore.

Many well respected established companies will split their stock 2 for 1 when the stock price hits 100. This is reasonable, but again, it is a meaningless event. However, you will constantly see gimmicky stock splits of splitting a stock when it hits 40 or even 20, and I have even seen companies split when it reaches 10! Then you have double gimmicky stock splits when they not only split well below 100, but they do a 3 for 2, or worse, a 4 for 3 or 5 for 4 stock split. Again, it really doesn't mean anything, even if it is gimmicky, but it does make you question whether the company is truly focused on its business when doing nonsense like this. Some companies even have the audacity to tell gullible investors that the stock split is a "Shareholder Friendly move" when it is no such thing.

Also, when they do a 3 for 2 split and you own an odd number of shares (e.g. 33 or 371, etc.), you are going to get **CIL** (cash in lieu of partial shares), which is annoying and complicates your tax filing if you own the shares in a taxable account. For example, if you own 371 shares and they do a 3 for 2 stock split, you will get 556 shares plus 0.5 shares worth of cash that you now have to report on your taxes that year, even if you never sold any shares. To prevent this minor annoyance, I always buy an even number (i.e. 2, 56, 788, etc.) of shares so I don't get into any CILs that I have to report on income tax.

Don't be fooled into believing that stock splits are part of being shareholder friendly, because in fact, any stock split below 100 is actually simply shareholder annoying. It is even more annoying when the company tells you they are doing the stock split to "increase liquidity" in the stock. First off, liquidity is meaningless to the fundamental stock investor and doubling the number of shares outstanding does not increase liquidity of the stock; liquidity is only increased if there is more interest in a stock. A company gets more interest in the stock by increasing sales and earnings, not gimmicks such as stock splits.

Chapter 68   More Details On Stock Investing: When Evaluating A Stock, Where The Stock Price Has Been In The Past Is Completely Irrelevant

When evaluating a stock to buy (or sell), it doesn't matter where the stock price was in the past. It doesn't matter whether the stock has recently doubled or lost half its value or gone sideways for years. You must evaluate its current fundamentals with respect to its current price. Only here and now matters. Just because a stock is way up doesn't mean you shouldn't buy it, and just because it is way down doesn't mean you should buy it. Always evaluate at its current price, not where the price has been.

Chapter 69 More Details On Stock Investing: Seek Out Shareholder Friendly Companies

Seek out shareholder friendly companies. Obviously, you want to buy stocks with strong solid fundamentals and balance sheets at fair or cheap prices. It is an added bonus if the company is also shareholder friendly. Here are some of the things shareholder friendly companies do. Typically, they do real stock buy backs, as opposed to phony stock buybacks. They pay dividends and they raise the dividend every year. They have high insider ownership of stock, so their motives are aligned with shareholders. They only make accretive acquisitions and avoid dilutive acquisitions. They don't shower themselves with excessive stock options that dilute existing shareholders and then immediately exercise (i.e. dump) those shares as soon as they can. They don't pay themselves excessive salaries and set themselves up with absurdly high golden parachutes. They don't waste money on excessively luxurious headquarters and corporate jets. They don't do gimmicky stock splits. Instead, they are focused on increasing the stock price and they make their fortune by actually owning the company stock and not through salary, golden parachutes and stock options they dump as soon as possible. They don't waste shareholder cash by doing one time cash dividends; they instead focus on real stock buy backs and increasing regular dividends, which actually help increase the stock price in the long run. They also don't sit on ridiculously large piles of cash forever; they keep what is necessary in case they fall on hard times and use the rest to buy back stock, pay and increase regular dividends and make accretive acquisitions.

Chapter 70   More Details On Stock Investing: Don't Bother Calling The Company

Peter Lynch was a huge advocate of calling companies and even visiting companies to get a feel for how their business was faring. Warren Buffett is always talking to senior management at companies. So if these investing legends always did it, why am I saying to not bother doing it? The main reason is that they are Peter Lynch and Warren Buffett, and you and I are Dick and Jane Nobody. When they called, they were immediately put through to the CEO. Here is my experience calling companies. I called hundreds of companies in the first half of my investing career. Keep in mind, back then those were expensive "long distance toll calls". For 100% of those calls, I of course did not get put through to the CEO, but not even once got put through to the head of Investor Relations nor even anyone in Investor Relations. For 100% of those calls, I got an administrative assistant whom 100% of the time told me, "They are in meetings and if you give me your name, the name of your firm and your phone number, they will get back to you." In 100% of those cases, no one ever got back to me the day I called. For most, someone actually did get back to me a day or a few days later. I used all the techniques Peter Lynch talked about in his book, and yet, not once did I ever get any useful information that wasn't already available in a press release or even a "feel" for the business. After the **Fair Disclosure** rule in the year 2000, companies provided even more information to investors in their reports. By then, and after my previous experience with calling companies, it was obvious that it was pointless to call any companies. I also believe that even Peter Lynch or Warren Buffett don't get any significant information, beyond what is already out there when they call a company today.

Chapter 71   More Details On Stock Investing: How Can The Little Guy Compete In Today's Market?

How can the "Little Guy" compete in today's market? Actually quite easily. In fact, it has never been easier for the Little Guy or Gal, also known as the **Retail Investor,** and in fact, I believe the Little Guy has advantages over the **"Big Players"**. Most of the obstacles for the Retail Investor have been eliminated, and not only that, some of the newer supposed advantages for the "Big Players" are actually disadvantages. There are 2 relatively new disadvantages for the Retail Investor, but in the big picture, they are not that big of a deal.

Up until 1975, to buy and sell stock you had to go through a "**Full Service Broker**" and pay over $100 commission per trade. Now you can pay $7 or less and trade online by yourself. You used to have to buy 100 share lots of stock; now you can buy any amount you want. You used to have to pay your broker service fees and had minimum balances that locked the Little Guy out of individual stocks. Now there are no fees at most discount brokers and most have no minimums. Until the year 2000, it was legal for companies to provide key information to selective people such as analysts, hedge fund managers and other money managers, and the Little Guy didn't get that information. Since the implementation of the **Fair Disclosure Rule**, companies cannot provide any information material to their business, without providing it to everyone. Initially, some companies did business as usual for a while, but now everyone gets the information. In the olden days before the internet, you had to make a long distance toll call to a company's Investor's Relations to just get the quarterly earnings reports, annual reports and press releases mailed to you, and you got them days or even weeks after the big institutions. Often you didn't even know when they came out. Now all those reports are available instantly on the internet to everyone for free.

I set up a **tracking portfolio** on Yahoo Finance and any news related to my stocks is instantly available to me on the screen below my portfolio. You can do the same thing on Yahoo or some other site that offers tracking portfolios. Every day before the market opens and after the close, I scan this screen for any information put out by companies of stocks I own or are thinking of buying. Of course I ignore all the info from stock gurus and other sources and strictly use only information from the company itself. I don't follow the market when it is actually open, because companies almost never put out key information while the market is actually open. Let the day traders and fast money types be glued to a computer screen all day studying meaningless short term stock price movements.

In the olden days, you had to call your broker and beg them to provide you key information, such as market cap, insider holdings, insider buying, % of stock held by institutions, dividend yield and earnings estimates and number of analysts following a stock and balance sheet data and press releases. Now, that is instantly available on your discount broker's website, Yahoo Finance, Google Finance and other sites at the click of a mouse or smart phone. The Big Players have no more information than you.

What about the fast money types trading in and out markets? Let them schizophrenically trade in and out of stocks long and short, options, puts, calls, straddles, commodities, using portfolio insurance, etc. Meanwhile, you can have a life, and invest in stocks for the intermediate term and long term, while they are staring at a computer screen all day, watching lines go back and forth on charts and looking over their shoulders wondering and worrying what direction the herd is going to go next and trading in and out of positions. Any money they make is going to be partially cancelled out by some complicated hedging instrument they are using, and every gain, when they actually happen, will always be a short term gain and taxed as heavily as possible and taxed as soon as possible. Meanwhile, you can ignore what everyone else is doing, have a full life outside of investing, holding most stocks from 1 to 3 years or longer, and your gains will be deferred until you actually sell stocks, and they will be mostly long term gains taxed at a much lower rate, the perfect way to build wealth over the long term. Even if a fast money type has significantly higher official average returns than you, you can build wealth faster due to lower tax rates and deferred payment of taxes.

What about **High Frequency Trading** (HFT) and the risk of another **Flash Crash**? I have to do everything I can to stop from bursting out laughing when answering this question. HFT is using "sophisticated" computer algorisms to move in and out of stock positions in fractions of a second. Let them mindlessly trade in and out of stocks in fractions of second and pay all that money to buy and maintain the trading equipment and pay all those commissions and pay the highest possible tax rates on any gains they may eek out. Meanwhile, go to the Forbes 400 list and see if you can find anyone on there who got there by HFT. Don't bother even looking; you won't find anyone.

The Flash Crash happened at 2:45 PM on May 6, 2010, and HFT contributed to causing the market to fall close to 10% in a few minutes. Some stocks, including a couple I own, suffered much bigger declines that lasted a few minutes. The market and affected individual stocks soon regained the majority of the loses by day's end. How did this affect the fundamental stock investor like me? Not at all, of course. I never use stop losses (more on that in **Chapter 80**) and never follow the market when it is actually open, and I was at the beach all day riding the waves and enjoying the sun, so when I came home it was all over, and it was as if nothing had happened at all, and in fact, as a fundamental stock investor, it was a non-event and absolutely nothing to worry about in the future. Let the day traders, Technical Analysts, fast money types, High Frequency Traders and people who are doing options, puts, calls and using stop losses worry about Flash Crashes.

Two relatively minor new obstacles have been put up by the powers that be to hinder the Retail Investor. The first was the repeal of the **Down Tick Rule**. Hedge funds are the biggest short sellers in the stock market, and they pushed hard to repeal the Down Tick Rule. The Down Tick Rule came into effect in 1938 to prevent short sellers from manipulating stocks down. The rule prevented shorting a stock unless the stock's previous trade was on an up tick. Otherwise short sellers could manipulate stocks down, by endlessly shorting stocks downward in relatively small 100 share lots on down ticks. Unfortunately, to the joy of hedge funds, the rule was repealed in 2007. There has been widespread and nearly universal opposition to this from nearly all quarters since then, but the big players have used their money, power and influence to successfully keep the rule from coming back. Since the rule was repealed, the short sellers have gone hog wild with coordinated one day short attacks on certain targeted stocks to drive them down by scaring out weak holders, and to trigger stop losses to trigger more selling, and to break trend lines and moving averages to trigger even more selling. Therefore, it gives them a huge advantage and allows them to drive down stocks 3-8% in a single day on no news. It also allows crooks to illegally manipulate stocks downward, by the crooks putting out anonymous (to avoid prosecution), and often slanderous accusations, masquerading as "Research Reports" on well known websites, to take advantage of the repeal of the downtick rule, to drive panicked selling by weak holders. However, as stated earlier, a fundamental stock investor can and should ignore these one day coordinated short attacks and short selling in general. In the big picture they are meaningless.

A second new obstacle for the Retail Investor involves same store sales for retailers and restaurants. As stated above, in the olden days before the internet and the Fair Disclosure Rule, the Retail Investor didn't get the information that big guys got, at least not in a timely or easy manner, so they were at a decided disadvantage. When this changed, some of the big players were pissed off at their loss of advantage, so they fought back. One way they fought back was to lobby companies, put out bogus studies, go on TV and whatever means necessary to try to get retailers and restaurants to stop putting out monthly same store sales reports, a critical fundamental piece of data for investors. They did this in the hope that they would still be able to use their positions of power to get this information from the companies for themselves, while the little guy would be shut out and have to wait until the quarterly earnings report. Most retailers and restaurants have followed suit and no longer provide monthly same store sales data, and the little guy has lost a key piece of data and has to wait until the quarterly earnings report to see how same store sales are going. Yes, it is a new obstacle for the Retail Investor but not the end of the world in the big picture.

Chapter 72   More Details On Stock Investing: How To Execute A Buy Order

For a fundamental stock investor, placing a buy order is simple. Place it any time you have a stock that meets the buy criteria outlined in this book. Before placing the buy order, always first check to see if the stock is thinly traded and/or if there is a big gap (i.e. more than 0.3%) between the **Bid Price** and **Ask Price**. When you buy a stock, you pay the higher Ask Price. When you sell a stock, you get the lower Bid Price. The middleman or **Market Maker** pockets the difference. If the stock is not thinly traded (i.e. stock trading pretty much continuously when the market is open), AND the bid/ask spread is less than 0.3%, simply place a **Market Order,** and you pay the Ask Price that is listed when you click the buy button. If the stock is thinly traded AND/OR the spread is larger than 0.3%, put in a **Limit Order**. In these cases, you can get badly ripped off by the Market Maker if you go with a Market Order. For example, a thinly traded micro cap stock could be selling for 20.74. But the bid could be 20.71, and the ask could be listed as 21.1, but that could be only for the first 20 shares, and you could end up paying 22.20 or some other ridiculously high price for the rest of the shares. In this case, you should use a limit price of say 20.8 or so, and wait for the trade to be executed. Therefore, when buying thinly traded stocks or stocks with a large bid/ask spread or too high ask price, use a limit order. There is no reason I can think of to ever buy a stock in pre-market trading or after market trading.

Chapter 73   More Details On Stock Investing: How To Execute A Sell Order

The same rule applies for a sell order. If the stock is thinly traded OR has a large bid/ask spread OR the bid price is ridiculously low, then use a limit price.

Also, when you decide to sell a stock, you have to decide the exact time to sell the stock, and I will explain the options. Normally, as a fundamental stock investor, you will be selling a stock, because the company issued a press release with its latest quarterly results. You will have evaluated the press release and have determined that the fundamentals are falling apart with respect to the current stock price. For example, you bought XYZ growth stock, because earnings were growing at 20-25% per year, and the Forward P/E was only 18. In the most recent press release, the current earnings growth or what the company has guided for the next quarter and/or full year, has now suddenly slowed to 8-10%, and the Forward P/E, based on this new lower reality, is about 20. You now are in a stock whose fundamentals are declining (growth is slowing down), and the stock is expensive with a 8-10% grower selling at 20 times earnings. This is a sell. As stated earlier, it is totally irrelevant whether earnings "beat" or "missed" expectations and the same for their guidance for the next quarter; you must always evaluate the earnings in absolute terms, as I just presented, and not whether the guidance is above or below expectations.

Normally these press releases are issued an hour or 2 before the stock market opens, or within an hour after the stock market closes. A few odd ball companies issue earnings reports while the market is open, but that is very rare. Say this company reported this earnings news at 4:05 PM after the market close of 4:00 PM. The news is going to put downward pressure on the stock; so say the stock closed at 56.75, you will be likely selling at a lower price than that. You have 4 options to use when selling, and none is necessarily better than others, and which of the 4 options is best, can be pretty much be luck, but I will lay them out now anyway.

Option 1) Sell After Hours - You can sell the stock in **after hours trading** that same night. The positive to this is that you don't have to wait to see where the stock will be in the morning; you know what price you will get right then by looking at the ask price. The negative is that this price could be worse than what you might get the next morning. Note that almost all discount brokers require you to use a limit order when trading after hours or in the pre-market. Also note, with a small and/or thinly traded stock, there may be little trading going on and with a huge and undesirable spread between the price the stock closed at and the after hours ask price.

Option 2) Sell Before Hours the next day - You can sell before the market opens in **pre market trading,** but you face the same pros and cons as selling after hours the night before.

Option 3) You can place a market order the night before but not have it executed until the open the next day. If you do this, you will be in the very first trade the next morning in the stock. That can be good or bad. Sometimes that first trade is only down a little before the stock really falls after the first couple of minutes. On the other hand, there are cases where that first trade turns out to be the low for day.

Option 4) You can wait a few days or a couple of weeks for a "**Dead Cat Bounce**". Sometimes when bad news comes out the selling is intense and the stock plunges as everything tends to be overdone on Wall Street and then 2-14 days later the stock bounces back a few percent, then you can sell. The downside of this method is that sometimes there is no dead cat bounce, and the stock continues downward for weeks.

None of the 4 methods work well, but when it is time to sell you must sell and put your money into a better situation with better odds of making money. You must choose one of the 4 methods, but which one works best seems to vary from time to time, and none is going to work best most of the time. You will have to make that decision. I tend to use Option 3 but with mixed results.

I will note that sometimes the hedge funds and other big players will play silly games like they did through most of 2013. When stocks reported bad news, they actually often rushed in to buy the stock after the initial sell-off, so that by the end of the day, the stock closed up despite the bad news. They were also rushing in to sell stocks that reported good news, so stocks would bounce up initially on the good news, and then the big players would rush in to sell or sell short the stock, so that is was down by the end of the day despite the good news. This was designed, I assume, to confuse and bewilder the retail investor trying to figure out the market, and get them to give up and get out of the stock market or to fulfill some silly Wall Street saying such as "Buy on the rumor and sell on the news." How did this work out for them? In 2013 the average hedge fund trailed the market by 22 percentage points, and I beat the market by 14 percentage points, so the silly strategy among other of their techniques, was failing pretty miserably. I point this out only so that you will be aware of quirky short term price swings that occur around earnings times. Of course for the fundamental stock investor, these things are meaningless and negligible in the big picture, if not annoying when they are actually happening.

Watch out for the **IRA 90 Day Trading Ban**. Beware of the infamous "Free Riding" violation when selling a stock in an IRA. If you buy a stock for your IRA account AND sell it within 3 business days, you cannot use the funds from that sale to buy another stock within the next 3 business days, also known as "T+3". This is a violation of the SEC's "Regulation T", and you will be banned in that IRA account from trading for 90 days. Even though these rules pre-date computers and no longer make any sense, the powers that be don't want to change them, because brokers don't mind holding your money for 3 additional days, meaning they want to do the free riding and don't want you to be free riding. Some discount brokers have built in systems to prevent you from doing this or at least warning you before you make such a trade, but others don't, and if you make this mistake, you get banned for 90 days. I have also heard of some brokers not enforcing the bans for some customers, but don't take the chance. Of course as a fundamental stock investor, it will be very rare for you to buy a stock and then sell it 3 days later. This could happen if you bought a stock, and then they issued an unexpectedly horrible earnings report or **earnings warning** 2 days later. An earnings warning is when a company is having a much worse than expected quarter, and they warn you in advance of the scheduled quarterly report date.

Chapter 74   More Details On Stock Investing: What About Corporate Raiders/Activists?

Corporate Raiders are primarily a short term annoyance for fundamental stock investors. These raiders are usually Private Equity or Hedge Fund managers, and they are often called "activist investors", because it sounds nicer than Corporate Raider. Just like with "activists" in politics, they try to force their agendas on everyone else for their own personal gain.

The current most famous Corporate Raider is known for using their great wealth to bully companies that have cash and/or valuable assets and make them blow it all on a one time dividend or to sell-off the valuable asset, so they can make a relatively quick gain over a 1 year period or as quickly as they can bully them into it. They will first quietly build a position in the stock until it gets to 10 to 15% ownership and has to file SEC ownership disclosure forms. Then they start publicly bullying the company to do what they want, such as getting their underlings elected to board seats, threatening to buyout the company or forcing them to sell off assets, publicly humiliating the company management, getting them to blow all their cash in a one time massive dividend to shareholders, etc. They often win, but sometimes companies will use the traditional tactic kids use against bullies and stand up to them and not give them their way.

As a fundamental stock investor, when these activists target a stock you own, it gives it a short term boost but does nothing for the company over the longer term, because once they make their quick gain either via one time dividend or sale of a valuable asset via spin-off or sale of company, they are gone and move onto their next target. They could care less about what happens to the company over the longer term. What they do is perfectly legal and should be, but this represents the underbelly of capitalism and gives free markets a bad name. I have often wondered if these activists would be failures at regular investing, simply because they can't make it at regular investing, and they can only make money by using these bullying "activist" tactics.

Chapter 75   More Details On Stock Investing: What About The Tax Implications Of Buying And Selling Stocks?

What about the tax implications of buying and selling stocks? As explained earlier in the book, the number one obstacle to wealth building is taxes. Therefore, it is critically important that you follow the steps outlined earlier in the book, such as buying a house when the timing is right, maxing out your 401k/403b/TSP and then maxing out your ROTH IRA contributions and only going to a taxable account after you have maxed the others out. Once you are in a taxable account, keep in mind, your losers will somewhat offset your winners as far as taxes go. Also, following the methods of this book, as a fundamental stock investor, most of your biggest winners will be held longer than a year, so they will be taxed at a lower rate. Also, because you don't pay taxes until you actually sell, and because as a fundamental stock investor your winners will often be held for years, you are putting off, i.e. deferring paying taxes. All of this adds up to greater wealth building. That being said, do not make a buy or sell decision with individual stocks based solely on tax considerations. Tax consideration should only be a secondary reason when buying or selling stocks in your taxable account. For instance, don't sell a stock that is down in December just to take the loss now if there is nothing wrong with the fundamentals of the company and it is undervalued. Also, don't wait to sell a winner until January if you own a stock whose fundamentals are clearly falling apart.

Also, be aware of the **Wash Sale Rule**. If you sell a stock at a loss in a taxable account and then buy it back within 30 days, you are not allowed to take that loss on your taxes. They do this to dissuade investors from selling all their losers on Dec 31st to take the loss for that tax year and then to immediately buy back the stock in early January.

Chapter 76 More Details On Stock Investing: Another Tax Savings Strategy

If you own individual stocks in multiple accounts including both taxable and sheltered accounts (IRAs, etc.), you can further reduce your taxes. What I do is when I find a stock that happens to also pay a dividend, I tend to put it in a sheltered account, so I don't have to pay any taxes on those dividends. I tend to put the non dividend stocks I like in a taxable account. Keep in mind, this often is not practicable for some people, because the relative size of the 2 accounts won't allow it to work. Also, as stated above, taxes should only be a secondary consideration when buying stocks for a taxable account, meaning, don't shy away from a bargain stock that also pays a dividend, just because you are buying it in a taxable account.

Chapter 77   More Details On Stock Investing: In A Down Year Look For Fantastic Bargains In Mid October To Early December In Small Stocks And/Or Cyclical Stocks

As stated earlier, the stock market goes up on average 2 years for every 1 down year. When a down year happens, especially a big down year, most stocks are beaten down, as weak holders get scared and just throw away their stocks. When this happens, they mindlessly and indiscriminately throw out cheap stocks with great fundamentals along with stocks that have lousy fundamentals and/or are overpriced. This is sometimes called "throwing out the baby with the dirty bath water". Then later in the year, there is even more selling as people foolishly sell these great stocks at cheap prices to take a **tax loss**. This relentless tax loss selling often beats down small stocks, more than big stocks, and cyclicals, more than growth stocks. Therefore, in down years in the mid October to early December timeframe, you can find some spectacular bargains in small stocks and cyclical stocks. Some will get so low you will think you must be overlooking something to cause them to get so cheap, but almost always it is just due to the silly tax loss selling.

In a down year, look for great small stocks that get crazy cheap during this time. Also, if in the early stages of recession, many cyclical stocks that have been declining for some time during the first part of a recession, also get beat down to ridiculously low levels. When these are down 50 to 90%, you will often see these cyclicals bottom in early December. During down years, always focus on small stocks and cyclicals beaten down to absurdly low prices in mid-October to early December.

Chapter 78   More Details On Stock Investing: Never Buy Drug Stocks With Only One Drug

Never buy drug stocks with only one profitable drug. In the olden days, it was perfectly fine to do so, back when patent laws were properly enforced, and before the appointment of so many non-Constitutionalist activist judges. Now patent laws are not enforced, and in cases where it should be perfectly obvious to everyone years in advance as to when the exact date a drug patent should expire, that is now no longer the case, due to the weakening of the rule of law in the USA. Along with other property rights, drug patents are routinely trashed and voided on a whim of an activist judge, and a drug company that spent millions of dollars and years and years of research developing and getting an important or even lifesaving drug approved, can basically see it lose its patent on the whim of a court without warning, and the stock instantly collapses due to the imminent launch of generic versions. Therefore, nowadays it is simply too dangerous to own stock in any drug company that has only one commercial drug on the market, no matter how good all the fundamentals look.

Chapter 79   More Details On Stock Investing: What About Buying Stocks On Margin?

Never buy stocks on **margin**. Buying stocks on margin is borrowing money from your discount broker in an attempt to get bigger returns via leverage. As stated throughout this book, never invest with money you will need in the next 5 years. When you invest in a regular "**cash account**", the maximum loss is simply 100% of what you invested. With margin, your losses can be much higher than 100%. There are 3 risks with buying on margin. One, if the stock you buy goes down, you can get a **margin call** in which your broker makes you put up more money. If you don't have more money, you are in big trouble or you have to sell another stock that you don't want to sell, and it is a bad time to sell. The second risk is that you are paying interest on the money you borrowed. The third risk is that the interest rate you are being charged can go up at any time. As stated repeatedly, stocks can go up and down in the short term, often with no rhyme or reason, so there is a good chance you can get a margin call. There is enough risk involved with regular stock investing; you don't need to compound it with margin investing.

As Bull Markets progress, the amount of margin buying invariably increases exponentially and usually peaks right before a Bear Market or Stock Market Collapse happens. When it happens, the typical fundamental stock investor is down 20 to 40%, but has no money they need within the next 5 years, and is not on margin, so they just have to sit tight and wait for the inevitable rebound. The margin investor, on the other hand, is completely wiped out and loses everything, and they have no money left for the rebound, and they usually never come back to stock investing for the rest of their lives.

Chapter 80   More Details On Stock Investing: What About Stop Loss Orders?

As stated repeatedly throughout this book with many great examples, never use **stop loss orders**. Stocks go up and down for no rhyme or reason in the short run. What drives stocks in the intermediate term and long term is earnings or specifically EPS. Therefore, if you are buying a stock, because you see higher earnings 1-3 years out, what a stock does in the short run, is completely meaningless, and if you put in a stop loss at 7% or 8% or 10% below the price you purchased the stock, there is a good chance you will get **stopped out** of a good stock and not only get stopped out, but ALWAYS get stopped out at a loss. Not only that, you will get stopped out at price below which you bought it, so it is at an even better price, such that you should be considering buying more, and here you are selling.

These stop losses are supposedly designed to protect you from a big loss, but with the typical volatility in the stock market and individual stocks, you will be slowly bled to death by getting stopped out of stocks over and over again.

Also keep in mind, they often don't protect you even at the pre-determined percentage you ordered. When the news is really bad, the stock will gap down and blow right through your stop point, and you can get stopped out at a 20% loss even though you had your stop loss set at a 7% loss. If a Flash Crash happens, you will be stopped out of your entire portfolio with losses way worse than 7%, and you won't benefit from the rebound from the Flash Crash. For all of my biggest winners and multi-baggers over the years, I would have been stopped out 100 times, and way before I made the huge profit.

Chapter 81   More Details On Stock Investing: What About Shorting Stocks?

Never short stocks. Shorting a stock is betting a stock will go down. How it technically works is you borrow the stock to short by your broker selling shares of that stock, and you "cover" the short by buying it. You have to have a margin account, and as I warned, you should never be using margin. When you buy stocks long, your maximum loss is limited to 100% of what you invested. When you short stocks, your maximum possible loss is much higher than 100% and in theory is limitless. Even if you are correct that a stock is overvalued, remember anything can and will happen in the short run, so if the stock goes up, you will get a margin call, which forces you to put up more money. Keep in mind the market goes up 2/3 of the time and down 1/3 of the time, so when you are shorting, you already have overall odds working against you. Again in the short run, anything can and will happen to stock prices, and if it goes up, you get a margin call. If it is a heavily shorted stock, there will be a massive amount of margin calls forcing shorts to cover by buying the stock, causing it to soar, which is called a **short squeeze**. The biggest "players" at shorting are the hedge funds, and as explained earlier in the book, they have a horrendous record on average the past 5 years. See **Chapter 11**. If an investor buys a stock long (not on margin), and the stock goes down in the short term, it is no problem, but if you short a stock, and it goes up in the short term, it is a problem, because you can get a margin call and can get caught in a short squeeze.

Chapter 82   More Details On Stock Investing: How Do I Know If The Stock Market Is Cheap Or Expensive?

How do you know if the stock market is cheap or expensive? As I have reiterated throughout the book, never try to time the market, it is futile. Also, you are not investing in "the Market", you are investing in individual stocks. As long as you can find stocks to buy and hold that meet the criteria of this book, you should do so. Sell individual stocks that no longer meet the criteria. Even in an expensive market, you can find bargains and in a cheap market, you will find lots of overpriced stocks.

Regardless of whether the market overall is cheap or expensive, always remember that that has no effect in the short run as to what will happen, and the market can and will go up or down or sideways in the short run at any time.

All that being said, you can determine whether the market is cheap or expensive and what the likely stock investing environment will be 2-5 years out, based on a study I did myself. Here are the results of the study. I found that when "the Market", as defined by the S&P 500, gets to very high valuations (i.e. high P/E), the next few years (2-5 years out) tend to not be good. When this happens, be sure to not become complacent with the easy gains you have made during the market rise into expensive territory and follow the rules of this book, and you won't be caught up in overvalued stocks. Also, you will likely find it harder to find stocks that meet the buy criteria of this book. On the other hand, when the Market gets to extremely low valuations (i.e. low P/E), the next few years (2-5 years out) tend to be very good. In that environment, you will likely find a lot more good bargains when shopping for stocks. In no way is this meant to be a market timing indicator, because overvalued markets can and often do continue to go higher for a long time, and undervalued markets can and do continue to go lower or stay cheap for a long time. Remember, everything the herd does on Wall Street is overdone both on the upside and downside. My study only shows you what the longer term market *may* look like 2 to 5 years out, so you know what you are up against.

Here are the conclusions of my study (see data below). When the Forward P/E of the market is 16, the market is fairly priced. When it is 17 or higher, it is expensive. When it is 15 or lower, it is cheap. When the Forward P/E is 18 or higher, the 2-5 year outlook for stocks is not so good. The higher the P/E, the worse the 2-5 year outlook is for the market. When the Forward P/E is 14 or lower, the 2-5 year outlook is good, and the lower the P/E, the better the outlook. Again, this study tells you nothing about what direction stocks may go in the next year, as anything can and will happen in one year, no matter how expensive or cheap stocks are; it is looking at the 2-5 year out period.

It would be a good idea to study this chart below and update it yourself which is easy. You simply look up where the S&P 500 index closed at today, and via a simple internet search get S&P 500 actual earnings for last year, estimates for this year and estimates for next year, and continuously update this table every few months or so, or at least once a year. Also, when you hear some talking head or "stock guru" say "stocks are cheap" or "stocks are expensive", do not trust them. They are often completely wrong out of laziness, ignorance or they have an agenda they are pushing, based on whether they are long or short the market. You can simply use this chart and tell if the so called guru actually knows what they are talking about or not. Also, other gurus try to greatly and unnecessarily overcomplicate things, by instead of looking at P/E, they attempt to use "discounted cash flow" or some form of what they call "normalized" earnings or "normalized margins" or "normalized sales" or "earnings to GDP ratio" or some other esoteric method that is going to fail.

Also note in recessions, earnings temporarily decline on average about 20%, (see data below), so the E in P/E can suddenly go down, resulting in a higher (more expensive) P/E, even if stock prices stay the same. The reverse is true, of course, coming out of recessions.

Effect of Extreme Market P/Es on Future Stock Market Performance

By John Molvar

Study Years: 1960 – 2013 (52 years total)

S&P 500 P/E Range: 7.4 – 28.4
S&P 500 P/E "Normal Range" (throw out 5 highest and 5 lowest): 9.1 to 21.2
S&P 500 Average P/E: 16.3

Earnings decline in recession. (38% in 2008-2009, 40% in 2001, 6% in 1991, 10% in 1982, 42% in 1975, 11% in 1970, 13% in 1966 and 12% in 1962, which works out to average earnings decline of 21.5%).

Extreme High P/E & Low P/E Outcomes

- When P/E rose to 21.2 at end of 1962, stocks fell 12.1% the next year and were only 12.1% higher 4 years later.

- When P/E fell to 14.9 at end of 1966, stocks rose 29.3% over the next 2 years and rose 47.0% over 6 years.

- When P/E rose to 19.1 at end of 1972, stocks fell 42% over the next 2 years and were only 3% higher after 10 years.

- When P/E fell to 7.3 at the end of 1974, stocks rose 57% over the next 2 years.

- When P/E fell to 8.1 at the end of 1981, stocks rose 35% over the next 2 years and were up 97% over 5 years.

- When P/E fell to 11.5 at end of 1988 (post '87 crash), stocks rose 50.7% over the next 3 years.

- When P/E fell to 14.5 at the end of 1994, stocks rose 34.1% over the next year and 220% over the next 5 years.

- When the P/E rose to 28.4 at the end of 1999, stocks fell 40.1% over the next 3 years and were still 24.1% lower after 10 years.

- When the P/E fell to 13.8 at the end of 2008, stocks rose 39.3% over the next 2 years and 104.6% over the next 5 years.

- When the P/E fell to 12.3 during mid 2012, stocks rose 53.2% over the next 18 months.

Year End Stock Prices and P/Es

Year	Dividend Yield	S&P 500	Earnings	P/E
1960	3.41%	58.11	3.10	18.8
1961	2.85%	71.55	3.37	21.2
1962	3.40%	63.1	3.67	17.2
1963	3.13%	75.02	4.13	18.2
1964	3.05%	84.75	4.76	17.8
1965	3.06%	92.43	5.30	17.4
1966	3.59%	80.33	5.41	14.9
1967	3.09%	96.47	5.46	17.7
1968	2.93%	103.86	5.72	18.2
1969	3.52%	92.06	6.10	15.1
1970	3.46%	92.15	5.51	16.7
1971	3.10%	102.09	5.57	18.3
1972	2.70%	118.05	6.17	19.1
1973	3.70%	97.55	7.96	12.3
1974	5.43%	68.56	9.35	7.3
1975	4.14%	90.19	7.71	11.7
1976	3.93%	107.46	9.75	11.0
1977	5.11%	95.1	10.87	8.8
1978	5.39%	96.11	11.64	8.3
1979	5.53%	107.94	14.55	7.4
1980	4.74%	135.76	14.99	9.1
1981	5.57%	122.55	15.18	8.1
1982	4.93%	140.64	13.82	10.2
1983	4.32%	164.93	13.29	12.4
1984	4.68%	167.24	16.84	9.9
1985	3.88%	211.28	15.68	13.5
1986	3.38%	242.17	14.43	16.8
1987	3.71%	247.08	16.04	15.4
1988	3.68%	277.72	24.12	11.5
1989	3.32%	353.4	24.32	14.5
1990	3.74%	330.22	22.65	14.6
1991	3.11%	417.09	19.30	21.6
1992	2.90%	435.71	20.87	20.9
1993	2.72%	466.45	26.90	17.3

Year	Dividend Yield	S&P 500	Earnings	P/E
1994	2.91%	459.27	31.75	14.5
1995	2.30%	615.93	37.70	16.3
1996	2.01%	740.74	40.63	18.2
1997	1.60%	970.43	44.09	22.0
1998	1.32%	1229.23	44.27	27.8
1999	1.14%	1469.25	51.68	28.4
2000	1.23%	1320.28	56.13	23.5
2001	1.37%	1148.09	38.85	29.5
2002	1.83%	879.82	46.04	19.1
2003	1.61%	1111.91	54.69	20.3
2004	1.60%	1211.92	67.68	17.9
2005	1.79%	1248.29	76.45	16.3
2006	1.77%	1418.3	87.72	16.2
2007	1.89%	1468.36	82.54	17.8
2008	3.11%	903.25	65.39	13.8
2009	2.00%	1115.1	60.8	18.3
2010	1.84%	1257.64	83.66	15.0
2011	2.07%	1257.60	97.05	13.0
2012	2.13%	1426.19	102.47	13.9
2013	1.94%	1848.36	109e	16.9
2014			121e	15.3
2015			134e	13.8
2016			143e	12.9

e - current consensus estimate by analysts

At the end of 2013, we are selling at 15.3 times 2014 estimated earnings, so the market is right in the middle of its historical price range, so stocks are neither cheap nor expensive, so one might expect average stock market returns in the 2-5 year out period.

Chapter 83   More Details On Stock Investing: How Many Stocks Should I Own?

How many stocks should I own? As stated earlier in the book, you should own at least 5 stocks. Less than that, and the risk is simply too great. There are approximately 5,000 non-penny stocks in the US Stock Market. Using the criteria of this book, I would estimate that in a typical stock market that about 400 stocks out of 5,000, or about 8% of all stocks, would meet the criteria of this book to buy/hold. After a big bear market that drives the P/E of the market below 10, I would guess you will find up to about 1500 stocks. In an extremely expensive stock market when the P/E of the market goes over 18, you will find only about 150 stocks worth owning. An important point to make right now is that even in an extremely expensive market, there are still plenty of stocks that are not expensive compared to their prospects; you just have to look harder and be more careful, which is why I always stayed fully invested (i.e. more than 98% of my money is invested in individual stocks at all times), and I recommend you do the same, if you are interested in building long term wealth.

So how many stocks should you own? Peter Lynch said to own 3 to 10 stocks in his book but went out and bought 1400 in his mutual fund, and in his own personal portfolio outlined in his second book, he owned about 50 stocks. Warren Buffett said to invest as if you can only make a total of 20 buys/sells your whole investing career, but he typically owned 20 to 50 stocks throughout most of his career. Early in my investing career, I owned about 10 stocks. However, I found it too upsetting when something fell apart on me. Also, I enjoy researching stocks and can do it very efficiently and quickly, so I am constantly finding things worth owning. For most of the past 15 years, I have owned 70 to 100 stocks. Because my primary job is investing (I do coaching on the side as a hobby), I have time to keep up with 100 stocks and I am very organized and know my system cold, so I can evaluate a stock in typically less than 4 minutes to determine if it might be worth buying or if it should be held or sold. When you first start out, it will take you much longer, until you know the system cold. The bottom line is that you should own as many stocks that meet the criteria of this book AND that you have time and inclination to keep up with. I would say someone with $2000 to $5000 to invest should own 5-10 stocks, and someone with more than $10,000 should own more stocks but a manageable amount for you personally. Diversification protects you from bad picks and the rare chance that you get taken by a company that is a fraud and you suffer a total loss. Don't just mindlessly buy more and more stocks, because often the best stock to buy may be one you already own. Once you get over 100K, you should be owning at least 20 stocks and more, if you have the time and inclination to stay on top of their fundamentals.

Chapter 84 More Details On Stock Investing: What Type Of Returns Should I Expect From Individual Stock Picking?

What type of returns should I expect? As we showed early in the book, the average long term return for stocks since 1926 is about 10%. To make investing in individual stocks worthwhile, you need to beat that 10% by at least a little. Also, as we showed earlier in the book, if you can beat the market by just a couple of percentage points, it makes a huge difference over the long term, as far as wealth building goes. Therefore, if you can average 11% or 12% over many years AND keep adding new money, especially when the market declines, you will be pleasantly surprised by how much wealth you can build.

I have been investing for 24 years and in individual stocks for 22 years, and as stated previously, I averaged 16.1% annual returns the past 15 years ending 12/31/13 versus 3.1% for the S&P 500. This was during a terrible stock market that included 2 out of the 5 Stock Market Collapses since 1926 (2000-2002 and late 2008/early 2009), which is why the S&P 500 performed so poorly during that time and the time frame became known as "The Lost Decade For Stock Investors".

The past 20 years I have averaged annual returns of 14.4% versus 9.2% for the S&P 500. However, I saved and kept adding new money and stayed fully invested in stocks the whole time through thick and thin. Even though I started investing late at age 28 and with only $8000 and made lots of mistakes, I was able to have my wife retire 9 years later when I was 37, and I was able to retire 14 years later at age 42.

Every year, you want to compare your performance to the S&P 500. Although the S&P 500 averages a gain of 10% per year, it has never actually gained 10%. It averages about 2 up years for every 1 down year, and the returns can be up 35% to down 40% and anything in between in any given year. Therefore, you need to judge your performance in comparison to the S&P 500. Even if you do very well, you will trail the S&P 500 some years but hopefully beat it more years than you trail it, and over the long haul, you want to aim to beat it by 1 to 5 percentage points per year on average. So your goal is to average about 11 to 15% per year over the long haul. If after 2 years in a row, you are failing to beat the S&P 500, you should consider abandoning doing individual stocks and just go with Index Funds or Stock Mutual Funds.

Chapter 85   More Details On Investing: What about Commodities?

What about commodities? Commodities are lousy investments over the long term compared to stocks. There will be periods where commodities have great runs such as 1974 to 1980 and 2003-2007, but if you look at the really big picture, since WWII that is just 12 years out of the last 70 years that commodities have done well. Compare that to stocks where the Dow has gone from 125 to 16,500 or up 13,100% ! Also remember that the commodity markets are relatively tiny markets compared to the stock market. Unlike stocks, when you buy a stock you own the shares, and when you sell a stock you give up the shares. In commodities, you don't have to take physical ownership of the material.

Because of the relatively tiny size of the markets and the fact that they don't have to take physical ownership of the commodity, a relatively small group of big players can easily manipulate these markets all over the place. As a little player you can't do that, so you are left to guessing which way they are going to be manipulating the market at any given time. Good luck with that one. Therefore, you won't be able to guess which way they will be manipulated in the short run, and in the long run, they are lousy investments, so you will likely lose no matter what happens. Those are terrible odds for success, especially when you consider how good the odds are in stocks over the long haul when using *Fundamental Stock Investing*.

Often you could do all kinds of fundamental research and correctly determine which way a commodity *should* go in price based on fundamental supply and demand, but if the big guys decide to temporarily manipulate it the opposite direction (and they often do that), you will go broke before you are proven correct. So if fundamental research won't help you, what about technical analysis, i.e. studying charts? Well guess what, all the players who study charts in the commodity markets are watching the same charts as you and drawing the same conclusions as you, so simple laws of averages ensures technical analysis will be correct about 50% of the time over the long haul, so in the end, you might as well be flipping a coin.

Many commodities are plentiful and recyclable and even for those that are not, humans are constantly seeking, finding, and developing new ways to find more sources of them, use them more efficiently and recycle the rest. Regardless of the direction short term manipulation takes these markets, the long term trend is always going to be lousy for commodities. For example, look at the grains. Every year we have fewer and fewer workers in the farm industry and fewer and fewer farms, but we produce more and more food due to efficiency and technology improvements. Grains are going to always be terrible investments over the long haul. For example, corn was selling at $400 a bushel in 1974 and 40 years later in early 2014, it was selling for $420 a bushel. Adjusted for inflation, corn is down 78% the past 40 years. Meanwhile the S&P 500 rose 2596% during that same time frame.

What about the most famous commodity which is gold? The gold market is a tiny market compared to the stock market, making it ripe for manipulation (silver is even worse!) by a few big players. Also, gold has zero intrinsic value, it cannot be used for any industrial application, it cannot be consumed so it never goes away, it has no practical use of any kind. It is expensive to store and protect, and miners are constantly finding more and more. In the last 70 years, gold had two big run ups each lasting 4 years in 1977-1980 and 2003-2007, so it has had 2 relatively brief spikes up and the rest of the time went nowhere or was in a big long term decline. During those long decades when gold goes nowhere or down, there will always be people saying "next year" will be a big year for gold. These people are called "Gold Bugs" and after many years of being wrong, they are someday right, but look at the gains in stocks they missed out on all those years. There are others who say you should always have 10% of your money in gold? Why on earth would you do that, given that gold is such a tiny market compared to stocks, and it has such a horrible long term record compared to stocks?

What about the fundamentals for gold? Well, actually there are none since it has no practical use. The only fundamental is supposedly fear, and how does one measure fear? If people are fearful, then gold will supposedly go up, but for gold to keep going up, people have to be more fearful next year than they were this year. How long can that go on? Even if you correctly guess which way the fear is going to go, what if the big players decide to manipulate the gold market in the opposite direction for the next couple of years? You will go broke long before you are proven correct. What about technical analysis? Again by simple law of averages, technical analysis will be correct 50% of the time and wrong 50% of the time. It basically works until it doesn't work, and often when it works, it is simply self-fulfilling prophecy, like a lover using astrology and selecting a mate with the correct "sign", only to find the relationship stops working shortly thereafter. In inflation adjusted terms, gold has gone from $600 an ounce in 1934 to $1200 an ounce in 2013, so it has only doubled in 80 years. Since then, the Dow has gone from 80 to 16,500 or a 20,525% gain. Here is a rhetorical question: "So, do you think you have a better chance at making money investing in stocks with good fundamentals at a good prices over the long term or from 'playing the gold market' ?"

The silver market is so tiny and so easily manipulated that 2 brothers - Billy and Nel Hunt were able to manipulate the whole market driving the price of silver from $11 an ounce to over $50 in just a couple of months in late 1979 and early 1980, before it collapsed right back down. Imagine what several big players can and will do with that market? Now 33 years later in 2013 it is at $19, again proving what lousy investments commodities are over the long term.

What about oil? Aren't we running out of oil, so therefore, it will be a good investment? In inflation adjusted terms, oil has gone from $115 a barrel in 1979 to $92 a barrel today in 2014. So despite the chorus screaming continuously the past 35 years that we are running out of oil, the price has fallen 15%, and in the meantime, the Dow has gone from 750 to 16,500 or up 2100%, despite the 1987 stock market crash, the 2000-2002 collapse and the late 2008/early 2009 collapse. Oil, like all other commodities, is a lousy long term investment compared to stocks. The first prediction that we were running out of oil was made in 1926, and these dire predictions have continued ever since. Humans are constantly seeking to discover new sources, get more out of existing sources, use it more efficiently, etc., which is why we have never run out of oil since the first so called "peak oil" warning alert was sounded in 1926. In the United States, oil production is actually increasing, despite being severely limited to mostly private areas with ANWAR, most of the rest of Alaska, the East Coast, the West Coast, the Eastern Gulf, the Rockies and other gigantic reserves locked up in Federal lands.

Here is information you will never learn in school or from the mainstream media sources because of their agenda. The **Rocky Mountain Green River Formation** has 3 trillion barrels of recoverable oil at prices below $120 a barrel. How much is that? To put it in perspective, it is more oil than all "proven reserves" in the entire world. At today's US only current consumption rate, that is several centuries worth of oil. While the Western philosophical thinking of the late 20th and early 21st century prevents development of this area, don't assume that will always be true and eventually that will be developed, especially when it is really needed. Therefore, forever forget about "running out of oil" as a reason to play the oil markets; it is simply never going to happen.

As with other commodities, remember the oil trading market is a tiny trading market that can easily be manipulated by a few big players, and you won't be getting a phone call from them telling you which way it will be going. They ran oil up to $150 a barrel in 2007 supposedly due to the following reasons: "We are running out of oil.", "China demand", "War in the Middle East", "instability in Nigeria", "hurricane threats", "Contango", "peak summer driving season", "backwardation", "the shoulder months refinery retooling shutdowns", "haven't built a new refinery since 1976", "Saudi Arabia's main oil field may be running out", "heavy A/C usage during summer heat waves", "refinery outages", "pipeline outages", "People in the Third World want to drive cars and eat steak too.", etc. Just 2 years later in 2009, we still had "We are running out of oil.", "China demand", "War in the Middle East", "instability in Nigeria", "hurricane threats", "Contango", "peak summer driving season", backwardation", "the shoulder months refinery retooling shutdowns", "haven't built a new refinery since 1976", "Saudi Arabia's main oil field may be running out", "heavy A/C usage during summer heat waves", "refinery outages", "pipeline outages", "People in the Third World want to drive cars and eat steak too.", etc., but suddenly oil was at $30 a barrel. Needless to say, the oil market is obviously tiny enough such that the big players can drive it in any direction they want in the short run, especially since they don't have to take physical delivery of oil. If they actually had to take possession of the oil they bought and give up possession of oil they sold instead of "playing the futures market", they would never be able to run up oil to $150 and then drive it down to $30 just 2 years later. What about technical analysis? Not to be a wise guy, but for oil and everything else, technical analysis will work until it stops working.

Chapter 86   More Details On Investing: What About Currency Trading?

What about currency trading? Currency trading in theory is a huge market, literally all the money in the world. However, only an infinitesimal percentage of currency actually gets traded every day, and the vast, vast majority just stays in its own country of origin. Therefore, like with the commodity markets, the currency markets are fraught with manipulation, and it can be done by just a couple of big players. In the late 1990s, for example, one big player was said to have manipulated the currency of Thailand so much that it sent the entire country into a tailspin. In 1992, they were said to have single handedly "broken the Bank of England" and caused that currency to plunge, and they made a 2 billion dollar profit in one day.

What about using fundamentals for currency trading? The fundamentals say if a country has a strong currency policy (i.e. low inflation policies and/or high or raising interest rates, trade surpluses and/or improving trade balance, etc.), the currency should go up, and if they have a weak currency policy (high inflation policies and/or low or lowering interest rates, trade deficits and/or deteriorating trade balance, etc.), the currency should go down. Sounds easy, but in reality the currency goes in the direction the few big manipulators want it to go in, and it may or may not be in line with the fundamentals. So as a small player, you have a 50/50 chance of guessing which way to "bet" on the currency.

A new perfect tool for fraud and manipulation and money laundering has also been created called "Bitcoin", a so called "virtual currency" backed by nothing and with no intrinsic value and miraculously created out of thin air for the gullible.

Stay clear of currencies, don't be a sucker for the big players. Just as I am writing this in 2013, authorities in the USA and several other countries announced yet another investigation into currency trading manipulation.

Chapter 87   More Details On Stock Investing: What About Options Trading?

Options are even worse. Not only do you have to get the price direction correct, you have to get it at the correct short term timing and the size of the move also has to be correct. So you could be correct on the direction of the security (i.e. whether it will go up or down) and the size of the move, but if your short term timing is off even by a day, you lose everything. I consider options the all time biggest sucker's bet. Unlike stocks where actual wealth is created at an average rate of 10% per year, options are a zero sum game where your odds of winning are 33% and losing is 66% because of commissions and middle man costs. Many experienced hedge fund traders use them as hedges, but overall they expect to, and actually do lose some money on their options bets, as they see them as the cost of "portfolio insurance". Inexperienced investors are all but certain to lose. This is the same as gambling in Las Vegas; stay clear of this mess. Again, there is no one in the Forbes 400 who got there by "playing" options. Someone may start out investing in stocks, but they find growing rich slowly too boring, so they branch out into options. Like a progressive gambler, they need more and bigger and more exciting bets, and soon all they do is options, completely forgetting about why they got into stocks in the first place. Don't fall down this slippery slope.

Chapter 88 More Details On Investing: I Just Heard About An Investment Where My Friend Is Getting 20% Annual Returns!

What do you do when a friend or family member tells you that they are getting 20% annual returns from a new investment or from a great money manager they discovered? Immediately hold onto your wallet and run for the hills as fast as you can!!! It is a scam. The type of scam is a **Ponzi Scheme** or just plain old fashioned theft.

Anytime anyone <u>promises</u> returns of 10% or greater, it is a scam.

Bernie Madoff, who was called "The Ace Of Wall Street" by the Wall Street Journal, also promised 20% annual returns, but it turned out to be a 50 billion dollar Ponzi Scam.

There have been nearly 100 episodes of the CNBC show <u>American Greed</u> on TV since 2007. It would be instructive for you to watch at least a handful of these episodes. The vast majority of them involve scams in which hundreds of investors were defrauded out of their entire life savings.

Most are Ponzi Schemes such as Madoff's and some were outright theft. They start out by promising fantastic returns based on their supposed great investing ability, and they initially target known acquaintances. They take money from these people and each month or quarter send them phony statements showing they are making the promised returns. In the theft cases, the perpetrator is just keeping the money for themselves and spending it by living a lavish lifestyle. In the Ponzi Scheme, they use money from new investors to pay existing investors and keep the rest for themselves. Some actually try to invest the money, but they are usually horrible investors and run up huge losses. Some operate without legally registering themselves, and others do legally register themselves as hedge funds or private equity funds.

Then they expand the scam to outsiders, and if anyone wants to get their money back, they pay them off with money from new investors. Everyone continues to get very authentic looking monthly or quarterly statements showing outstanding returns. Obviously these scams are not sustainable and always collapse. The worst part of these cases is people not only get taken by these scams, but they put all their money into them, because once they start getting the phony statements in the mail, they believe they are real, and they believe the scammer is the great investor they claim to be. Even worse, they get all their friends and family to invest in the scam, and most of them also put their entire life savings into it. The scammer tends to have a good deal of charisma, that along with the phony statements and praise from others, easily fools the unsuspecting investors.

Almost all of the scams collapse when the next big stock market decline happens. This is because when people see the news on TV about the declining stock market, they get scared and ask for some or all of their money back. Of course the fraudster can't pay them back, because they don't have the money; it was all spent on themselves and/or lost in poor investments. Very quickly the scam collapses. Warren Buffet has a great saying: "When the tide goes out, we get to see who is swimming naked." What the saying means is that when the market has a big decline (i.e. The tide goes out.), the legitimate money managers survive, while the illegitimate money managers (and legitimate managers who really didn't know what they were doing) fail completely and are exposed for what they are (i.e. are found to have been swimming naked).

Investors desperately try to get their money back. However, the scammer either doesn't return calls or makes a hundred excuses, the most common of which is: "There is a delay in the bank clearing the money.", and often the scammer sends out checks that bounce. When people finally realize they were ripped off, they contact the authorities, but it is always way too late.

The bad guy then grabs what money is left and portable valuables and tries to flee to a country that has no extradition treaty with the USA. Some make it out and get away with it, and their stories end up being profiled on CNBC and are titled <u>American Greed Fugitives</u>. Some get caught and a few surrender to authorities and try to take their chances in the court system by trying to con jurors and judges like they did to investors all those years. A few try to cut deals, and many of these stories end up being profiled on CNBC <u>American Greed</u>.

The only certainty is that the investors loose everything or at least 95% of their money. I warn you, these scams are everywhere, big and small, and some are so clever and devious, they not only appear perfectly legitimate, but the scammers become famous and politically connected, and some even have the audacity to pretend they are great philanthropists before the scam ultimately collapses. Don't get taken by any of these schemes. Any time you hear of an investment *promising* 10% or greater annual returns, hold on to your wallet and run for the hills.

Chapter 89 More Details On Stock Investing: How Long Do I Stay Fully Invested In Stocks?

How long do I stay fully invested in stocks? This is more of a philosophical or moral or lifestyle type of question. The default answer is that you should stay fully invested in stocks forever (i.e. the rest of your life). It is by far the best way to build wealth. I have been fully invested with more than 98% of my money in stocks for about 99% of the time the past 22 years. How much wealth do you need is a personal question with a different answer for all of us. All of us have different goals and reasons for building wealth. Not that there is anything wrong with it, but my goal was never to build wealth to live an extravagant lifestyle or to be richer than someone else. My goal was to buy financial independence and freedom to pursue the things I really like to do. Fortunately for me, all the things I enjoy in life (doing stuff with my wife and kids, running, lifting weights, coaching, relaxing at the beach, helping other people, watching track & football on TV, watching movies on TV) are all free or very cheap. This made it easier for me to build wealth and maintain it.

For someone building wealth for an extravagant lifestyle, you are obviously going to need more to do that. For other people, it is a contest to keep blowing up that balloon (increasing their net worth) more and more until the day they die. Some would say these people such as Warren Buffett are a slave to their stocks/net worth, and I don't plan on going down that path. However, it is wonderful that America is still a relatively free place to pursue our own form of happiness and if Buffett wants to keep blowing up that balloon until the day he dies, it is wonderful that he is free to do that.

Chapter 90   More Details On Stock Investing: How Much Money Do I Need To Retire?

To retire without a pension or social security or any other income, I would say you need an absolute minimum of 700K, and to own your house outright (no debt), and to be living in a relatively low property tax city, and to own your cars outright, and have no debt of any kind, and no big expenses of any kind in the future (college costs, big medical costs, new additions, expensive traveling, etc.), AND most importantly to live a frugal lifestyle. You may ask, "Who wants to build wealth and live a frugal lifestyle?" Well me, but that is just me. Also, I know of a few people who have successfully retired on much less than that, but I don't recommend that because of the risk involved.

For most people, you need at least a million dollars. If you plan to live high off the hog, then you need more like 2 million. If you want an extravagant lifestyle, you are looking at 3 million or more.

Chapter 91   More Details On Stock Investing: How Long Does It Take To Retire Early?

How long does it take to build wealth to the point you become financially independent? There are so many variables, it is very difficult to say. It depends on how much money you start with and what the investing climate is like. For example, are you starting your investment career in an easy market such that the market P/E is less than 13, or are you starting in a tough market environment e.g. the market P/E is greater than 17? See **Chapter 82** to make this determination about the current market environment. Are you married and have 2 incomes or just one income? Are you savers or big spenders? Do your jobs have good 401k/403b/TSP plans or no plan at all? Are you in a high tax state and/or city or low tax state and/or city? How much does your job pay? What type of lifestyle do you want in retirement?

With all those variables, it is very tough to generalize, but it would be a cop out to not provide a rough answer. Let's assume you are married, and both work and have average paying jobs and have 401k or 403b plans, and both are pretty good savers, and you are starting with no significant debt and have about $5000 in cash to start with, and you are starting investing in an average market environment (e.g. S&P 500 Forward P/E is 15, which is exactly where we were at the end of 2013), and let's assume you are fundamental stock investors and you are successful at it, i.e. you beat the market by 2 percentage points on average, and therefore, average 12% average annual returns over the long haul. I would say you could have 1 million dollars in about 14 to 20 years. That sounds like a long time, and it is, and it requires unending disciple and sacrifice and patience and especially requires that you never get scared out of stocks by the doomsayers and when there is a big stock market decline. However, never forget, that 14-20 years is going to go by whether you save and invest or not, so you might as well be a millionaire at the end of that 14-20 years. So say this theoretical couple starts investing at age 25, they could be millionaires by age 39-45.

There is certainly no guarantee to any of this, but doing nothing as far as saving and investing goes (which 99% of people do) is the surest way possible to never build wealth.

Also, if you are young and/or naive and/or fresh out of the insulated fantasy world of a liberal arts college campus and easily seduced by populist politicians preaching the politics of envy/victim hood and consuming Mainstream Media news, you could spend your whole life bemoaning the 1% who did save and invest successfully or worked hard to start their own business and talk about how those so called "One Percenters" are screwing you and everyone else. You don't want to wind up down that dead end path. A life of envy and thinking you are a victim (even if you are a victim) is harmful for you both emotionally and physically. Negative thinking will never get you anywhere in life. The instant you start thinking of yourself as a victim, you will never accomplish anything significant the rest of your life. You would be amazed at the power of positive thinking once you are armed with the right knowledge to accomplish a goal and have the positive mindset to pursue your goals and insulate yourself from negative people and negative ideas and the politics of envy.

Chapter 92 More Details On Stock Investing: Completely Ignore Politics

Completely ignore politics. All politicians do is tax and spend other people's money and run up more and more debt. The Republicans and Democrats fight viciously over spending with the Republicans calling for a big run-up in debt, and the Democrats calling for an even bigger run-up in debt. In the end, they are all just out for themselves, and they always do take care of themselves.

Ever notice when the politicians come up with some new gargantuan government program or new law, they always make a point to slip into the legislation that they are exempt from the law? For example, congress made themselves exempt from illegal insider stock trading laws. When it became public information, they passed the STOCK Act in 2012 to make it illegal for them to do insider trading. However, they sleazily overturned the law by amending the Act less than one year later to make it impossible for regulators to track their financial moves. Just how sleazy was this? They cowardly waited for the hours shortly after the Boston Marathon Terrorist bombings, and they "unanimously" passed the amendment by "voice vote", so that no one's name was recorded as having voted for the amendment, and the President quickly signed the amendment into law, which effectively continues to allow them to conduct illegal insider trading.

Following the political process will depress and frustrate you and won't help you one iota with your investing. There is nothing worse than focusing your efforts on something you can't control, such as politics. You must be positive and put your positive energy into things you actually can control. Politics is just the opposite; it is negative and pretentious and the process is completely out of your control.

Also, it will actually hurt your investing, because you will be distracted from carefully evaluating the fundaments of your individual stocks and instead focusing and wasting precious time and emotional energy on whether the Republicans will succeed and increase the national debt from 17 trillion to 22 trillion over the next five years, or the Democrats will succeed increasing the debt from 17 trillion to 25 trillion. The only thing you need to know is, no matter what happens and who "wins" or who the mainstream media declares "the winner" during the next "budget crisis" or "debt limit crisis" or "government shutdown", the politicians always win and take care of themselves, and the dwindling percentage of people who still pay taxes lose, and spending goes higher and the debt goes higher, and you can be 100% certain that they will never address any of the government Ponzi Schemes (Social Security, Medicare, Medicaid, public employee pensions, student loans and now ObamaCare), and the governments come closer to eventual bankruptcy.

As I write this, the politicians are playing with the 19th "Government Shutdown" since 1976, and I am completely ignoring it, because I know the result will be exactly the same. Instead, I am focused on my company's earnings reports this quarter and things that I can actually control in my life, and you should be too.

Chapter 93 A Different And More Positive Take On The Out Of Control Growth Of Government Debt

I have a unique, and I believe, more accurate and positive take on the spiraling out of control growth of government debt. As anyone with an IQ above room temperature knows, the entire Western World (USA, Western Europe and Japan) governments are headed for bankruptcy. In America, it is at all levels of government. Federal, state and city all have unsustainable retirement system and healthcare system liabilities, and they are all going broke. It is inevitable, and it is only a question of when. As I am writing this, the USA Commonwealth of Puerto Rico is said to be about to default or partially default (restructure) on its debt (bonds) and is going to declare bankruptcy. Despite a population of only 3.7 million people, they have run up a staggering 70 billion in debt, including a mind boggling 40 billion in unfunded government union worker retirement liabilities from absurd contracts politicians gave to these employees over the decades.

So how can one continue to invest in stocks and maintain any optimism if we are going broke? Here is where I have a decidedly unique, and I believe, accurate and more positive take on things. Yes, we are going broke, but it is only governments that are going broke. Individuals' debt, as measured by **Household Debt and Household Debt to Income Ratio,** peaked in 2006 and has plunged since then, and is now the lowest it has been in 10 years. When you look at debt servicing costs (i.e. annual payments) and debt servicing cost to income ratio, the story is even better. Due to low interest rates, the ratio has plunged to the near all time lows set in 1994 and 1981. This means monthly debt payments by individuals are actually near the lows set 20 and 35 years ago. Corporate debt levels are extremely low. The **Corporate Cash Per Dollar Of Debt Ratio** has soared to the highest levels since the late 1950s and early 1960s.

Therefore, we have this dichotomy where individuals have their lowest monthly debt payments in 20 or 35 years, and falling and corporations have their lowest debt levels in 50 to 60 years, but the government at all levels has skyrocketing and out of control debt with no hope in sight of getting it under control.

Obviously, something has to give. The politicians will never stop spending other people's money, and they will try to progressively increase taxes on the dwindling percentage of the population still paying taxes. Currently, out of 195 countries, the USA already has the 2nd highest corporate income taxes in the world behind Japan, and as far as individuals go, half the population already pays all the Federal Income taxes, and the other half pays nothing. The top 1% already pay nearly 40% of all Federal Income taxes, and the top 10% pay nearly 75% of all Federal Income taxes. The politicians could raise the taxes on corporations and the wealthy to 100%, and it wouldn't come even come close to stopping the spiraling rise in government debt. Ultimately, it will end as it has in all governments around the world facing bankruptcy in the past 70 years or so.

What happens is that bond investors (i.e. the people loaning all this money to governments at all levels) finally realize the situation is hopeless and stop buying the bonds. This causes bond interest rates to explode to very high levels, and quickly the governments can no longer make the interest payments. The governments have only 2 options, deflate the currency by printing more money to cause inflation to soar so the debt appears smaller, or to default i.e. fail to pay the interest and principle on the debt (i.e. the bond holders lose everything). Inflation kills the average man in the street, and the default kills the wealthy bondholders and foreign bond holders. In this battle, history has always shown, inflating doesn't work well and soon fails, and they default on the bonds. Let's look at recent history:

Russia (1998) - When Russia went broke, they first tried to inflate their way out by devaluing the currency, but that failed and ultimately they defaulted and bond holders lost nearly everything. Since they were too big to bail out and couldn't borrow any more money, they had to sharply cut spending, and they cut spending by a stunning 20% down to a more sustainable level. By defaulting, they overnight went from drowning in debt to completely debt free. Shortly afterwards, they completely scrapped their complicated tax system and replaced it with a simple 13% flat income tax. Suddenly, they owed nothing AND had a balanced budget, and government spending was finally under control. Not only that, Russia's economy rebounded with stunning speed. Due to the default crisis, GDP fell 5.3% in 1998, only to soar after the default to up 6.4, 10.0, 5.1 and 4.7% the following four years, the best growth in the nation's history. As is the case in America, it was only the government that was going broke in the 1990's in Russia, not individuals and not businesses.

Latin America (1982) - In the 1970's and early 1980's, Latin American socialist government spending exploded out of control with debt soaring at an unsustainable 20% per year. In 1982, bond holders finally realized the debt could not be paid back, and interest rates soared out of control. In August of 1982, Mexico announced it would default on its debt. Instantly, all bond sales in Latin America ceased. One by one the rest of the Latin American nations' governments defaulted on their debt, and bondholders lost nearly everything. After defaulting/restructuring debt to pennies on the dollar and forced reduction in government spending, Latin American governments today have extremely low debt with not a single Latin American country in the top 25 countries in the world in debt. Today, on a per GDP basis, Latin American government debt is a tiny fraction of the horrendous government debt situation in the United States. America's **Total Government Debt to GDP ratio** is an unsustainable 105% of GDP, whereas Brazil's is 15%, Mexico's is 20%, Paraguay's is 13%, Bolivia's is 15%, Costa Rica's is 24%, Uruguay's is 33%, Peru's is 22% and Chile's is 38%. Despite the default, the largest Latin American economy which is Brazil, managed to average 3.1% average annual GDP growth during the 1980's, and other countries had similar growth rates.

Southeast Asia (1997) - Due to reckless government spending, the Debt to GDP ratios in the Association of Southeast Asian Nations (ASEAN) exploded to an unsustainable 100% to 160% (The USA is currently in that range at 105%.). Initially, they tried to devalue their currencies and inflate their way out, but this resulted in rioting in the streets of Indonesia and Thailand and the ouster of the sitting governments in both of those countries. Bond holders stopped lending, and interest rates skyrocketed. The governments would have defaulted, but they were bailed out by the International Monetary Fund (IMF) and forced to dramatically reduce government spending as part of the IMF bailout. Of course, the USA is too big to be "bailed out." GDP plunged in Indonesia 13%, but again, the economy quickly rebound growing 0.8, 4.9, 3.6 and 4.9% in the following years. In

Thailand, it fell 10.5% but quickly rebounded growing 4.4, 4.8, 2.2 and 5.3% in the following years. Debt to GDP ratio is now only 44% in Thailand and 23% in Indonesia.

Greece (2010) - Out of control government spending in Greece caused the Debt to GDP ratio to rise to 113% by 2008, an unsustainable level, which caused bond buyers to flee and interest rates to explode up to 47%, and by 2010, the Debt to GDP ratio exploded to 170%, and the government defaulted on their debt and was bailed out by the rest of Europe. Knowing they would continue to be bailed out, the Greeks still refused to actually cut spending, even though they promised they would, and Debt to GDP remained over 150%, resulting in further defaults and bailouts. At some point, the rest of Europe could decide to stop bailing out Greece which would force the Greeks into reality and make them follow the examples set by the other nations described in previous paragraphs.

Note that in all of the above cases, the politicians were completely useless and were never able to solve the problem. Nothing happens until the bond holders realize that they won't get their money back, and panic selling in the bond market triggers soaring interest rates, precipitating the government to default on their debt. This can happen quite quickly, and the politicians are useless and are just spectators during this crisis, although they will continue to give speeches and pretend to be helping, but they will just take care of themselves.

In summary, when governments spend recklessly such as has happened in the USA, the debt to GDP levels rise above 100%, which is an unsustainable level, which eventually results in soaring interest rates, and bond buyers flee, and then governments try to inflate their way out of the debt by printing money, which the man in the street won't stand for, so they then ultimately default on their debt (if they are too big to be bailed out), as was the case with Russia and Latin America and obviously the USA. This results in bond holders losing everything or nearly everything, forced huge reductions in government spending (because they can't borrow anymore) resulting in a temporary plunge in GDP (short but deep recession) and a temporary stock market collapse.

However, the country emerges debt free because they defaulted, meaning they won't pay the money back, so they start over debt free with much lower government spending levels, because they have to balance their budget every year, because no one will loan money to them (i.e. They can't sell bonds.), and they have a quickly rebounding economy and stock market in the ensuring years. Although this will be a harrowing and tumultuous event with lots of short term pain for all, in the end, we get a fresh start with governments back to operating with a sustainable economic model. The current economic models of the Federal, state and city governments are completely unsustainable and make no economic sense. In fact, if a private group tried to set up a system like this (taking money from the new people to pay off the people who got in earlier), they would be prosecuted for running an illegal Ponzi/Pyramid Scheme and would be thrown in jail. Of course, you will hear all the politicians and those desperate to keep it going until the bitter collapse say that it isn't a Ponzi scheme, but a variation of the old saying goes: "If you have to say it isn't a Ponzi Scheme, then it is."

The key is to not panic and sell you stocks in great companies with great balance sheets during the panic sell-off that happens when the government defaults. I would expect a typical Stock Market Collapse on the order of 40 to 50%, which is similar to the 4 most recent Stock Market Collapses. As always, I would not try to predict when this will occur; you will never get it right, and even if you do, you will not get back in at the right time, so it will do you no good. I will ride it out and stay fully invested, knowing that just a couple of years later, we will be better off, and the market will rebound as happened in Russia, Latin America and Southeast Asia. Remember, it is only governments that are going bankrupt, not companies and individuals. Of course, bond holders get slaughtered, and anyone counting on government entitlements (transfer payments from working to non-working people) will see 10 to 30% reductions in entitlements, along with 10 to 20% reduction in pay/benefits and/or lay-offs in the government sector.

Chapter 94 More Details On Stock Investing: What About Other Investing Techniques?

This book is about *Fundamental Stock Investing*. The reason *Fundamental Stock Investing* works so well is that it is the only method that attempts to correlate a company's future profits (over the next 1-3 years) to the current stock price and determines if the stock is cheap, fairly valued or overpriced. In fact, it uses the exact criteria one would use when deciding if you were going to buy a business or not. It is the only method that makes actual business sense. In the short run, anything can and will happen to a company's stock price, but in the long run, a company's stock price correlates exactly with its profits. This difference between a stock's price in the short run and the long run is where you make money by *Fundamental Stock Investing*. Not only that, because the method generally involves holding stocks for longer time periods, transactions costs are lower, but most importantly, gains are taxed at much lower rates, and the gains are also deferred, all of which results in much higher increases in wealth than the official gains compared to ALL other investing methods. There are many systems you can use to make money in stocks, but when you combine the returns with the huge tax advantages, *Fundamental Stock Investing* becomes the superior method. It is also the simplest and easiest to learn method and the only method that uses common sense.

What about other investing methods? There are many different systems/methods/techniques one can use to make money in stocks. This is possible, because the stock market has averaged 10% annual returns over the long term, so even if you are using an inferior method, as long as it isn't a seriously flawed method, the odds are on your side, even using methods that are inferior at building wealth to *Fundamental Stock Investing*. Examples of these methods and why they are inferior are as follows:

The *Price and Earnings Momentum* method completely ignores price. Who would buy a company while ignoring the price it is selling for? *Technical Analysis* is studying charts and graphs of stock prices and completely ignores how the actual business is doing and ignores the price! Who would buy a company while ignoring how the business is doing and the price it is selling for?! The *Options* method is treating stock investing as if you were playing a game and is essentially gambling. The *Price Momentum* method also ignores both how the business is doing and the price. The *CANSLIM* method ignores price and tries to time the stock market and tries to use technical analysis with some fundamental analysis simultaneously, that has you constantly jumping in and out of the market and in and out of stocks, suffering endless stop losses, in the hope you might catch a big momentum winner to make up for all the constant losses from jumping in and out of the market and in and out of stocks. The *Buy And Hold Forever* method is like buying a business and then never once checking on how the business is actually doing for the rest of your life. How dumb is that? The *Value Investing* method does consider price but ignores how the company is actually doing and the future prospects for the company. The *Hedging* method attempts to balance investing long in stocks with short investing against stocks, which almost guarantees mediocre or worse returns, which explains the horrendous performance by Hedge Funds the past 5 years. None of these methods make any "business sense". *Fundamental Stock Investing* makes perfect business sense, and that combined with the huge tax advantages, it is always superior to all other methods over the long run. While other methods come in and out of favor, *Fundamental Stock Investing* is ageless, because it treats stock investing as if you were actually buying a business.

Chapter 95   Saving Money Is Critical For Building Wealth

Saving money is critical, and the rest of the book will be devoted to techniques on how to save money. As stated repeatedly throughout this book, the key to building wealth is through a combination of both investing AND saving.

To build wealth, you must invest and save. Doing one without the other will fail to build significant wealth over time. I know of many very good investors who fail to build significant wealth. The reason is simply that they are not saving enough money to have enough to invest to reach a critical mass such that they really start building wealth. Many of them blow any investment gains by taking the profits and spending it as soon as they make it. Others never have enough savings to begin with.

Through experience and research over the years, I have identified all the major areas where people waste money, and I cover them all in the chapters that follow. In no way am I saying you need to live like a monk to save, or that you have to follow all of the advice to succeed. In fact, I have at various stages of my life failed to follow several of the techniques that are listed. The key is to be at least aware of all of them and to follow as many of them as you can, for as often as you feel you can. With half an effort or more, you will do ok.

"If you can't save money, the seeds of greatness are not in you."

- billionaire W. Clement Stone from the book <u>The Wealth Choice: Success Secrets Of Black Billionaires</u>

Chapter 96   Saving Money: The Ultimate Savings Tool Is The 401k/403b/TSP

The single most important savings technique is always working at a job with a good 401k/403b/TSP Plan.

As shown earlier in the book, the quadruple advantage of "free" matching funds, federal tax deductibility, state tax deductibility and tax deferred growth makes them the ultimate savings vehicle. If at all possible, pick a job that has a plan, and if possible, one that has a great plan. A good plan will match up to 3%. A great plan will match up to 5% or more.

Additionally, when you max out your 401k/403b/TSP and Roth IRAs, then the money is not available to spend, so it is likely you will spend less. As the saying goes, "pay yourself first".

All things considered, a great plan is far more important than salary when building wealth. A good plan must be one of your highest priorities when seeking a job.

Chapter 97   Saving Money: If Practicable, Pick A Low Tax State To Live And Work In

If practicable, pick a low tax state to live and work in. As stated repeatedly throughout this book, the number one obstacle to wealth creation is taxes. Don't unnecessarily pick a high tax state to live and work in. You will build wealth at a far faster rate in a low tax state.

In general, Red States are much easier to build wealth in than Blue States. However, you can find good situations in some Blue States and some onerous situations in Red States. NEVER live in a city that has a city income tax. As stated earlier in the book in the real estate section, avoid buying a home in cities that have relatively high real estates taxes. These taxes are going to be much higher as times goes on due to the unsustainable benefit packages given to public employee unions. This is especially critical if you don't have a very high paying job, in that case low property taxes are more important than low state income taxes. Some Blue States have high income taxes but actually have relatively low property taxes. If you are a high income earner, it is more important to be in a low income tax state than a low real estate tax state. Of course, many Blue States are horrible in every regard, with outrageously high taxes of every kind, including fees and fines. Many of these Blue States are also very expensive to live in from a cost of living standpoint. Some Red States have generally low taxes overall but have high investment taxes on capital gains and dividends, so if you have a lot money in taxable accounts, these taxes can hurt you. You have to research all this and weigh all these options versus where the jobs are and family considerations, and if practicable, choose a state with a low tax burden for your personal situation.

I can give you a bad example of what not to do. I knew hundreds of people who worked in the state of Maine which has outrageously high income tax rates, and yet, these people chose to live in what was, at the time, the Red State of New Hampshire with no income or sales tax but some of the highest property taxes in the nation. I should know, because I was one of these foolish people for 3 years until I wised up. Keep in mind, when you work in a different state than you live in, you effectively pay the higher of the two states' income taxes. So needless to say, these people, including me for 3 years, were getting simultaneously killed by the high Maine income taxes and the high New Hampshire property taxes. They would have been better off living in Maine, which has far lower property taxes or Massachusetts, which has high taxes for everything but low property taxes, and they could have avoided the Mass sales taxes by buying most items in New Hampshire with no sales tax. Most of them never gave any thought to what they were doing in that regard, and most of course, faced huge obstacles to wealth building. Avoid a situation like that when practicable.

Chapter 98 Saving Money: Cars Are The Single Biggest Money Sink

Cars are the single biggest money sink. Nothing in the world depreciates more quickly in value than a car, and nothing has so many ongoing costs (gas, insurance, maintenance, excise taxes, tolls, fines, parking, inspection, registration, driver's license, etc.) associated with it. Therefore, you need to do everything you can to keep these costs down.

Most people unnecessarily buy cars that are way too expensive and expensive to operate, and they don't keep them long enough. According to Kelley Blue Book, the average transaction price paid at a dealership in February 2014 was $32,160. The difference between them and people who buy cheap cars that are also cheap to operate and keep them a long time and invest the extra money, can amount to literally becoming a millionaire, compared to just going from paycheck to paycheck the rest of their lives, with little or no real savings, which most people end up doing.

Obviously, sports cars are the biggest possible waste of money, and unless you are already a millionaire, you can forget about ever building wealth if you insist on blowing money on a sports car.

What I am talking about is the typical middle or lower middle class person who feels they (and their lover) "need" to have an SUV or Van and/or a Pick-up truck like everyone else. Building wealth is not about being like everyone else; it is the antithesis of being like everyone else. The typical new mid sized SUV or Van, when you add up everything, is going to cost $30,000 or more. Not only that, the high cost means higher insurance, higher maintenance costs, higher excise taxes and gas mileage below 25 MPG, which means an extra $500 to $1000 per year in gasoline costs.

New midsized pick-up trucks are going to be close to $25,000 and get even worse gas mileage, averaging 20 MPG or less, meaning an extra $1000 to $1500 every year in higher gas costs. They are also the most underutilized piece of light equipment ever invented, with the vast majority of pick-up owners using them as passenger vehicles most of the time, as opposed to hauling material as part of running a business.

If you are serious about building wealth, and even if you have a family of 4, you should be looking at a compact sedan with 4 doors. These cars cost only about $15,000 to $18,000 and get about 35 MPG. These cars also have much lower insurance costs, maintenance costs and excise taxes. Better yet, consider buying a relatively new and/or low mileage used or "pre-owned" vehicle. In just the first 5 years, a 4 door compact sedan is going to save you a total, including the initial purchase price, of $15,000 to $20,000 dollars versus an SUV or Van and $10,000 to $15,000, compared to a pick-up truck. If you buy used or pre-owned, you save even more. If you have to get a car loan to pay for your vehicles, the extra costs goes much higher.

The **Opportunity Cost** is huge. It is very important that you become familiar with the concept of opportunity cost. When you spend/waste money on something, it is not only the actual cost of the item, but what that money could have made if, instead of spending/wasting it on something, you invested the money in the stock market and earned say the typical average annual return in stocks of 10%. When you do this, you realize the opportunity cost lost is far greater than the actual money you spent/wasted. In all of these savings chapters, I provide the opportunity cost of failing to save money, and you will be shocked by how simple expenditures that people take for granted are so costly in the long run when you are trying to build wealth.

If you invested the extra savings from the first 5 years of let's say approximately $15,000 at a 10% average annual return from investing in stocks, that money would be worth $160,000 after 25 years (of opportunity cost), and that is just the savings on the first car you buy! Each successive car you buy compounds that amount, and if you are talking you and your lover, double those amounts.

The next biggest mistake people make is getting a new car every 3-5 years. Cars last much longer than they did in the olden days, and you should aim to keep a car for 12-15 years or at least 200,000 miles. The past 25 years, my wife and I have owned a total of 4 cars. During that same time a couple I know has owned 12 new cars, and that is typical of many couples. The upfront extra cost of those extra 8 cars is

$160,000. However, that is nothing compared to the opportunity cost. If that extra money was invested in stocks earning 10% average annual returns, the opportunity cost is nearly $700,000 over 25 years. Contemplate that. By keeping my cars longer and investing the savings, I made nearly 3/4 of a million dollars more than that other couple. If you are serious about building wealth, stop buying new cars every 3-5 years and keep them 12 to 15 years.

Some people ask, "What about the extra maintenance costs of keeping a car longer?" Look at it this way, the typical new car owner has a $500 monthly car payment. (According to Experian, the average monthly auto payment was $471 in early 2014). Even if your old car is breaking down every month, the cost would be less than a new car payment, and even the worst lemon/clunker doesn't break down that often.

Here is another example. I know of another couple of modest means that buys new "his and her" Grand Jeep Cherokees every 4-6 years. Here is a rhetorical question; how much money do you think they have in savings and investments?

In summary, cars are huge money sinks, and you got to aggressively act to keep these costs down to save and use the saved money to invest and build wealth. Forget the "me too" SUV/Van/Pick-up truck, and instead, buy 4 door compact sedans and/or consider buying used or pre-owned cars. Stop getting a new car every 3-5 years and keep them 12-15 years. These 2 strategies will result in invested opportunity cost savings in the ballpark of a million dollars over a 25 year period. What follows is chapter after chapter on money savings techniques, but following the advice of this chapter alone can make the difference between becoming a millionaire and going from paycheck to paycheck with little savings/wealth accumulation like everyone else.

Chapter 99   Saving Money: Buy A House When The Timing Is Right

A key component to saving and building wealth is to eventually buy a house, PROVIDED it is at the correct part of the real estate cycle. As stated earlier in the book, owning a house over the long term is far better than renting. The key to buying a house is to buy it at the right time in the real estate cycle. See **Chapter 6** to ensure that you are at the right time in the real estate cycle when you buy your house. There are numerous reasons, the main one being that you are gaining equity in the house with each payment opposed to renting, where the money is just going out the window. Also, over the long run, a house is an appreciable asset (4-8% per year over the long term), so your equity is growing, so you are building wealth. Thirdly, the government subsidizes home ownership, allowing you to be able to deduct the interest payments, and when you sell the house, generally you pay no capital gains tax. Of course, do not buy such an expensive house, that you have no money left over for savings and investments.

Chapter 100   Saving Money: The Effect Of Marriage And Divorce On Wealth Building

Obviously, whether you should get married or not, and if you do, picking the right spouse, are way out of the scope of this book (and I know little about the topic myself), and one should never get married for financial reasons alone, and once married, no one should stay together just for financial reasons alone. That said, there are financial advantages to being married. However, before I talk about the financial advantages of getting married, I must first talk about the other side of the coin, which is divorce.

A divorce is always a devastating set-back for both parties, so do not get married, if you can see yourself getting divorced at some point. If you get divorced, you are looking at massive legal fees, usually tens of thousands of dollars. Not only is your income about cut in half, costs going forward for both people increase greatly. Child support payments are extremely high with some activist judges deliberately setting them impossibly high, which does the spouse receiving child support no good, if the one paying stops paying, because the payments are too high. You are single again, and singles tend to spend more money per person. Needless to say, divorce will be the single biggest financial setback you will face in your lifetime.

The American divorce rate soared after the 1950's before peaking at about 50% in the 1980's. It has declined since then to below 40%, but only because fewer people are getting married and getting re-married. Again, I am no expert on marriage and wouldn't advise anyone either way, but since this book is about wealth building, I needed to point out the devastating consequences of divorce on wealth building, and I also am providing below a list of the risk factors for divorce from some highly respected studies (see references below) on the subject. Of course, there are literally tens of millions of exceptions to these risk factors, so they may not mean anything in your personal case, but if you have multiple risk factors and wealth building is an important goal for you, you may want to be extra careful when it comes to marriage, even if you are "madly in love".

Here are the risk factors, in no particular order, according to the referenced studies:

1) If you and your lover argue about finances more than once a week, you are 30% more likely to get divorced.

2) If your parents divorced, you have a 40% higher chance of getting divorced. If your parents re-married after getting divorced, you have a 91% higher chance of getting divorced.

3) If one of you smokes and the other doesn't, you have a 86% higher chance of getting divorced. If both of you smoke, you have a 140% higher chance of getting divorced.

4) If one or both spouses drink more than 2 drinks a day, you have a more than 200% higher chance of getting divorced.

5) If you are a practicing Christian/Catholic, you have a 19% lower chance of getting divorced.

6) If both of you have been previously divorced, you have a 92% higher chance of getting divorced.

7) If the woman is more than 2 year older than the man, you have a 53% higher chance of getting divorced.

8) If the man is more than 9 years older than the woman, you have a 105% higher chance of getting divorced.

9) If your IQ is below average (i.e. below 100), you have a 50% higher chance of getting divorced.

10) If you have lived with your current lover or a previous lover for more than 2 years before getting married, you have a 55% higher chance of getting divorced.

11) If you are a male homosexual, you have a 50% higher chance of getting divorced and if a female homosexual, you have a 167% higher chance of getting divorced.

12) Getting married before age 18 increases the risk of divorce by 48%.

13) Getting married before age 25 increases the risk of divorce by 24%.

14) If you have no children, you are 66% more likely to get divorced.

15) If you have daughters, you are 10% more likely to get divorced than if you have sons.

16) If you are a woman actively serving in the military, you are 250 times (24,900%) more likely to get divorced.

17) The more you spend on the wedding, the more likely you are to divorce. Eight out of 10 couples that divorce within 5 years cited wedding costs as a major contributor to divorce.

18) If one of your careers is in the performing arts (music, acting, dance, etc.), you have a 43% higher chance of getting divorced.

19) If you are a farmer, you are 7 times less likely to get divorced.

20) If you are an engineer, you are 4 times less likely to get divorced.

Sources: Anneli Rufus "15 Ways To Predict Divorce" The Daily Beast 5/19/10, Deborah Mitchell "21 Factors That May Increase The Risk Of Divorce" 7-17-10 published in eMax Health

So what are the advantages of getting married? After reading those scary and depressing stats above, it is hard to talk about marriage positively, but according to the stats, tens of millions or more than 50% of married couples are still together and likely to stay together. As far as the topic of this book goes, which is wealth building, getting and staying married offers the following significant advantages:

1) The majority of marriages have more than one income during part or all of their marriage, and this increased income leads to more potential savings, and therefore, more potential money to invest, resulting in quicker wealth building.

2) Living under one roof greatly reduces expenses and increased savings efficiencies.

3) Married people spend less money per person on average than single people on average.

4) The government subsidizes marriage via significantly lower income tax rates, and as stated repeatedly throughout this book, taxes are the number one obstacle to wealth building.

5) Married people live much longer than single people, with men living 8-17 years longer and women 7 to 15 years longer, leaving more time for wealth building, and more importantly, more time to enjoy the wealth you have built.

6) Married people are more healthy on average than single people, resulting in lower medical costs on average.

Chapter 101   Saving Money: Don't Marry A Big Spender

Don't marry a big spender. I have stated that I offer no advice on whether one should or shouldn't get married and have only pointed out the positive effects of marriage and negative effects of divorce on wealth building and what the studies have shown as the risk factors for getting divorced. Here is one thing I do feel comfortable on giving advice: Do not marry a big spender.

If you are serious about wealth building, you will have a much harder, if not impossible task of building wealth, if your spouse is a big spender. No matter how much money you and your spouse make, it won't matter if one or both of you are big spenders, because no matter how high income is or goes, the big spender will simply increase their spending by an equal or greater amount. It is simply the way big spenders operate. We are all flawed and have bad habits and like all bad habits, big spending is something that only the big spender can overcome. You can't help adults with bad habits; they can only help themselves. Don't think going into a marriage that you are going to change the big spender's habits. On the other hand, if YOU are the big spender, this second half of the book is full of information on how to change your ways by saving money.

Chapter 102 Saving Money: What If I Am Already Married To A Big Spender?

What if I am already married to a big spender? You are in a tough spot but there are a few things you can do to mitigate their spending:

1) Max out their 401k/403b/TSP. The money will be taken out before they even see it, so they will probably spend less, and of course, you will build wealth quicker.

2) Fully fund their ROTH IRA on January 1 every year or when you get your tax refund. Again, less money available to spend and more money saved and invested.

3) Normally, you want to adjust your **Income Tax Withholdings** via your **W-4,** such that you owe money on April 15th. That way you defer paying taxes as long as possible, and over the long haul, you will in theory build wealth quicker, because every year that money will have an extra 3.5 months to grow before the taxes are paid. That is, of course, if you have the financial discipline to make sure the extra money is invested/saved, and you have the money available to pay the taxes on April 15th, so you don't get hit with interest and/or fines. With the big spender, you want to use the exact opposite strategy. You want to claim on their W-4 zero allowances AND have extra money withheld each paycheck. This makes the money unavailable to the big spender, and more likely, they will spend less. Then when you get the big tax refund, immediately invest it in a Roth IRA or other taxable account that is off limits to the big spender.

Chapter 103   Saving Money: Don't Pay Too Much For College

Don't pay too much for college. From the end of World War II through the 1980's, going to college was almost universally a wise investment. Since then, college costs have spiraled out of control due to massive government subsidies and the badly mistaken belief that there is no limit to how much one should spend on college, both of which have allowed colleges to raise tuition, room and board, fees and book costs to astronomical levels. However, just like anything else in life, you must do a **cost/benefit analysis** on anything you purchase including college.

We have now reached the point that the cost of most majors at most private colleges no longer makes any sense for someone interested in wealth building, and in fact, not even close to making any sense. Of course, getting a practical degree for the purpose of wealth building is not the only reason people go to college. Some of the non-practical reasons people go include the prestige, the image/status, "everyone else is going", the reputation, to party and get laid, to take a 4 year break from growing up, to simply "get an education" as an end in itself and not as a means to a viable career, to play sports, etc., and there is nothing wrong with any of that, depending on your priorities. The same also applies to the parent who is contemplating funding their kid's college costs.

However, if you are interested in building wealth, and you wouldn't be reading this book if you weren't, you need to forget about those traditional non-practical reasons for going to college and look at it as simply an investment. If you want to build wealth, forget about the traditional college path for you or your kids of going to a private college "with a great reputation" charging between 150K and 250K over 4 years for a liberal arts or other major with poor employment prospects upon graduation. You will never, ever, recover that initial "investment" and will be saddled with debt working in a job that likely didn't require a college degree or shouldn't have required a college degree, and you also lost those 4 years of opportunity cost, where you would have been working and making money and saving and investing and building wealth.

Instead, you need to be thinking only about practical majors in engineering, pure sciences, the healthcare field and education if you want to be a teacher or other such practical majors. Furthermore, you want to go or send your kid to an in-state state school if possible or a cheaper private school. If you are going for something else or paying for a child to major in something else and going to an expensive private college, then you are not serious about wealth building. If you or your child are not capable of making it in one of those practical majors or are not interested in one of those majors, then you need to seriously consider not going to college and pursing a career that doesn't require a college degree. Although out of the scope of this book, there are numerous careers that one can pursue without a college degree or with a cheap short term technical or trade degree. Also keep in mind that if you truly want to be educated in the liberal arts such as languages, philosophy, psychology, history, government, political science, etc. there are now infinite and free or cheap resources available on the internet to educate yourself in these areas later on.

This may sound like radical advice compared to what everyone else is advising but consider these stats. Currently more than 50% of recent college grads are not working or working in jobs that don't require a college degree. This doesn't even count the tens of millions who went to college and didn't graduate. Most are still living at home upon graduation or upon dropping out. Most have massive amounts of debt from going to college. Combined they now have 1 trillion dollars in college debt, and this is saddling the overall economy with yet another huge government created Ponzi scheme in addition to Social Security, Medicare, Government Pensions, ObamaCare, etc. These stats are a stunning indictment against the long held myth "that everyone needs to go to college".

Compare the hypothetical example of two twins, one who goes to a "Big Name" private university with a "great reputation" and majors in business or psychology or communications, which are three of the most popular college majors. The other goes straight to work at Wal-Mart at age 18 as an entry level "Sales Associate". At the end of 4 years, the college twin has graduated, has zero savings, owes over $100,000 in student loans and is unable to find a job in his major and winds up in a job that doesn't require a college degree. The Wal-Mart twin has no college education but has the basic skills that are very useful in the working world (He shows up every day he is supposed to; he shows up on time; he follows simple instructions to the letter, and he is the so called "go-getter".). Within 2 years, the Wal-Mart twin has been promoted to Customer Service Supervisor, because most people are unreliable and/or consider it a dead end job, and employees come and go like a revolving door, so it is easy to get promoted if you have half a brain and simply do your job and stay in the job for a while. By the time the college twin graduates, he has been promoted to Assistant Store Manager and is now making $45,000 per year. Not only is the Wal-Mart twin making way more than the $25,000 the college twin is making (while forever searching for a job "in his field"), he owes nothing and has been putting in 10% of his pay into the Wal-Mart 401k plan to which Wal-Mart matches 6%. The Wal-Mart twin puts his money into an S&P 500 index fund and has averaged 10% annual returns. He already has $18,000 in his plan by age 21. Assume the Wal-Mart worker never gets promoted beyond Assistant Store Manager, and he averages 2% raises per year and he continues to contribute 10% of his pay and Wal-Mart matches 6% and he continues to put it all in the S&P 500 index fund, which has averaged 10% average annual returns since 1926. By age 39, the Wal-Mart twin has a staggering half a million dollars in his plan. By age 50, the Wal-Mart twin will have 1.5 million dollars and will have probably retired well before age 50. Meanwhile, the college grad is crushed by his 100K in college loans, struggling to keep up as he bounces from job to job (that don't require a college degree), while still searching to find a job in his field. The loans won't be paid off until at least age 30, and he will of course have zero savings. By age 39, he will have a tiny fraction of the wealth of the Wal-Mart twin and will never catch up, even if he eventually finds a good paying job in his field.

In no way am I advocating someone go to work at Wal-Mart versus going to college. In fact, people should do whatever they want to and pursue what is important to them. However, this book is about wealth building, and if you are interested in wealth building, my whole point is simply this: Don't do what everyone else is doing when it comes to college, only do what is going to help you achieve your goal of building wealth.

Chapter 104 Saving Money: Saving For College Using Coverdell ESA Accounts And 529 College Savings Plans

As I just explained in the previous chapter, the key when it comes to college is: don't pay too much for college. Don't go to college and major in something, where you wind up in a job that doesn't need a college degree, and don't go to an expensive private college as tens of millions of people are doing. Don't go to an expensive private school to get a degree when you can get the same degree at an in-state state school for just a fraction of the cost. All that said, if you have a child that you think has the ability and inclination to get a degree in engineering or science or healthcare or education/teaching or some other practical field, then it might be a good idea to save some money for college in a **Coverdell Education Savings Account (ESA)** or **529 College Savings Plan**.

I say "might be a good idea", because of the massive and ever increasing involvement of Federal and state governments into subsidizing education with tax dollars, the whole thing has become a convoluted expensive mess. Not only that, the landscape of financial aid is constantly changing. Therefore, I cannot offer any definitive advice on the subject but will point out some things to consider:

1) The problem with saving for college in an ESA or 529 is that they will count it against you, i.e. they will punish you by, in general, giving you less financial aid. However, if you don't save, and you don't get much aid, you may be stuck with huge expenses, you are not ready for.

2) Never sacrifice your own retirement savings for your children's education, especially in light of how overpriced most "college educations" have become.

3) Don't save more than you plan to spend. In my own case, I put $2000 per year into each of my children's ESA's for the first 5 years of their lives. Then I never put anything else into those accounts, based on the assumption that it would grow enough by the time they go to college (at an in-state state school pursuing engineering/technical

degrees), which looks like it is going to be about the right amount or about 75% of what it will cost.

4) The ESA has the advantage that you can put the money anywhere you want including into a brokerage account investing in individual stocks, which is what I did. The 529 is limited to what is available in your state.

5) The 529 has unlimited contributions, while the ESA is limited up to $2000 per year or less, if your income is what the government considers "too high". Then again, you don't want to save more than you need and/or so much that it will hurt the financial aid you are eligible for.

6) The 529 is tax deductible IN SOME STATES, and the ESA is not.

7) Both the ESA and 529 grow earnings tax fee.

8) You pay no taxes on the ESA when you take it out, provided you use it for education expenses, and you use it by age 30, or transfer it to another family member for their education expenses. Otherwise, you are taxed on the earnings, AND you pay a 10% penalty tax. The 529 has no age limit to use the money for college, and you pay no taxes when you withdraw the money.

9) The ESA can be used for K through 12 private school expenses and college. The 529 can only be used for college expenses.

10) The 529 remains in the parents' custody. The ESA is legally turned over to the child at age 18 and then the child is in control.

You will have to decide for your own situation, how much you are willing to pay for college, how much you will save for college, and how it will affect your financial aid package, and whether you go with an ESA or a 529. The only firm advice I can give you is: don't pay too much for ANYTHING including college, if you are serious about building wealth.

Chapter 105 Saving Money: Do It Yourself When It Comes To Home Maintenance

Do it yourself. As discussed earlier in the real estate chapter, when you buy a house you need to do as much work yourself as possible. Mow your lawn, clean your house, shovel your snow, and don't hire people for chores. If you have kids, get your kids involved early in chores around the house and yard to build character, teach them basic skills and save money. Teach them the principle that everyone living under a roof must work. If you live in the North, don't have a pool; it excludes 40% of buyers and costs a lot to maintain. If you live in the South or Southwest, you need a pool, or you will exclude a large number of buyers, but use the cheapest possible treatments to maintain your pool, and do it yourself. Fertilize your lawn yourself. If you have city water, don't water your lawn unless absolutely necessary. Plant your own trees and shrubs.

When something breaks at home, you can fix it rather than hiring someone, way more easily than you used to be able to do in the olden days. For many years, I failed to do this, but after getting burned a few times, I wised up. Every time you fix something, if you have children, have them watch/participate, so they learn these basic skills. It doesn't matter if you are not a handyman or good with your hands or you lack experience or confidence to fix things. Everything has changed with the advent of the internet. No matter what breaks such as toilets or sinks or screens or whatever, there are now websites and/or videos on the internet, often complete with videos, on how to fix everything. Furthermore, the replacement parts and products to fix these thing are now readily and extremely cheaply available from Home Depot, Lowes, Amazon, etc. You can have zero skills and experience and replace leaking heating system parts, pumps, valves, etc. There are repair discussion websites, where people love telling other people how to fix things, and if you are not sure, they will tell you how.

Say for example, your central air unit has failed. You can go on a heating/cooling/HVAC website discussion group, go on the Central Air forum, post your symptoms on the site, and within a couple of hours, people will be telling you what is wrong, and then you can do a search on how to replace the part and will find a site that says how, and then you can do a search for your model number and find the manual online and get the replacement part and then order it on Amazon or some other site. This all takes less than 20 minutes to do. We are in a whole new era, so you should take advantage of it. You can save hundreds of dollars each repair, and you will gradually gain confidence in your ability to fix things, and you will feel good about your newfound self-reliance, and your kids will learn right along with you.

Chapter 106 Saving Money: The Cost Of Smoking

Don't smoke. A lifetime of not smoking versus smoking, and the opportunity cost difference invested in stocks, results in a shocking amount of money. Not only that, smoking is bad for you, so your quality of life is lower; you have higher medical bills, higher dental bills, higher clothes replacement costs; you die sooner and your health later in life is likely to be severely compromised, and as shown earlier, you have an 86% higher chance of getting divorced. You are paying outrageous taxes on those cigarettes, and remember, taxes are the number one obstacle to wealth creation. Because of those ridiculous taxes, some people call smoking a poor, dumb man's tax. You are also in America, which means getting treated like second class citizen with all the anti-smoking laws. In addition, according to the American Journal of Medicine, the average smoker pays an extra $3500 per year in healthcare costs.

Let's just look at the cost of the cigarettes alone. If you are a pack a day smoker, you are paying approximately $2500 a year. If instead you didn't smoke and put that extra $2500 per year into an S&P 500 index fund in a Roth IRA from age 20 to age 50, you would have an extra $435,000 in savings or nearly half a million dollars. If you are serious about wealth building, ditch the cigarettes.

Chapter 107 Saving Money: Pack A Lunch

Pack a lunch. Take the extra 10 minutes to pack a lunch, instead of eating out at work. The cost of packing a lunch at home is about $3.00. The cost of eating out for lunch, even at a cheap place such as a sub shop, when you add in the drink, is about $8.00. By packing your own lunch, instead of eating out, you save about $1300 dollars per year. Over 30 years invested in stocks, this amounts to $225,000 or nearly a quarter of a million dollars. I failed to follow this advice for several years but eventually wised up.

Chapter 108   Saving Money: Attention Coffee Drinkers

Skip that morning coffee stop, and make it at home. Better yet, stop routinely drinking coffee; the caffeine is bad for you, and you don't need it. A Starbuck's Tall coffee is $2.00, the equivalent is $1.75 at Dunkin Doughnuts and $1.50 at McDonalds, and the cost to make it at home is $0.15 per cup. Therefore, making coffee at home versus getting it at Starbucks saves $675 per year. If instead, you make your own coffee and put that extra $675 per year into an S&P 500 index fund in a Roth IRA from age 20 to age 50, you would have an extra $120,000 in saving. If you are serious about wealth building, make your own coffee at home.

Chapter 109 Saving Money: Eating Out

Cut back eating out to once per week or once every other week. It is far cheaper to eat at home than eating out. The cost of a typical restaurant dinner, including tax and tip and drinks, is about $23. The same meal at home is about $11. I also wasted too much money going out to eat too often over the years. If a family of 4 cuts back eating out from twice a week to once a week the savings is about $48 per week or about $2500 per year. If instead, you eat out once a week and put that extra $2500 per year into an S&P 500 index fund in a Roth IRA from age 20 to age 50, you would have an extra $435,000 in saving or nearly half a million dollars. If you are serious about wealth building, eat out only once a week or less.

When eating out, find a cheaper place that you like, that is nearby you. Many restaurants break even on the meal and make all their profits on the drinks and deserts. Order water instead of a drink, and eat ice cream when you get home for desert. Go out to lunch, instead of going out for dinner, and you often can get cheaper prices. Consider ordering take out by phone. In the olden days, just fast food and Chinese restaurants had take out, but now, almost all top restaurant chains have take out, and you can bring it home and have your own drinks and deserts and save on tip, which normally is 15-20%. A big spender actually clued me into this advice, proving the old adage to always separate advice from the person giving you advice, meaning don't accept or reject advice, just because it is coming from a particular person; consider the advice on its own merits.

Chapter 110 Saving Money: The Cost Of Going Out To The Movies

Don't go out to the movies. This is one of the biggest money wasters out there. I too wasted money on this when I was younger. First off, most films these days are over hyped agenda ridden crap. Most importantly though, all movies come quickly to online services (Netflix, Amazon Instant Video, Cable and Satellite, On Demand, etc.) and quickly to video rental and then to regular TV. Also most local libraries are loaded with films that you can rent for free. Going out to the movies cost between 7 and 20 bucks, depending on when and where you go. If a family of 3 goes to the movies once every 2 weeks, you are looking at spending on order of $1000 a year. If instead, you watch movies at home, and put that extra $1000 per year into an S&P 500 index fund in a Roth IRA from age 20 to age 50, you would have an extra $175,000 in saving. If you are serious about wealth building, stop going out to the movies.

Chapter 111   Saving Money: The Club Scene

Don't go out to clubs with high cover charges and expensive drinks. This is the trap the 18-25 age group falls into. I too fell into this trap from age 21-23. They go to the latest "hot club" which charges you 10-20 dollars to wait in line, just to get into the jammed club, where people are bumping into each other and losing some of their hearing from the blurring loud, crappy, pop/rap music, that will be completely forgotten in less than 2 years and never be heard again, and you pay outrageous drink prices, including a tip of about 8 dollars, and you have to pretend you are having a good time. If you are over 30, admit it, and say, "been there, done that". A young adult can easily drop 50 dollars or more at one of these places, until they grow out of it. That is $2600 a year by "clubbing" every Friday Night. If instead, you go to a local place with no cover and cheaper drinks, or better yet, ditch the whole bar scene, and have small parties at home, and put that extra $2600 per year into an S&P 500 index fund in a Roth IRA from age 20 to age 25, and then you stop going to the club scene when you grow up at age 25, but keep the money in the account and never contribute again, you would have an extra $280,000 in saving or more than a quarter of a million dollars. If you are serious about wealth building, skip the expensive club scene.

Chapter 112 Saving Money: Vacations

Don't go on expensive vacations. An expensive vacation can run you $1000 per person when you factor in flight, rental car and expensive eating out. For a family of 3 that is $3000 for just a one week vacation. You can go on much cheaper vacations by driving and staying out of the touristy areas or doing day trips to see attractions in your area. You would be surprised about the quality of local attractions that are near you that you have never visited. If instead, you go on local day trips, and put that extra $3000 per year into an S&P 500 index fund in a Roth IRA from age 20 to age 50, you would have an extra $510,000 in saving or more than half a million dollars. If you are serious about wealth building, stop going on expensive vacations, until you have built significant wealth.

Chapter 113 Saving Money: Don't Cheat On Your Income Taxes

Don't cheat on your income taxes. Avoid this temptation. Not only is it illegal and unethical, it will never get you rich. Furthermore, you don't want to have to worry about getting that letter from the IRS saying they are auditing you when you know you have cheated. It can result in years of government harassment, financial ruin and even jail time. Taxes are the number one obstacle to wealth creating, and you must do everything you can do to legally minimize your taxes, but never cheat on your taxes; it is not worth it. I made a point of paying every single penny I owed on time and kept excellent, organized records, so I never had to fear an audit.

Chapter 114   Saving Money: Life Insurance

Only buy **Term Life Insurance** and only if you need it. Never try to combine life insurance with investing by buying whole life or partial life or annuity plans. Your investing returns will always be lower, and you will pay too much for the insurance. However, do consider investing in the companies that do sell these plans, because they are very profitable. See **Chapter 32** on investing in insurance companies.

Also, children don't need life insurance; they have no income for anyone to count on. Non-working spouses and other family members who don't work also don't need life insurance. Only working family members need life insurance, and you must insure them. Insure them with term life insurance and search for the cheapest policy you can find. Also, you don't ever need more than $700,000 in life insurance, and that is only if you have children still living at home. With no children and if both spouses work, you don't need more than $500,000 or more than your home mortgage, which ever is less. As soon as the kids are gone, or if you have a net worth of more than $700,000, get rid of life insurance; you don't need it anymore.

Chapter 115 Saving Money: Don't Be An Upgrader

Don't be an **Upgrader**. An Upgrader is someone who has to have the latest hot new gadget and the latest new upgrade to that gadget. When new innovative products come out, they are several magnitudes more expensive and far less capable than what will be available just 2 years later. An upgrader is someone who was the first to get a VCR, the first to get a CD player, the first to get a PC or Mac, the first to get a DVD player, the first to get a cell phone, the first to upgrade their computer every 2 years, the first to get an MP3 player, the first to get a Blu Ray player, the first to get the biggest big screen TV, the first to get a smart phone/i-phone, the first to get a tablet, the first to upgrade their phone, etc. The worst of the upgraders are those people you see camping out overnight in line to buy the latest Apple product. The upgrader blows thousands of dollars every couple years on these products, and that first thing they get is vastly inferior to what becomes available just 2 years later and at just a fraction of the cost. Upgraders never build wealth. Don't be an upgrader.

Chapter 116 Saving Money: Gym/Club Memberships

Don't waste money on expensive gym/club memberships. I made this mistake for a few years. Work out at home. For the cost of just 1 year's membership, you can put together a nice basement or garage or other space gym. In less than 2 years, you will have paid for it and will save a ton of money every year on gym memberships and a ton of time and gas, so you don't have to drive back and forth and wait for people using equipment or worry about inconvenient hours to work out. Also, free weights are generally superior to machines anyway. The average monthly cost is $55, so you will save $660 per year. If instead, you work out at home, and put that extra $660 per year into an S&P 500 index fund in a Roth IRA from age 20 to age 50, you would have an extra $115,000 in saving.

Chapter 117   Saving Money: Additions And Other Home Improvement Projects

Don't put on that addition or other "home improvement project". Contrary to popular mythology, unless you are doing most of the work yourself, the cost of the addition/home improvement project will never come even close to "paying for itself" in increased home value. Raw material prices and labor costs have soared in the past 2 decades. The contractors always come in over cost and take much longer than expected to complete. The classic situation is a young couple that buy a smallish house, then have kids, and it is crammed living, and then when the kids are age 14, they decide to build an addition, that is finished when the kids are 15 - and will be moving out in just a few years. Don't fall into this trap. If you plan to have kids, buy the right sized house before you even have the kids. Don't buy the small house, then waste money on the addition. The same applies when someone decides they need a whole new kitchen; it will never pay for itself. On the other hand, if you are skilled at carpentry, plumbing and wiring, and do it yourself and with family members, it is actually worth it, and they will increase the value of your home.

Chapter 118 Saving Money: Change Your Life Philosophy

Change your life philosophy. Especially if you are a big spender trying to change your ways to become a better saver, take a hard look at the very big picture of your life. Firstly, think about how I have shown in this book how many places there are to save money, and if you are patient and persistent with your savings and investing, you ARE going to build significant wealth over the next 10 to 20 years and beyond.

Think about the freedom that financial independence will allow you to be able to do what you want to do, and if you are very successful, the freedom of being free of bosses and "the workplace". Think about how the time is going to go by whether you save or not, so you might as well save and invest. Secondly, think about the good things in life. A lot of the best things in life are free or nearly free. Things such as exercise - aerobic exercise (running, swimming, cycling, walking, etc.) and resistance exercise (weights, etc.) and the benefits of being fit and how much better you feel. Think about enjoying a good movie at home with family and friends, enjoying your favorite sports at home with family and friends and a good home cooked meal. Think about going to beaches, parks, mountains and trails, having a loving mate, reading, cheap hobbies, etc. Think about having good relationships with the people close to you and having a spiritual life. These are the good things in life.

Now compare those good things in life to materialism. Now I will be first to admit, I enjoy nice things and have a few, but they are not all that important to me. Materialism is a dead end, whether you are into it because you are trying to impress someone else, or you just feel you need expensive things to make you happy. Whether you are a Christian, follow Eastern religion or for example the great German philosopher Schopenhauer, they will all tell you materialism is an illusion and a dead end. As soon as you get over the initial thrill, you will want more, better, bigger, faster, etc. If you crave materialism, you will never be satisfied.   It never ends and will never make you happy. God forbid if you actually get poorer, and materialism is important to you; what are you going to do then?

Don't live to impress other people, which is why some people pursue materialism. Be your own person, and have the confidence to do so. The pursuit of materialism is illusory and destructive for your psyche and will kill your wealth building plans. Break free from the materialistic pursuit trap, and think of the big picture. Think of wealth building for the freedom and security, and sure, to own some nice things, AFTER you build wealth, but even then, look at those material items sort of like a nice extra, but nothing you "need" or "crave". Focus on things that are much more important than materialism, such as faith, physical fitness, good personal relationships with the people close to you, getting outdoors and enjoying nature, cheap hobbies and entertainment etc.

Chapter 119 Saving Money: Home Equity Loans

Avoid home equity loans. Taking out a home equity loan is going backwards, as far as wealth building goes. Sure they are convenient, nice to have, have lower interest rates in general and are tax deductible, but NEVER lose sight that when you take one out, you are going backwards in wealth building, because you are adding debt that is taking away from your net worth. Remember, unless you are doing most of the work yourself, that addition or new kitchen is not going to pay for itself, even though the contractor and home improvement chains and others will tell you so. The only time to use one is if you use it to reduce debt payments from other high interest credit card or student loan debt that you are rolling into your home equity loan, or you are putting on a new addition and doing most of the work yourself.

Chapter 120 Saving Money: If You Lack Discipline, Get Rid Of Your Credit Cards

If you lack discipline, get rid of your credit cards. Credit cards are an excellent tool for the disciplined person who is a saver, never overspends and always pays off the balance at the end of the month. I personally use credit cards for basically everything. The fact I am using a card has absolutely no effect on how much I spend; it would be exactly the same amount if I didn't have a card. This is unfortunately not the case for many, many people. Because they have a card, they spend more. If that is you, get rid of the card. If you do not pay it off at the end of the month, you are paying outrageously high interest rates and falling deeper and deeper into the hole. If that is the case, get rid of the card. See **Chapter 8** for dealing with existing credit card debt.

Chapter 121 Saving Money: Don't Replace A Car/Heating System/Central Air/Refrigerator/Room Air Conditioner/Etc. That Is Still Operating Fine With A More Energy Efficient Model

Don't replace a car/heating system/central air/refrigerator/room air conditioner/etc. that is still operating fine with a more energy efficient model. Sure the manufacturer or the government may try to convince you to do this, but it will never pay off. The wasted life of the old unit, the high cost of the new unit, and more importantly, the opportunity cost lost (the money for the new unit could have been invested.) will never make up for the spread out over the long run annual savings in reduced energy costs. The initial purchase cost of the new unit and opportunity cost lost can never be overcome. The correct way to do it, is when the car/heating system/central air/refrigerator/room air conditioner/etc is at the end of its useful life, then buy the much more energy efficient replacement model.

Chapter 122   Saving Money: Before You Buy Anything, Always Check Online First

Before you buy, always check online first. One of the great benefits for consumers is the age of the internet for shopping. Before you buy anything, quickly go online on Amazon, Wal-Mart.com, etc., and search to see how cheap you can get it online. Always include shipping costs, because some sites/sellers try to trick you by selling a tiny item for $5.99, then charging you $8.99 for shipping when you check out. Many retailers have "site to store" options, where they will ship it for free to the store nearest you. Also, in many states you can still avoid sales taxes by buying online, but the ever expanding growth of government is closing out that option.

Chapter 123 Saving Money: Buying Groceries

Buy from the cheapest grocer. The supermarket industry is highly competitive, and most shoppers have 2 to 4 rival stores in their area to choose from. Scope it out, and you will typically find one that has significantly cheaper "every day" prices than others. Only go to the others for specific items when they are having promotional sales in the flyers you get in the mail. Buy cheaper generics whenever the quality is close to the same. Study ingredients and labels and cost per unit on the labels. Sometimes you find big discrepancies in prices between similar items. Sometimes they trick you and charge you more per pound when you buy the bigger container. Stock up on sales (by the way, just as a fundamental stock investor would do with a company with sound fundamentals when it goes down in a market sell-off and gets even cheaper).

Don't fall for the organic/natural food fad. You will pay much higher prices for organics/natural and generally get lower quality food if you do. There is zero benefit to eating so called "organic" and "natural" foods; it is just a sales pitch for the gullible. The only thing that matters is the actual nutrient make up of the food, not whether it is "organic" or "natural" or "free range". If you truly want to be healthy, exercise every day and exercise more, get more sleep, don't smoke, don't drink alcohol to excess, keep your percent body fat low, reduce stress in your life, and minimize sugar, fat and salt intake. Those things make you significantly more healthy, while eating organic/natural food does nothing for your health and hurts your wallet. Don't get conned by this new booming industry. Anytime something is booming such as the organic/natural food fad, hedge funds and ETFs, ask yourself who is getting rich, the seller or the buyer of these products?

Chapter 124 Saving Money: Clothes

Don't waste money on expensive clothes. Many off price retailers such as TJ Maxx/Marshalls and other similar stores have clothes that are just a fraction of the price of other retailers. In fact, I am astounded how cheap they can actually sell some of their stuff and still be so profitable, and yes, I have owned the stock (TJX) for many years. Buy end of the season clear outs, etc.

Chapter 125 Saving Money: Don't Waste Money On Energy Bills

Don't waste money on energy bills. Get yourself and your family in the habit of turning off lights when you are not in the room. When in heating season, have thermostats with timers that go lower at night and when you are not there. Do the same for cooling during the air conditioning season.

Chapter 126 Saving Money: Barter With Telecommunication Companies

Barter with telecommunication companies. Few people realize that you don't have to pay the advertised price for cable, satellite TV, internet, phone and cell phone service. Once you have been with a company for a while and have been paying your bills on time, they don't want to lose you. Yes, it is a pain and will take 15 minutes of your time every 6 months to a year, but you've got to get on the phone with them and ask for the "retention representative" and politely and calmly say you want to stay with them, but XYZ competitor is offering a lower price if you switch, and is there any way they can give you a better deal. It is basically a game, but you can lower you cable, satellite, internet, phone and cell phone bills by 10 to 30% by playing the game. What these companies do is routinely raise rates for everyone every 6 months to a year. They hope you don't notice or are just resigned to paying more or don't want to take the time to barter or to switch to someone else, and that is true for 80% of their customers. You want to be one of the 20% who gets on the phone and asks for the "retention representative" and starts bartering for a lower rate.

Chapter 127 Saving Money: Change Electricity Providers

Change electricity providers. Some states let you chose your electricity provider. You still have the delivery company monopoly that is half your bill, but you can pick the source of your actual electricity. For some strange reason, these provides don't advertise or market much, but you will find there are vastly lower rates out there, up to 50% cheaper, which is especially important if you live in the North and have electric heat or live in the South and are using A/C. If your state allows source competition, go online and research the provider rates and change providers to the cheapest. Most have contracts of 6 months to 2 years, so once you switch, you have to mark your calendar, so you remember to plan to switch again when your contract expires, because they jack up your rates automatically when the contract expires, and they don't warn you in advance.

Chapter 128 Saving Money: Draw Up A Budget

Draw up a budget. When you start saving and investing, and at least once a year, such as the end of the year, draw up a budget that shows all of your spending. If you don't know where the money is going, you won't know where you can save. Include all the major categories. Go through your last 12 months of credit card statements, last 12 months of your checking account, and last 12 months of monthly bills. Add them up and rank them. Then take a hard look at each category, and figure out how those can be cut back. Update it every year to see what costs are rising, what is falling, and where you need to work on to save money.

Chapter 129   Saving Money: Don't Speed

Don't speed. I fell into this trap when I was young and dumb. The politicians and auto insurance companies have set up sweetheart deals via regulators in most states that not only can increase your insurance premiums if you have an at fault accident, which is reasonable, but also can raise your insurance rates if you get a moving violation. You will be shocked how much money these sweetheart deals allow the insurance companies to take from you. You might get a $100 speeding fine which is outrageous enough or even $150 to $300 in many Blue States, but the real killer is the insurance rate hike that comes later. This hike is also masked from you, so you won't realize how much it costs. It doesn't get added to your bill for many months later, and to further mask the true cost, they spread it out and punish your for some ridiculous length of time typically 3-7 years, and the total extra cost is typically in the range of $1000 or more. Most people don't realize just how bad this is. You can get less than 7 years for murder in some cases, yet for just 1 speeding ticket, they can punish you for 7 years. To squeeze even more money out of you, some Blue States are now classifying things such as expired inspection stickers, registrations and driver's licenses, as a "moving violation". Massachusetts has gone so far as to stop reminding you when your drivers license expires, in the hope you will forget, and they can fine you for that, in addition to the speeding ticket they will give you, when they pull you over. More states are likely to follow the lead of Massachusetts.

Therefore, every speeding ticket/moving violation is actually going to cost you about $1000 over about 5 years. Remember, states and towns are running up massive debt to keep their unsustainable public employee union benefit systems going, so they are really going after working people driving to and from work as a revenue source.

That best way I know of to prevent getting a ticket is to use cruise control whenever possible, and set it for 5-9 MPW over the posted speed limit. Most of the time, they won't pull you over for that, and you can relax when you drive and not be in fear. It is a shame the politicians have directed so much of law enforcement's efforts towards taking money from honest, hardworking people driving to and from work, rather than going after the bad guys, but of course they know you won't get violent and resist, and they know you will pay the money. There is no "revenue" in going after the bad guy committing traditional crimes, and it is dangerous pursuing and arresting bad guys, especially in the inner city. It shouldn't be this way, but it is, so you have to be very careful not to get speeding tickets because of the extremely high cost of them.

You can also expect more and more states to institute fines for talking on cell phones and not wearing seat belts and driving in the "passing lane" and driving in the right lane when a police car is in the breakdown lane and going from doubling to tripling fines near construction sites and anything they can think of to get more tax revenue out of you. Whenever you hear a politician tell you "it is a safety issue", hold onto your wallet, because it means a new tax/fee/fine and another freedom taken away. Desperate to keep the unsustainable spending going as long as possible, several Blue States will soon be charging you a new tax for every mile you drive by tracking your odometer readings when you get your car inspected.

Chapter 130   Saving Money: Watch Out For Cameras At Intersections And On Highways

Watch out for cameras at intersections and on highways. Despite the fact states and cities are struggling to fund their runaway spending, they are spending even more money to install cameras at intersection lights and extremely expensive combination cameras/radar guns on highways to get even more money from you. Don't even think about running a light with these cameras. As stated above, that is a $1000 cost to you over 5 years, if you run a light.

Even more insidious are the combo camera/radar guns on highways. You could be driving home after a hard day's work and simply moving with the flow of traffic and dealing with pressures of work and kids and relationships etc. and making ends meet. Then, 4 weeks later in the mail, you get a $300 speeding fine followed up by a couple of months later, a big hike in your insurance rates for the next FIVE years, and you will likely not even remember the speeding occurrence. Meanwhile there are 6000 new unsolved homicides in the USA every year (35% of murders now go unsolved compared to only 9% in 1963.), so be very aware as to where the politicians have the law enforcement's efforts focused on. I point out all this, so that you understand the scope and magnitude of the effort the politicians are directing at you, the working person, driving to and from work, to get more and more tax revenue out of you through fines going forward. A series of tickets/insurance rate hikes can cost you thousands of dollars in actual costs, that add up to hundreds of thousands of dollars in opportunity cost lost over a lifetime, so don't get caught.

Chapter 131   Saving Money: Attending Pro Sports Games

Don't go to pro sports games, watch them on TV. Pro sport athletes are paid astronomical salaries, and to compensate them, the teams charge outrageous ticket prices, well beyond the means of ordinary people, but like anything else, it doesn't stop ordinary people from paying these crazy ticket prices to fund the lavish lifestyles of pro athletes, making 100 times what they are making.

With today's big screen HD TVs and tremendous camera technologies, you can see far more at home on TV from 10 different angles, as if you were right on the field, cheaply eat and drink whatever you want and as much as you want, pause your DVR to go to the bathroom or eat dinner or take a phone call or enjoy the good weather outside, and black yourself out from the score, and watch later when convenient for you. At the game, you have people crowding you, spilling drinks on you, standing up and getting in your way. You wait in line to get frisked to get into the stadium, have people complaining about you standing up, are missing action to wait in line to go to the bathroom or buy a drink or food. You pay $12 for a watered down stale low end draft beer, waste hours battling traffic in and out, risk getting assaulted by some drunk, pay $30 to park and $10 for a lousy hotdog that the team buys in bulk for 35 cents a piece, worry about leaving the game early to beat the traffic, and then you spend the entire next day recovering from the tailgate hangover.

Pro football ticket prices now cost an average of $200, pro baseball $60, pro basketball $90, and pro hockey $150 dollars. If Joe Sixpack goes to 4 baseball games, 2 football games, 1 basketball game and 1 hockey game a year with his wife and 2 kids, and they get just one drink each and 1 hot dog each, the total bill for the year is $4400, and then Joe Sixpack wonders why he is just scraping by, and railing on about how the so called "1 percenters" are screwing him. If instead, he watches all the games on TV, and put that extra $4400 dollars per year into an S&P 500 index fund in a Roth IRA from age 20 to age 50, he would have an extra $760,000 in savings or 3/4 of a million dollars and will have joined the so called "one percenters" instead of complaining about them. As I write this in early 2014, a tiny but important crack may have finally appeared in the whole pro sports spiraling up salaries empire. For the first time in 40 years, 3 teams were having trouble selling-out their home NFL playoff games in time to lift the NFL TV blackout, and in one case, a corporation bought out the unsold tickets to lift the blackout. Joe Sickpack may be finally smartening up when it comes to pro sports games. If you are serious about wealth building, don't be a sucker going to pro sports games; watch them on TV.

Chapter 132 Saving Money: Never Pay Too Much For Anything

Never pay too much for anything. This should be a golden rule for you. Everything you buy from $5 items to big ticket items such as cars and appliances, it is important you get in a habit of never paying too much for anything. If something is priced higher than it is worth, don't buy it. The same of course applies to stocks. You need to do it on principle and for the obvious practical reason that the key to building wealth is a combination of savings and investing. You need to be both pennywise and especially pound wise, so it becomes automatic. Here is a personal example. I love going to the beach and have since I was 2 years old. The past 30 years, I estimate I have gone to the local beach about 2000 times. The parking at this beach varies from 5 dollars to as high as 30 dollars, for a close spot during the peak summer holidays and weekends. Instead of paying to park all those years, I simply parked a mile away in a free spot and jogged the 8 minutes it took to get to the beach. Assuming an average savings of 6 dollars, I saved $12,000 in parking costs. The stock invested opportunity cost saving works out to approximately $70,000. Not only did I save 70K, I also got a little extra exercise.

Chapter 133 Summary Of My Stock Investing Returns

As stated earlier, I foolishly waited until I was 28 before I started investing, and only had $8000 when I started, and made lots of mistakes, yet, I was persistent and patient in my savings and investing, and my wife was able to retire 9 years later, and I was able to retire less than 15 years later at age 43.

For 2013, I was up 48.4% versus 29.6% for the S&P 500 (31.9% including dividends), 38.3% for the NASDAQ, 26.5% for the Dow, 36.9% for the Russell 2000, 32.3% for the average US diversified stock mutual fund, and 9.8% for the average hedge fund.

Since I started doing individual stocks in 1992, I have been up 19 out of 22 years and have beaten the S&P 500 11 out of the past 14 years.

In percentage terms, 2013 was my 3rd best year ever. Relative to the S&P 500, it was my 6th best year ever. It was the most money I ever made in a single year.

The past 5 years I have averaged 24.7% annual returns versus 17.8% for the S&P 500.
The past 10 years I have averaged 10.5% annual returns versus 7.3% for the S&P 500.
The past 15 years I have averaged 16.1% annual returns versus 3.1% for the S&P 500.
The past 20 years I have averaged 14.4% annual returns versus 9.2% for the S&P 500.

Chapter 134   Epilogue

A sizable minority of the population (i.e. tens and tens of millions of Americans) are capable of becoming wealthy slowly by saving and investing. The vast majority of course never will, because one or more of the following reasons will prevent them:

1) They give up before they start or never get started, because they think that the 12 to 20 years it takes to grow financially independent is too long, and they don't have the patience and persistence and the mental toughness to stick with it for that long. Ironically, the guy who first talked me into doing individual stocks and *Fundamental Stock Investing* principles in 1992, gave it up less than 2 years later, while I persevered onward.
2) They lack the discipline to save.
3) They are excellent savers, but don't invest, so they never build wealth.
4) They have the discipline to save but have not read this book and don't know where and how to go about saving and cutting costs.
5) They are good savers and invest, but have not read this book, and therefore, do not know how to use *Fundamental Stock Investing* and are using other inferior systems.
6) They are aware of *Fundamental Stock Investing,* but are easily distracted and get impatient and keep trying all kinds of different investing systems that don't work very well over the long run, especially when you look at after tax returns. They try day trading, market timing, using margin, precious metals, start listening to "experts", such as the raving guy on TV, options, penny stocks, shorting stocks, ETF trading, currency trading, technical analysis, price momentum trading, earnings momentum trading, CANSLIM, etc.
7) They are good savers and invest and use *Fundamental Stock Investing,* but they don't have the stomach to ride out big market downturns, and they get scared out of stocks, and sell at exactly the wrong time after the bulk of the decline has already happened, and they never get back in on time or are scared permanently out of stocks. When the inevitable stock market collapse comes about half of all "retail investors" (aka the little guy) get permanently scared out of stocks. A friend of mine went into stocks for the first time in his life

after age 50 in 2006 and had the misfortune of a 3-4% drop on his first day. Even worse, he had the misfortune of getting into stocks just 18 months before the 2008/2009 stock market collapse, which was one of the five worst collapses in the past 100 years. However, he did not panic and never sold and hung in there and has more than doubled his initial money, despite getting into stocks at the worst possible time. Even better, he added significant new money after the collapse and is very happy with all the wealth he has accumulated the past 8 years.

If you can get over those roadblocks and save well and invest well using *Fundamental Stock Investing,* you will slowly build wealth over time and be on the road towards financial independence. There are no guarantees, but the odds are in your favor.

Back Cover Of Book

This book will set you on the path towards achieving financial independence. It is for both the beginner and the experienced investor who has been burned in investing by using popular but foolish methods that treat investing as if it were a game. This book is unique, because it is the only book that addresses how to build wealth over time with techniques for saving money and investing in stocks using *Fundamental Stock Investing*. Stop wasting time and negative emotional energy complaining about the so called "One Percenters" and start working towards financial independence!

Fundamental Stock Investing, which is defined as buying stocks as if you were buying a business, is a simple and common sense method that is vastly superior over the long haul as proven by investing legends Warren Buffett, who became the richest man in the world, and Peter Lynch, who averaged staggering 29.2% annual returns over a 13 year period and beat the S&P 500 by an average of 13.4 percentage points per year during that period. That 29.2% remains unprecedented for any money manager over such a long period of time. Using *Fundamental Stock Investing* the past 15 years, I have averaged 16.1% annual returns versus 3.1% for the S&P 500, also beating the index by 13 percentage points per year. Not only that, because the method generally involves holding stocks for longer time periods, transactions costs are lower, but most importantly, gains are taxed at much lower rates, and the gains are also deferred, all of which results in much higher increases in wealth than the official gains compared to ALL other investing methods. There are many systems you can use to make money in stocks, but when you combine the returns with the huge tax advantages, *Fundamental Stock Investing* becomes the superior method. It is also the simplest and easiest to learn method and the only method that uses common sense. What is unique about this book is that it also explains how you must combine savings with successful stock investing to build significant wealth over the long haul, and it outlines critical techniques to save money so you have more to invest. This book will set you on the path towards achieving financial independence.

www.ingramcontent.com/pod-product-compliance
Lightning Source LLC
Chambersburg PA
CBHW051854170526
45168CB00001B/99